ON THE RUN

The American Civil War: execution of a deserter in the federal camp.

ON THE RUN

DESERTERS THROUGH THE AGES

GRAEME KENT

The Robson Press

First published in Great Britain in 2013 by
The Robson Press (an imprint of Biteback Publishing Ltd)
Westminster Tower
3 Albert Embankment
London SE1 7SP

Frontispiece © Getty Images

Every reasonable effort has been made to trace copyright holders of material reproduced
in this book, but if any have been inadvertently overlooked the publishers would be
glad to hear from them.

ISBN 978-1-84954-570-9

10 9 8 7 6 5 4 3 2 1

A CIP catalogue record for this book is available from the British Library.

Set in Garamond and Grotesque

Printed and bound in Great Britain by
CPI Group (UK) Ltd, Croydon CR0 4YY

MIX
Paper from
responsible sources
FSC
www.fsc.org
FSC® C020471

CONTENTS

ACKNOWLEDGEMENTS

I would like to thank my agent Isabel White, a patient, never-ending source of encouragement, inspiration and expertise, and Hollie Teague, my editor at The Robson Press. Decades too late, I give my thanks to all those squaddies I accompanied 'under escort' back to camp – even the one who made a break for it at Leeds railway station – for their pragmatic tolerance on their interminable journeys to face retribution.

INTRODUCTION

There have been many books written about valour in battle. This is not one of them. *On the Run* deals entirely with those men and women who, over thousands of years, have departed with alacrity and for multifarious reasons from life in the armed forces.

As long as there have been military units and organised martial bodies of any kind, there have been men and women who decided that they were out of place in them, did not like serving in them or, for other reasons, chose to walk away from their places of duty.

While deserters have usually been treated by the general public with contempt, sometimes good-natured, sometimes not, this condemnatory view is, tellingly, not always shared by those who have served in the armed forces and appreciate that the line between staying put and fleeing is sometimes a fine one. This was exemplified, not long after the Second World War, in the iconic radio comedy *The Goon Show*, when its principals, all of them ex-servicemen, could come up with such heartfelt lines as 'I was in the 4th Armoured Deserters' and know that the pusillanimous boast would receive a wryly sympathetic reception from the millions of former soldiers, sailors and airmen listening in.

I first came into professional contact with absentees as an 18-year-old National Service conscript in the early 1950s, when for several months I was detailed to accompany a corporal to pick up recaptured absentee soldiers at police stations around the country and escort them back to their units to face courts martial and possible terms in a 'glasshouse' or military prison. The only solace the sympathetic, cadaverous corporal and I could offer to our charges from the shallows of our experience on these long, often tearful, return train journeys was to urge our distressed prisoners to plead guilty to going absent without leave, implying that all-important intention to return, rather than desertion, as the sentence for the former was much lighter than for the latter. An absconder found guilty of being absent without leave would be sentenced to a period of detention in his unit's cells. Depending upon the discretion of his commanding officer, this could be roughly for the same length of time as the original length of absence. Offenders found guilty of desertion would be sent to a military correction establishment. A typical sentence here would be from a few months to a year, often followed by dismissal from the service, although much longer penalties could be imposed.

It soon became apparent that many of our absconders were not the rough-hewn, heedless lawbreakers of fiction, but for the most part homesick, contrite and frightened youths. Their inherent gloominess was leavened by the occasional inadequate, slightly older renegade regular soldier who regarded a term in a house of correction as a reasonable, almost inevitable payment for a brief and hectic period of freedom on the loose.

One particularly hardened and incorrigible character of this sort, who had gone on the run and been recaptured on at least half a dozen occasions, had but one complaint. At the time, convicted escapees were liable to be sent to one of the two main military prisons in Great Britain: Colchester or Shepton Mallet. This particular serial absconder had served time alternately at both prisons and regarded the fact with comparative equanimity.

Unfortunately, so our serial deserter would complain to us bitterly on our journeys, each establishment decreed that a different shade of Blanco, the cleaning and colouring compound, should be used for scouring the webbing belts, straps, anklets and packs of their inmates. This meant that, to his enormous chagrin, as soon as he was discharged from Colchester prison he had to spend a great deal of time applying a whole new set of colouring to his equipment if Shepton Mallet were his next destination.

It soon became apparent upon our periods of escort duty where the sympathies of the general public lay. Most men at that time had served in the Second World War or had completed a post-war period of National Service. As soon as some of them caught a telltale glimpse of the handcuffs around our prisoner's wrists there would be howls of antipathy directed at his custodians and shouts urging the deserter to make another run for it.

Since those odd days over half a century ago I have sometimes wondered what happened to the callow boys and insouciant old lags who found service life all too much for them and as a result went 'over the wire'. Doubtless upon their discharge the great major-ity went on to live lives of complete respectability and usefulness, regarding their departed nightmarish period of military service with bewildered amusement.

These thoughts led me to an examination of deserters and deser-tions in general and in turn to some of the more unusual and interesting absconders down the ages, which has culminated, decades later, in this book. Over the years I have spent much time in many countries reading the transcripts of courts of inquiry and discussing life on the run with one-time deserters and those close to them. These range from a former colonial civil servant who befriended the film star and deserter Errol Flynn in his wild, hedonistic Papua New Guinea days in the 1930s, to a great-grandmother who, in Second World War London, frequently harboured, sometimes simultaneously, her three wayward sons, who deserted regularly from two different branches of the armed forces. This redoubtable lady received so many visits of inquiry from the military police that when she opened the door to her uniformed, red-capped visitors she would merely ask resignedly, 'Which one do you want?'

There have been relatively few books written about the history of desertion. A number of individuals have written or had writ-ten for them accounts of their abrupt departures from service life and there have been a handful of books about British deserters in the First World War in particular, in addition to several academic studies of desertion in the American Civil War. Generally, however, any investigations into desertion necessarily have involved at some stage the study of contemporary accounts, regimental records and transcripts, and the files of newspapers.

In these, through the ages, there have been many justifications and pleas in mitigation from those who have abandoned their posts. It is very difficult, however, to establish just why some people desert and others in similar circumstances stay put. In most cases there seem to have been a multiplicity of reasons. The natural desire not to be killed or maimed occurs often; even so, other causes often combine to push the deserter over the edge, or over the wire, in war or peace. Discontentment with military life and boredom feature large, as does homesickness. Personal and domestic problems may weigh heavily, as well as opportunism and bloody-mindedness. Location, climate and weather sometimes influence whether someone remains or goes. Ambition can occasionally impel a desertion, if something better or more lucrative seems to be just over the horizon. Greed was a considerable factor in the days when bonuses were paid to volunteers, causing bounty hunters to skip avariciously from one military paymaster to another. Indifferent and unhelpful officers play their part, as do heavy defeats recently sustained in battle, with subsequent loss of morale leading to defections among the vanquished troops. Coercion by the enemy sometimes provides the deciding factor.

All these motives and others will be found among this trawl through the accounts of deserters and desertions. One or two semi-iconic figures, unfortunately, logically enough, seem to have escaped my hunt through history. Even with the exercise of due diligence it has not always been possible to track down every example of deserter history and folklore. I particularly regret not being able to verify perhaps one of the most fascinating tales of the Second World War. Two Tibetan yak-herders were supposed to have been kidnapped by the Russians in their homeland and forced to fight on the Eastern Front, where they deserted and were recruited in turn by the Germans, before finally freeing themselves again and then being taken prisoner by a Canadian unit in France towards the end of the war. A similar story has also been told about a group of Korean soldiers supposedly buffeted by the winds of war halfway across the world from their Asian homeland to Normandy in 1944.

Regardless, there have still been plenty of authenticated accounts of desertion from which to select, across thousands of years and over forty different countries. Among their number are poets and pugilists, thieves and thugs, lovers and lunatics, princes and politicians, comedians and conspirators, film stars and fanatics, and even the occasional pope, all bound by the simple fact that at one time or another they went on the run.

THE FIRST DESERTERS

When they saw His Majesty prevailing against them they fled headlong
to Megiddo.
– Annals of Thutmosis III, Egyptian Pharaoh

The first men known to have deserted the field of conflict did so
out of sheer panic. They were warriors of a coalition of tribes
from Palestine and Syria who had risen against the young Egyptian
Pharaoh Thutmosis III. In 1479 BC, Thutmosis led a large, well-
equipped army into central Palestine, near Mount Carmel. The
Egyptian force was armed with spears, axes, javelins and swords. The
young pharaoh also had a special force of charioteers.

The two forces met outside a hill-top fortress called Megiddo. In
an early example of psychological warfare, Thutmosis first lined up
his force of 10,000 men within sight of the defenders of the town
and slowly reviewed them as they marched and drove past him in
magnificent array. The pharaoh then led a charge through the heart
of the Palestinian force. The rebels, already bewildered and cowed
by the magnificence of the vast Egyptian force, turned and ran.
They were impelled by that most basic of motives: the ominous,
fearful realisation that they had bitten off more than they could
chew. An Egyptian account stated, 'When they saw his majesty
prevailing they fled headlong to Megiddo in fear, abandoning their
horses and their chariots of gold and silver.'

Many of them scrambled for the safety of the town walls, but
the sight of the pursuing Egyptians intimidated the inhabitants
of Megiddo equally and they refused to open the town gates.
Only some of the deserters were able to enter the fortress when a

few courageous inhabitants threw ropes and knotted sheets over the side of the wall for them to scale. The others were cut down outside the stronghold they were supposed to be defending. After a brief siege Megiddo surrendered and paid tribute to Pharaoh Thutmosis III.

The Egyptians of this period were already well aware of the dangers posed by deserting troops – among them the loss in discipline and fall in troop numbers – and did their best to deter their soldiers from leaving. One contemporary account of the vicissitudes of a recruit's life, the first of many down the ages, commented gloomily, 'If he joins the deserters, all his people are imprisoned.'

That was only one of the deterrents facing a deserter. Leaving a tribe when danger threatened was never going to be an easy option. All the same, for the next 3,000 years and more this surely did not prevent a lot of people from trying.

As cities and states developed in the ancient world, so did armies and the need to fight in self-defence as well as in pursuit of aggressive expansion. It all culminated in a peace that could best be described as mere breathing space between wars. Some of the soldiers were professional warriors, but others were pressed into service by their communities. The professionals had a pragmatic attitude to warfare – it was their business – but pressed men were not nearly as sanguine when conscripted. Many of them had no heart for conflict. As a result, stories of desertion start to become more and more detailed and self-justifying.

They also begin to enter the mythology of the ancient world, with stories such as the defection of the inventor Daedalus, who murdered a rival in a fit of rage and fled for the protection of King Minos of Greece, before deserting again, this time on wings he had designed with his son Icarus, only to see the boy ascend too high and plummet to his death.

In the real world, conscription was introduced early in the classical era. The city-states of the Greek world would frequently fight one another over the years but, from 499 BC, they temporarily lay aside their differences to fight a common enemy: Persia. Ancient

Athens required all its male citizens to perform nine months' service in their country's army. Many of the aggrieved citizens left their homeland to take up residence in far-flung regions to avoid recruitment. Of those who remained and were pushed into service, many proved to be extremely reluctant warriors.

Amid the various sub-sections of desertion, the impulse for self-preservation remained the most common, even among professional warriors charged with guarding settlements. A typical example was recorded in 701 BC, when the invading Assyrians with their infamous two-horse chariots bore down on the front gates of the town that later became known as Jerusalem. The defenders of the hill-top fort poured out of the rear exits, callously leaving the citizens to their fates. 'The fertile valleys were full of chariots,' bemoaned one despairing inhabitant of the doomed town.

Paradoxically, the better-trained deserters were also much sought after. No state or nation ever had enough trained soldiers, so they began poaching those from other armies. Each leader of the time had his own method of persuading troops to desert from other forces and joining his army instead.

Themistocles, who led Athens successfully against the Persians at the naval Battle of Salamis in 480 BC, relied heavily on recruiting disaffected Persian warriors to his ranks. He would leave messages at oases and watering places where deserters might congregate, detailing the advantages of coming over to the Greek side. A year later when the Spartan ruler Leotychides sailed off the coast of Mycale to pursue the campaign against the Persians, he stationed in one of his craft a herald with a very strong voice, whose duty it was to keep bellowing, 'The Greeks, having conquered the Persians, are now come to liberate the Greek cities of Persia!' The herald went on to announce that at the very least Leotychides expected those on the shore to remain neutral during the impending conflict, while those who forsook their allegiance to the Persians and joined the Spartans would be well rewarded for their efforts.

Ptolemy I of Egypt, who reigned between 323 and 283 BC, refined the concept of heralds coaxing and cajoling deserters in his conflict against the Macedonian invader Antigonus, when he sought to re-establish the former empire of Alexander the Great. Ptolemy had built a number of small vessels designed to sail dangerously close to enemy vessels. Before retreating, the crews of these vessels would detail the scale of bribes available to anyone deserting and joining the Egyptians. These sums ranged from two minae for ordinary soldiers, to a talent for each officer. Two minae represented half a year's wages for an unskilled worker of the time, while a talent was worth roughly sixty times as much – these were appreciable sums. As a result so many took advantage of the Egyptian terms that the greatly depleted force of Antigonus was forced to retreat. As a vindictive parting shot, the Macedonian ordered that any of his deserters who were recaptured should be tortured to death.

There may have been many procedures in existence to lure deserters across, but making the actual bid to reach enemy lines in safety presented its own difficulties.

In theory everything should have gone according to a simple, preconceived plan. Deserters would slip unobtrusively over to the lines of their opposing nation of choice, be debriefed, praised, rewarded and re-enlisted. In practice, it did not always work out as smoothly as this.

Reaching the enemy camp in safety proved increasingly difficult. When Agathocles, the tyrant of Syracuse, was besieging Carthage in 310 BC, a large force of his Libyan mercenaries, amounting possibly to several thousand, decided to desert en masse. They chose a moonless night for their act of treachery and, on a signal, slipped away from their own forces across no man's land towards their perceived new haven.

Unfortunately, the Libyan deserters had omitted to give the Carthaginians notice of their impending arrival. An alert sentry on the walls of the beleaguered city saw the shadowy figures approaching and gave the alarm that Carthage was about to be attacked. Torrents of spears rained down upon the hapless would-be new adherents to the cause of Carthage, killing many of them before they could be identified. The Libyans had only one choice. They turned and fled back towards the area occupied by Agathocles. By this time the forces of Syracuse had been alerted by the confused sounds of battle in front of their lines. As their former allies fled back in disarray they assumed that Agathocles in turn was being attacked under cover of darkness. Now it was their turn to slaughter the trapped Libyans, which they did with a vengeance.

An added complication to the art of deserting lay in the fact that wily leaders developed the awkward habit of sending loyal followers over to the other side, in the guise of absconders, in order to reconnoitre, give false information or even resort to surreptitious acts of sabotage in their new habitat once they were settled in.

As a refinement of this dissembling, it was not long before generals started to send out spies posing as deserters in the direction of opposing camps, hoping that they would be able to spread misinformation and confuse the other side. In 1274 BC, the Egyptian Pharaoh Ramesses the Great was leading a force against the Hittites in Syria when an Egyptian patrol captured two Bedouin Arabs who admitted to being deserters from the Hittite Army. They informed their captors of the location of the main Hittite force, several hundred miles from the town of Kadesh. According to a contemporary inscription, the courageous Arabs assured the Egyptians that 'the enemy from Hittite is in the land of the Khaleb'.

However, the so-called deserters were agents of the Hittites. The brilliant but sometimes impetuous Ramesses led his army into an ambush, from which he only extricated himself and his army by an impressive display of physical bravery and leadership, augmented by the timely arrival of a relief force.

Where military discipline prevails, official punishments and penalties cannot be far behind. Armed forces of the Ancient Greek world showed such concern at the trouble being caused them by absconders that they agreed upon official deterrents for anyone caught trying to leave camp without permission. These punishments began to feature in written records, but not all of them were as serious as the tortures prescribed by Antigonus.

Egyptians were less punitive than some of the other states in their treatment of deserters, although attempting to evade conscription was regarded as a particularly heinous act. They compelled common-or-garden deserters to wear some public mark of their transgression and stationed them in unpleasant areas until such a time as they had redeemed themselves in public, when they could be readmitted into the military fold.

The ancient Athenians had their own method of shaming troops who left their posts: they published the names of absentees. In many armies persistent offenders were punished with branding or were tattooed. Spartan deserters were deprived of their civil rights and shunned by their fellow citizens. A warrior returning from a campaign without his shield could be a shameful sign that he had deserted and had brought disgrace among his family. Spartan mothers warned their warrior sons leaving home, 'Come back carrying your shield, or lying on it!'

Over the centuries the names of one or two ordinary deserters from the ranks began to be recorded in military reports, together with a few details of their flight. In 480 BC, as the 300 Spartans and their allies prepared to make their heroic stand against the invading Persians at Thermopylae, they were betrayed by Ephialtes, a man from Malis who was said to have been a deserter from the Greek coalition of forces. He showed Xerxes, the Persian general, a goat-path that took the invaders behind the Greek lines. Herodotus writes: 'As darkness fell, the Persian king sent his best troops to follow the hidden path and so come up behind the Greeks. At dawn on the third day of battle, the Greeks discovered that they had been betrayed.'

Now beset on several fronts, the coalition of Greek forces, including Thespians and Thebans, held on bravely before the Spartan king Leonidas was killed and most of the defending force, including all the Spartan contingent, with him. However, in turn, the Persians were defeated at Salamis in 480 BC and could not press home any advantage gained at Thermopylae. The Spartans put a price upon the head of the fleeing deserter Ephialtes; some time later he was killed in a brawl unrelated to the events at Thermopylae. All the same, the Spartans paid the killer his reward.

One so-called deserter from the ranks was immortalised, although in myth rather than history – Sinon. In the Homeric tradition, when the Greeks leave the wooden horse and its contingent of concealed warriors outside the walls of Troy, Sinon, reputed to be the greatest liar in the Greek ranks, is charged with the task of persuading the Trojans that he is a deserter and that it will be all right for them to open their gates and tow the horse inside. At first the Trojans were suspicious but, according to the second book of the *Aeneid*, Sinon was glib enough to persuade the citizens that he had fled the Greek ranks because Odysseus had nominated him as a human sacrifice in order to propitiate the gods and ensure the Greeks a safe voyage home. The self-proclaimed absconder declared that the rest of the army he had once served was on the high seas: 'at this moment they are running free'. The Trojans believed him, dragged the edifice into their city and that night Sinon released the Greek warriors inside so that they could destroy the city.

Another ordinary deserter to emerge briefly from the mists of obscurity was Scyllias, a local man serving with the Persian fleet when it attacked the Greeks. Scyllias was famed for his prowess as a diver. Shortly before his desertion he had been employed to salvage treasure from a shipwrecked Persian vessel. In the process the diver had put aside several valuable items for himself, looking for an opportunity to make off unseen with his loot. The chance came when the Persian fleet sailed to take on the Greeks under Themistocles at what became the Battle of Artemisium.

Scyllias deserted his vessel with his appropriated goods and rowed across in the dark (although some accounts claim that he swam clutching his booty) to the Greek ships. The Persian seaman informed Themistocles of the situation and of the Persian battle plans. Armed with this knowledge Themistocles was able to win the battle and with that Scyllias disappeared from history, together with his booty.

An increasing number of desertions were recorded not just from the humble rank and file but from leaders of varying titles. Any officer with sufficient military skills and charisma who had at his disposal a substantial number of fighting soldiers realised that these men immediately under his command could be utilised for his own advancement or profit, as long as he could persuade or intimidate them into throwing in their lots with him.

As a result, it was not long before some leaders, for different reasons, were negotiating terms with opposing forces with some enthusiasm and no little skill. There are numerous accounts of such desertions in the Old Testament of the Bible. One of the first occurs in about 1000 BC, when David, the future King of Israel, hid from his former master Saul in the fortress of Ziklag. He was joined there by Amasai, a Levite soldier previously in command of thirty soldiers of Saul's army. The First Book of Chronicles states that the Holy Spirit descended upon Amasai as he pledged his band to David with the words, 'We are yours, O David, and with you, O son of Jesse!'

The first example of a royal desertion also occurs in the time of David. Absalom, the third son of King David, was horrified when his brother Ammon raped his half-sister Tamar. Their doting father, now a patriarch, did nothing about it. For years Absalom brooded over the injustice. Eventually he deserted King David with a number of followers and at Hebron declared himself the new King of Israel.

David sent three armies to crush his renegade son. Job, David's general, routed the army of Absalom, who fled from the field of battle. David had ordered Job to spare his son's life but the general knew that as long as Absalom lived he would be a threat to his father. The story went that as the vain Absalom fled on horseback his long tresses became entangled in the branches of a tree and he was left hanging. The Second Book of Samuel, verse 17, recounts what happened when the pursuers arrived and Job approached the still struggling Absalom. The general 'took three darts in his hand and thrust them through the heart of Absalom while he was yet alive in the midst of the oak. And ten young men that bare Job's armour compassed about and smote Absalom, and slew him.'

Ironically, a number of leaders from the Greek world who

encouraged deserters to come over to them ended their own days in exile. Themistocles of Athens and Leotychides of Sparta both became involved with political factions in their respective countries and were driven into exile, taking refuge with their former adversaries, the Persians. Another Athenian, Hippias, was also driven from his state. He joined the Persian Army and in 490 advised its leader Darius I to invade the Greeks at Marathon. The attackers suffered a great defeat, presumably making Hippias as unpopular in Persia as he was in Athens.

As written records became more plentiful, more names of the first deserters were recorded, appearing briefly on tablets and then disappearing again. In 538 BC, when Cyrus, the Persian emperor, invaded Babylon, a general called Gobryas, a former vassal of Babylon, deserted and entered Babylon unopposed, now as a representative of Persia.

A more premeditated form of military desertion was practised by the Athenian nobleman Alcibiades who used a series of planned flights to secure both career advancement and self-preservation. Born in about 450 BC into a noble family, the son of a general killed in battle, Alcibiades was brought up by a kinsman, the orator and statesman Pericles. As a young man the ambitious Alcibiades used his wealth to promote himself as a politician in Athens, gaining considerable personal publicity by entering seven chariots, including the eventual winner and second and fourth place takers, for the races at Olympia.

In the Assembly, Alcibiades pressed successfully for Athens to enter into an alliance against Sparta. He was given joint command of a force sent to Sicily to pursue the campaign against the Spartans and their allies. However, Alcibiades had made enemies. He became involved in a scandal when throughout Athens a number of statues of Hermes, the messenger of the gods and patron of road travellers, were mutilated. Alcibiades was accused, probably falsely, of engineering this vandalism, but his opponents saw to it that he was dispatched with his army to Sicily before the general could face his accusers.

Once he had reached Sicily, Alcibiades was recalled to Athens to be tried for the desecration of the statues. On the return voyage he learned that he had been sentenced to death *in absentia* for his alleged crime. Alcibiades hastily abandoned his position as an Athenian general and entered into negotiations with Sparta, the enemy of Athens. In *Alcibiades*, Plutarch describes the events leading up to the general's defection: 'Seeing himself utterly hopeless of return to his native country, he sent to Sparta desiring safe conduct, and assuring them he would make them amends by his future services for all the mischief he had done them while he was their enemy.'

He persuaded the Spartans to grant him a safe passage, then, with a few companions, sailed in a trading ship to Sparta, where he became an adviser to King Agis I.

Alcibiades soon fell out with the Spartan monarch. Circumspectly he continued on his travels, next placing himself under the protection of a Persian governor called Tissaphernes.

By this time the Athenian forces were not faring well in their campaign against the Spartan alliance. Swallowing its collective pride at approaching one who had only recently deserted the cause, the Assembly begged Alcibiades to return and command the Athenian fleet. The former commander agreed. He set to work to rebuild the weakened Athenian forces. Unfortunately he was so dogmatic in his approach that he was soon being denounced in the Assembly as a tyrant, while the temples of Athens were said to resound to the prayers of mothers begging the gods not to let Alcibiades take their sons to the war.

At first the commander's campaign went well. In 410 BC, he won a great victory over the Peloponnesian fleet, but four years later the Athenians were defeated at Notium. Alcibiades was blamed for this. He was dismissed by the Assembly and exiled to his castle on the western shores of the Hellespont. From this remote fastness he continued to meddle in politics. In 404 BC, at the instigation of Lysander, the Spartan commander, Alcibiades was murdered.

Even the mighty Alexander had to avert threatened desertions during his efforts to conquer much of the known world. In 327 BC, having fought his way across Syria, Egypt and Persia, he finally led his bedraggled, exhausted troops into India. It proved to be a conquest too far. Alexander fervently desired to cross the holy river Ganges but his veteran soldiers stopped and begged their revered leader to take them home, drawing attention to their pitiful condition. 'We have conquered all the world but are ourselves destitute of all things.' There was a great debate over the matter but Alexander sensed that if he did not lead his men back there was a strong possibility that there would be mass desertions. Reluctantly he began his great retreat.

The armies of ancient history varied greatly in their composition, but without exception they were affected by constant desertions from their ranks. Military authorities of all types did their best to forestall these absences with punishments and threats. There are even records in existence of how some civilisations tried to retain their more skilled soldiers and technicians by branding them, so that they could be recognised in any general sweeps of the populace. Nothing seemed to work. Then, as now, warriors of all sorts were prepared to defy authority by leaving their posts arbitrarily.

Towards the end of this period, seven years before the death of Alexander in 323 BC, the Roman Empire began its rise. The Romans adapted some of Alexander's military strategies but they owed much of their success to the awesome efficiency of their army, the first professional, full-time, regularly paid military force in the world. But even this great institution suffered desertion from its military ranks.

2

'LET NO ONE SPARE A SOLDIER!'

To seduce the enemies' soldiers from their allegiance and encourage them to surrender is of special service, for an adversary is more hurt by deser- tions than by slaughter.
– Epitoma rei militaris, Vegtius, c. 390 AD

In 146 BC, Rome conquered and occupied Greece after the Battle of Corinth. For hundreds of years, until the fourth century AD, Rome possessed the greatest empire in the world, comprising some 60 million people. At its zenith, its borders extended from the Mediterranean, across Europe and parts of North Africa, and as far as Assyria and Mesopotamia in the east.

Much of Rome's power was due to its magnificent, highly organ- ised army. But even these superbly trained, disciplined and closely monitored troops were as liable to desert as any other soldiers – if provoked enough. Over the next 300 years the Roman forces and their allies and adversaries threw up more than their share of unusual and ingenious absconders.

A major problem in retaining the strength of the legions lay with the strict internal discipline invoked. More culprits fled to avoid punishments such as flogging for disobeying an order than for any other reason. So many legionaries went absent without leave that Roman deserters even initiated the practice in battle of announcing their imminent defection by approaching the enemy with their shields, spears and swords extended before them in a conciliatory manner.

In an attempt to quell desertions the ruthless Roman Army stead- ily reinforced the number of cruel and harsh punishments in force for any men attempting to abscond, reflecting the concern that such attempts created for their superiors. As early as 214 BC, the Roman Marcus Claudius Marcellus captured the stronghold of Leontini in Sicily during the Second Punic War between Rome and Carthage. Marcellus found hundreds of Roman deserters hiding in the town and had them all beheaded. The action was of such enormity that it even caused some concern in Rome itself although, in *Marcus Claudius Marcellus*, Plutarch concluded that, all things considered, the general had been quite magnanimous: '...he violated none of the townsmen, only deserters, as many as he took.'

Indeed, punishments for Roman deserters were always harsh. Soldiers swore an oath upon enlistment to be faithful unto death. If an individual broke this oath and was recaptured after deserting, he could be subjected to the punishment of *fustuarium*. In this, a tribune would touch the condemned man lightly on his shoulder with a stick, a signal for his fellow soldiers to beat the victim to death with sticks and stones. The few hardy or lucky former legionaries to escape with their lives from such a thrashing were never allowed to return to Rome nor be aided by their families. In 391 AD, the Emperor Theodosius issued an edict giving permission for ordinary citizens to use force to defend their lands and property against any deserters: 'Let no one spare a soldier when he becomes a robber.'

If a whole unit should desert or mutiny, the captured troops could be sentenced to decimation, whereby one man in ten was executed and the rest forced to live outside the military camp. Nevertheless, those deserters who stuck together and maintained their military discipline could occasionally present an impressive show of force. In 275 BC, a body of Campanian mercenaries employed by Rome mutinied at Rhegium and deserted, capturing the stronghold of Messana and holding it for some years, despite all the efforts of the regular Roman Army to retake it.

Rome took enormous pride in the ruthless results of its military training and found it difficult to believe that any untutored warriors could prevail against its forces. Little is known, for example, of the antecedents of Spartacus, the former slave and gladiator who led a revolt against the might of Rome between 73 BC and 71 BC. After his initial successes the Romans declared, on meagre evidence, that in order to have been so successful in battle against them, Spartacus must have learned his trade in some remote outpost of the Roman legions before deserting.

Two or three centuries later there were similar legends that St Paul had deserted from the Roman Army and changed his name from Saul of Tarsus in order to escape recapture, but there is no word of this anywhere in the Bible.

Nevertheless the Romans acknowledged the concept of desertion from an early period and even included a number of runaways in their abundant folklore. A story went that one of the city's leaders in 390 BC, Marcus Furius Camillus, was so vilified by his rivals, who accused him of taking bribes from a defeated enemy and depriving his troops of some of their booty, that he left Rome in disgust and went into voluntary exile. However, when Rome was threatened by Gaul, Camillus, at the age of seventy-nine, returned with an army and defeated the barbarians, displaying his inherent loyalty to his homeland.

Among the early records of desertions were accounts of Roman uprisings and defections in occupied Britain. During the reign of Emperor Commodus from 177 to 192 AD, there was a great deal of discontent in the Roman Army, leading to a revolt of the legions in England, alarmed at news of the plotting and counter-plotting taking place in Rome in their enforced absence. Agitators stirred up trouble among the legions and, for a brief period, 1,500 soldiers left their posts. There were many other desertions all over the empire.

While the aristocracy was plotting and planning in ancient Rome, many ordinary soldiers were still doing their best to find ways of permanently detaching themselves from military servitude. One of these was Maternus, an obscure foot soldier fugitive with grandiose plans, which even extended to conquering Rome itself.

He gathered a small army of deserters, attacked and looted cities in Gaul and Spain, releasing any prisoners he found, many of whom joined his company. The Emperor Commodus was greatly concerned by the unexpected, and extremely unwelcome, effectiveness of Maternus. He ordered his provincial governors to hunt the Roman deserter down and kill him. Maternus then put his plan into action. He ordered his force to disband and to cross the Alps in small groups and meet up with him in Rome itself, where he hoped to assassinate the emperor and take his place.

Most of the force managed the long and hazardous journey and assembled in Rome during the festival of Cybele, the goddess of the fertile earth, held in March, but the plot was betrayed to Commodus by one of Maternus's men, jealous of his leader's success. Maternus and his men had to leave the city hastily, fortunate to escape with their lives. Nothing is known of what became of them afterwards.

In an era of treachery, many noble Romans also employed desertion as an important part of their strategies. One of these major defections occurred in 33 BC. A close friend of Julius Caesar and supporter in the Senate, for a time Mark Antony was left in charge of Italy while Caesar was fighting abroad. In 44 BC, Caesar was assassinated by a group of senators, including Brutus and Cassius, who feared that Caesar was on the verge of overthrowing the Republic in favour of a tyranny with him as tyrant. After the death of Caesar, Mark Antony joined with Lepidus and Octavian, Caesar's great-nephew and adopted son, to hunt down Caesar's killers. The three men formed the Second Triumvirate in 43 BC and began their rule of Rome.

The empire was divided among the three. Mark Antony became leader of Rome's eastern provinces. He needed gold and grain and invited Cleopatra, the Queen of Egypt, to visit him in Tarsus to discuss possible trade. Cleopatra arrived in a burnished barge, dressed as Aphrodite, the goddess of love, and accompanied by boys representing Cupid and girls in the guise of nymphs.

From that time, Mark Antony made Alexandria the centre of his activities, ignoring Rome. He fell in love with Cleopatra, thus antagonising Octavian, whose sister Octavia had earlier married Mark Antony. Antony spurned Octavia and sent her back to Rome, later divorcing her. Octavian declared war on Egypt, and Mark Antony threw in his lot with Cleopatra, thus deserting Rome.

His liaison with Cleopatra had lost Mark Antony the respect of the Roman people. He was defeated in several battles against the forces of Octavian. Finally he was outfought at the sea battle of Actium in 31 BC, when his own vessels deserted *him*. Cleopatra's vessels broke through the Roman lines. She and Mark Antony then fled to Egypt, where they lived together for almost a year before Octavian and his forces reached them. Mark Antony committed suicide and, upon hearing the news, Cleopatra followed his example. A representative of Octavian's broke in to Cleopatra's chamber only to find the queen and one of her servants dead and another, Charmion, dying. According to Plutarch's *Life of Antony*, Octavian's man asked angrily: 'Was this well done of your lady, Charmion?'

The servant replied quietly with almost her last breath: 'Extremely well done, and as became the descendant of so many kings.'

Another Roman general to turn against his homeland during the same period was Quintus Labienus, in a desertion prompted mainly by envy and self-pity. Labienus was a Roman general and friend of Julius Caesar. He eventually turned against his patron, deserted Caesar's cause and fought against him, believing that Caesar had not promoted him sufficiently.

Labienus first caught Julius Caesar's eye as a fighting man and military administrator during the latter's campaigns in Gaul from 58–50 BC. The general was quickly promoted to become Caesar's right-hand man and chief of staff. He was second-in-command when Caesar invaded Britain. Labienus then went on to become governor of Cisalpine Gaul.

Unfortunately, Labienus, who was unsure of himself because of his lowly origins, proved to be an arrogant and harsh ruler. Although he owed so much to Julius Caesar he began to grow jealous of Mark Antony, feeling that Caesar preferred him. In time Labienus even began to criticise Julius Caesar in public.

Labienus blundered in his treatment of Commius, the King of the Atrebates tribe in Gaul, believing that the leader was plotting

against Rome. Instead of marching on Commius, Labienus chose
to send some troops to the king on pretence of holding discussions
with him. Acting on the governor's secret instructions the delegates
then tried to murder Commius.

Commius managed to escape, vowing vengeance on Rome. The
king launched a number of attacks and Mark Antony met him
in battle. Commius lost much of his force but again managed to
escape. He then contacted Mark Antony, promising to send him
hostages and remain at peace, as long as he never had to make face-
to-face contact with the Romans again.

Mark Antony agreed that, under the circumstances, these were
reasonable conditions and agreed to them. Still not trusting the
Romans, Commius left for Britain, where he founded a dynasty.
When Labienus heard what had happened he was furious. He
regarded Mark Antony's pact with Commius as an implicit criticism
of the manner in which Labienus had conducted negotiations with
the king. Labienus was sure that Julius Caesar would condone Mark
Antony's attitude, and this made the governor even more rebellious.

For some time Labienus had been attracted to the cause of
Pompey, Julius Caesar's rival for the leadership of Rome. When civil
war broke out between Caesar and Pompey, Labienus abandoned
his old master and went over to Pompey. The defection meant a
great deal to Pompey, who relied upon his new ally's knowledge of
Caesar's forces. Soon Cicero was writing to a friend that Pompey
'has Labienus at his side, who has no doubts about the weakness of
Caesar's forces'.

Even after Pompey had been defeated and killed, Labienus
continued to oppose his mentor. His hatred of his old superior
officer had intensified. When it was suggested that peace might be
made between them, Labienus declared, 'There can be no peace
between us until Caesar's head is brought back!'

When Julius Caesar was assassinated, Labienus feared that he
would be hunted down and arrested by his heirs, the triumvirate
of Mark Antony, Octavian and Lepidus. Crassus, who had become
Governor of Syria, invaded Parthian territory but was killed. Mark

Antony took over the invasion. Labienus became a general in the Parthian Army. He invaded Roman territories with some success, conquering Asia Minor, but was killed in a sudden counter-attack in 39 BC. Without Labienus's leadership the Romans took back the lands he had won from them.

Other leaders besides Labienus began to use defections for their own ends and desertion became an accepted and approved military strategy. Even the Roman war machine could be outwitted at times, especially by mercenaries apparently prepared to switch allegiance in the heat of the conflict. This occurred at the Battle of Cannae in 216 BC, regarded as one of history's great military encounters, in which Hannibal very nearly annihilated a powerful Roman Army.

Two years earlier, Hannibal, the Carthaginian enemy of Rome, had crossed the Alps from Spain into Italy and inflicted several defeats on the Romans. The Romans regrouped and sent an army of around 80,000 infantrymen and 6,000 cavalry to repel the invaders. Hannibal had 40,000 foot soldiers and 10,000 mounted men. The battle was conducted on an open field, with a river on one side and low hills on the other.

Among the Carthaginians were 500 Numidian mercenaries, warriors from north Africa. Before the battle had got under way, according to a pre-arranged stratagem, the Numidians ostentatiously refused to fight the massed Roman Army. As the Roman troops jeered, armed Carthaginians, simulating great concern, conducted the Numidians to the rear of their force and left them there. In his *History of Rome*, Livy wrote: 'About 500 Numidians, carrying, besides their usual arms and missiles, swords concealed under their coats of mail, rode out from their own line, with their shields slung behind their backs, as though they were deserters.'

The battle started with a sudden Carthaginian cavalry attack, which broke the Roman right wing. The Roman infantry pressed forward in the centre but was halted by more Carthaginian horsemen. Suddenly the massed, hitherto inert Numidian 'deserters' produced the swords from beneath their tunics and fell upon the Romans, who were taken by surprise. The Roman soldiers were encircled and slain in their thousands. Over 47,000 infantrymen were killed and 10,000 mounted troops. Almost 20,000 were captured. The surviving Roman soldiers and officers, who had fled, were regarded as deserters and were formed into two new legions and sent in disgrace to garrison duty in Sicily.

Soon afterwards, Hannibal's forces began to run short of supplies. The Romans launched attacks on Carthage and Hannibal had to return home to defend his country. He was defeated and fled, subsequently reduced to a life of wandering exile before he committed suicide by poison in 183 BC.

Rome often did its best to befriend and even train some of the princes of the lands it conquered, but it was a policy that had its dangers, as was evinced by the desertion of Arminius in 9 AD. The scion of a German noble family, Arminius had been educated in Rome as a part of the Roman policy of trying to bind its remoter lands and peoples together in the capital. He had been allowed to serve as an officer in the Roman auxiliary forces and had even been granted Roman citizenship.

However, none of this had diminished Arminius's loyalty to his people. In his campaigns against the enemies of Rome in Thracia, Macedonia and Armenia, the young German had noticed that some of these oppressed tribes had fought bravely and occasionally had even come close to defeating the physically and numerically superior Roman forces. Arminius studied the ways in which the Romans deployed their forces and fought, and began to wonder whether his own people, the Cherusci, could rise successfully against the distant power of Rome. When he returned home he decided to abandon his allegiance to Rome. While they prepared their plans, Arminius and his father Segemerus took care to convince the local Roman governor Publius Quinctilius Varus that they were loyal servants of Rome.

In 9 AD, Arminius lured Varus away from the Rhine deep into the marshy forests of his own tribe's territory by telling the governor that there were uprisings in the area that he would help the Romans put down.

The gullible Varus, more of a lawyer and administrator than a soldier, believed Arminius and set off in late summer into the thickly wooded area with three legions, three squadrons of cavalry and six cohorts of auxiliaries, accompanied by baggage wagons and even women and children. Before long the force became hopelessly extended along the slippery route, while the wagons came to a halt in the mud.

Varus had been warned what would happen in the forest by Segestes, Arminius's father-in-law, who hated his daughter's husband because Arminius had eloped with her. The Roman governor refused to believe that a Roman auxiliary officer would desert him in such a fashion, and thus would not abandon his plans.

At a pre-arranged time, the Cherusci leaders who had been guiding Varus disappeared into the trees of the Teutoburg Forest, and Arminius launched a massive attack at different sites along the track upon the bogged-down Romans. Arminius had fewer men than Varus, but he possessed the element of surprise and convinced the Romans that they were being attacked by a vastly superior force by ordering his men to clash their shields and shout as they appeared and disappeared among the trees.

The battle lasted for three days before the Romans were utterly defeated. Varus committed suicide by falling on his sword rather than become a prisoner of the Germans.

The defeat in the Teutoburg Forest had a traumatic effect upon the Romans. They virtually abandoned their plans to advance eastwards through Germany. Writing 100 years after the event the historian Suetonius remarked on the impact the defeat had had on the Emperor Augustus: 'He was so greatly affected that for several months in succession he cut neither his beard nor his hair, and sometimes he would dash his head against a door, crying, "Quintus Varius, give me back my legions!"'

Today, under the name of Herman, Arminius is celebrated for having freed Germany from Roman rule, but he failed in his efforts to unite the German tribes. His efforts to assume command were treated with suspicion and in 21 AD he was murdered.

Even the Romans could not maintain their control forever. By the fourth century AD their empire in the west was beset on all sides. Barbarians encroached on almost every border. The German tribes advanced from the north. In the west, the Saxons, Jutes and Angles overran England. Desperately, Rome increased its army to a force of 600,000 men, diluting the standards of the once proud legions and causing one writer to complain: 'Among us, deserters are frequent, because soldiers are the vilest part of each nation.' Desertions and mutinies were rife, and skirmishes and then complete battles were lost. Across the whole crumbling Roman Empire, groups of deserters roamed in bandit hordes. In vain the authorities threatened to punish anyone harbouring such a fugitive, with massive fines being administered and some culprits even sentenced to hard labour. Young men of conscription age who cut off their thumbs to avoid military service were threatened with burning at the stake, or arrested and forced to serve anyway. Some of them were even conveyed to their units in wooden cages as a mark of shame for trying to avoid military service.

As unrest spread throughout the Roman Empire more and more troops were needed to combat revolts and invasions. For a time new recruits were paid only in clothing and equipment, not currency, leading to resentment and defections among newly arrived conscripts.

When an army was in the process of being raised, a red flag would be hoisted over the Capitoline Hill in Rome, a call to all those subject to conscription that they had thirty days in which to report to arms. Once this had been regarded as a clarion call to duty, but in the closing years of the empire it was merely a signal to many to put as much space as possible between themselves and their city.

Throughout its existence, the Roman Army, by virtue of its power and importance, had devoted more time and thought to its military procedures than any other civilisation before it – but even the Romans could not prevent their troops from deserting.

Finally, in 410 AD Alaric and his Visigoths invaded Rome, with over 30,000 Roman deserters in his ranks, bringing much of its empire to a close and causing the contemporary St Jerome to write elegiacally, 'The city which had taken the whole world was itself taken.'

The Roman Army devoted considerable efforts to solving the problem of desertion among its ranks, but to no avail. Over its long history it had experimented with both punishments and coercion, from crucifying troops who deserted in battle to currying favour with more experienced legionaries by placing them in the rear ranks in battle, so that younger and thus expendable troops bore the brunt of the first attack. But nothing had prevented the steady exodus of those who preferred to serve no longer.

3

PEACE AND NORTHUMBRIA

One by one the companies closest to him, one after the other, settled to flight, without giving battle.
– Michael Attaleiates, who was present at the engagement, confirms the effectiveness of Andronicus Ducas's strategic desertion from the Battle of Manzikert in 1071

For hundreds of years after the breakup of the western part of the Roman Empire, Europe descended into wild lawlessness. Across the Continent in these Dark Ages, bands of marauding outlaws were increasingly reinforced by contingents of deserters, trained in the arts of war by the Romans and their adversaries and successors. In Britain, starting in about 360, the Picts and Scots renewed their forays from the north. Tribal leaders struggled for supremacy, while various military usurpers struggled to re-establish the remaining Roman garrisons for their own ambitious purposes. Later, Muslim armies swept across North Africa into Spain, while Arab armies occupied Roman Palestine and Syria. It was an age where every man had to look after himself, in which self-preservation ranked high and deserters were common, as were professional mercenaries, who transferred their allegiances effortlessly to the highest bidders.

The Scandinavian Vikings started attacking the coast of England in their clinker-built longships in the eighth century AD. In 793, they swooped on the monastery of Lindisfarne off the north-east coast. Monks were murdered, valuable items stolen and buildings burnt to the ground. This is often regarded as the beginning of the Viking Age and many attacks by the Norsemen on the shores of England; the scholar Alcuin wrote: 'Never before has such a terror appeared in Britain.'

In April 991, a Viking leader called Olaf Tryggvason led a large fleet of ships to the river Blackwater near Maldon in Essex, and fought a battle against the English force waiting there for the invaders. Details of the battle are given in a fragment of an old English poem, 'The Battle of Maldon'. Whether the poem is a piece of contemporary factual reporting or not is debatable, but the existing stanzas do deliver what is probably the first description of an English deserter.

The battle allegedly took place on an old causeway linking Northey Island to the south bank of the Blackwater estuary, near Maldon. The English defenders refused the Vikings' shouted demands for tribute, and prepared to fight. The English, probably overconfident, refused the opportunity to block the causeway and keep the attackers at bay. Instead, contemptuously, they invited the Vikings to cross and fight them on the dry ground.

Several thousand Vikings were believed to be attacking the area at the time, but it is uncertain how many invaded Maldon. Those present at once charged across to fight the smaller English array waiting on the firm footing. At first the fighting swayed both ways, but when the English leader Ealdorman Byrhtnoth was killed the English forces started to panic. The first man in the poem recorded as taking flight is one Godric, the son of Ossa, who 'leapt into the saddle of his lord's own horse...' and fled, followed by others, including two of his brothers. As a consequence, the thane Offa is recorded as shouting, 'Godric, the cowardly son of Ossa, has betrayed us all!'

The existing form of the poem breaks off before reaching the end of the battle but it is plain that Godric was not the only English deserter on that day. Having reached the shelter of a wood, he was soon joined as the day progressed by other fugitives from the battle. The poet mentions drily that some of these skulking figures had at the council of war before the battle been the progenitors of 'many a boastful speech'.

Fewer than a hundred years elapsed before the first English leader is recorded deserting his cause and his troops. In 1065, Harold was the Earl of Wessex and one of King Edward the Confessor's supporters. His quick-tempered brother, Tostig, was the Earl of Northumbria and ruled his lands with such a heavy hand that his noblemen rose against him and deposed the earl. King Edward sent Harold with a small force to try to smooth matters out in the north. The royal emissary found the insurgents keen for peace but adamant in their refusal to have Tostig as their overlord again. They let it be known that they were willing to go to war rather than once more to be subjected to the iron rule of their former earl.

Despite his regard for his brother, Harold believed that the proposed civil war would do great harm to England. Acting on his own initiative, he agreed to the demands of the thanes and informed Tostig that in the cause of peace his exclusion was to be permanent.

Tostig was furious at his treatment and left the country with hatred in his heart for his brother. While the earl was abroad, King Edward died, naming Harold as his successor. Still incensed by his treatment in Northumbria, Tostig offered his services to Harold Hardrada, King of Norway, the last of the great Viking leaders, who was planning a bid for the English throne based on his distant blood ties with the former English ruler, Canute.

In September 1066, Hardrada sailed with a fleet of 300 vessels to make his challenge for the crown of England. He joined up with Tostig at the mouth of the river Tyne and the Norwegian force, augmented by Tostig's supporters, landed further up the river, not far from York, defeating an English army at Fulford.

Hearing of the landing, King Harold of England force-marched his army to the north in a few days and met Hardrada's force at Stamford Bridge on the river Derwent. Harold arrived so quickly that his army took the thousands of Norwegians by surprise. The English overpowered the contingent guarding the bridge across the Derwent and poured across the river to attack.

The battle was a fierce one. The Vikings rallied, with Hardrada leading by example, but then the Norwegian king was struck in the throat by an English arrow and died at once. Tostig took up the Viking banner and refused his brother's proposal of a truce. In vain, Harold even offered Tostig, through an emissary, a third of his kingdom: 'Your brother sends you greetings. He offers you peace and all of Northumbria.' Fighting was resumed and the Norwegians were defeated with great slaughter. Tostig was one of the rebels to die.

It was becoming obvious to the leaders of subsidiary forces everywhere that they could exert a considerable influence on a battle by the manner in which they deployed their troops, even if this sometimes meant circumspectly galloping away from the combat.

In 1071, the armies of the Christian Byzantine Empire were defeated by the nomadic Seljuk Turks at the Battle of Manzikert. As a result, the Turks occupied the area of Anatolia, which is now known as Turkey. The Byzantine defeat was largely due to the desertion of one of its generals, Andronicus Ducas.

The Byzantine Emperor Romanus IV Diogenes was trapped with his army by the Turks in a valley near Manzikert, in what is now eastern Turkey. He called upon his reserves to come to his aid. The Byzantine reserves were commanded by the ambitious Andronicus Ducas, a general fiercely jealous of the Emperor Romanus. He realised that if he were to withdraw from the field with his army, not only might Romanus be killed but, in addition, Ducas would be able to get safely back to Constantinople to conspire to seize the vacant Byzantine throne.

At once Ducas gave the order to retire, setting a conspicuous example by spurring his mount from the field. As he headed for Constantinople he took care, a trifle prematurely in the opinion of some, to let everyone know en route that Romanus had been defeated.

Upon his return to safety Ducas joined in the plotting for power with a will. Emperor Romanus was captured by the Turks and ransomed for a huge sum. After a time the unfortunate emperor was released into the care of the unfeeling Ducas and died soon afterwards. The Seljuk Turks continued their advance and occupied and settled in Anatolia. The once powerful Byzantine Empire was reduced to its European component and a narrow strip of land along the Bosphorus.

The actions of would-be deserters were becoming less important to commanders, but the movements of whole units, plotted in advance by their chiefs, from one side to another, were about to become an important component in the strategy of war. While individual deserters continued to trouble their leaders, mass defections could affect the courses of whole battles and even campaigns.

4

QUICK OR DEAD

Yon men will win all or die. None will flee for fear of death.
– Before the Battle of Bannockburn in 1314, Sir Ingram de Umfraville warns King Edward II that there will be no deserters among the opposing Scots

It was bad enough when members of the rank and file deserted, but another bane of the lives of military commanders was noble and well-placed followers who took their military commitments lightly and went off on in groups or on their own whenever the fancy took them.

During the Middle Ages, a nobleman-deserter responsible for the humiliation of a king was Piers Gaveston, a favourite of King Edward II of England and often regarded as a bad influence on the monarch. Gaveston, the son of a Gascon knight, had been a playmate of Edward II's from an early age and their increasingly close relationship was regarded by his father Edward I's strictly heterosexual noblemen as decidedly unhealthy.

In 1306, Gaveston and Prince Edward accompanied King Edward I on his campaign against Robert the Bruce in Scotland. The monarch was uneasy at the prospect.

Finding enough troops with which to march over the border had always been a problem. In 1299, Edward I had been so outraged by the rate of desertions when he strove to raise an army to go north, that he instructed all local officials to imprison anyone who refused to join this army. Such objectors were sometimes left to languish in captivity for long periods.

During the 1306 campaign, winter quarters were established at

Lanercost. Soon many of the noblemen in the army grew bored with the lack of action. A number of them requested leave of absence in order to attend a great tournament in France. Unwilling to deplete his force, King Edward refused to let them go. Twenty-two of the highborn supplicants promptly left the army anyway and made their way to France for the tournament. The handsome and reckless Gaveston was one of the knights among their number.

The furious monarch ordered that the lands of all the deserting knights be confiscated. Later he relented and returned their estates, except in the case of Gaveston, already in Edward's black books. In 1307, Piers Gaveston was exiled.

In the same year, Edward I died. On his deathbed he made his heir swear never to allow Piers Gaveston back into the country, but as soon as Edward II was crowned he sent for his friend. Gaveston was created Earl of Cornwall. He was even made Regent when Edward II left for France. However, he antagonised the barons to such an extent that eventually they seized and executed him.

Kings and princes have been as ready to desert as their lowliest subjects if the situation seemed dangerous enough or some political award was in the offing. With Robert the Bruce continuously defying the overlordship of England, in 1314 King Edward II of England invaded Scotland to assert his country's supremacy over the border. The English were decisively defeated at the Battle of Bannockburn and Edward fled in ignominy.

Edward II's first intention was to relieve the besieged Stirling Castle, whose English defenders had agreed to surrender to the Scots if they were not reinforced by Midsummer's Day. Robert the Bruce intercepted the English Army by positioning most of his force on a mile-long front along a plateau above the river Bannockburn and a muddy valley. He was protected by a marsh on his left and a forest on the right. The Scottish leader further guarded his troops with a series of pits three feet deep containing camouflaged sharpened stakes.

Bruce's 10,000 men waited for the arrival of Edward with 3,000 heavy horses, 5,000 bowmen and 15,000 foot soldiers. The English force struggled through the heavy mud and laboriously built a bridge over the river, before resting for the night.

The following morning Edward gave the order for his cavalry to charge. Bruce unmasked his sharpened stakes and many of the English horses and their riders were impaled on them. The Scots then charged in their turn on foot. The massive English force was suddenly in a state of chaos. Many men were killed underfoot by the retreat of the surviving English cavalry. A premature order was given for the English archers to fire. The resulting shower of arrows killed as many Englishmen as it did Scots. Hundreds of the fleeing invaders were drowned in the river. The troops at the rear could not get through the retreating advance guard to strike a blow at the enemy.

Suddenly, a hastily formed group of Scottish non-combatants, including cooks, grooms and even priests, charged at the English from one side, issuing wild cries. Edward thought that a fresh Scottish army was attacking him and lost his composure. Believing that all was lost, he turned his horse and fled from the field, abandoning his men. He was followed by a guard of fifteen noblemen and a small detachment of cavalrymen. In their haste, the retreating men left behind much treasure and the Great Seal of England. Edward reached what he thought would be the sanctuary of Stirling Castle but was refused admission by the governor, who explained reasonably enough that he was on the point of surrendering to the advancing Scots.

Resuming his flight, the exasperated English monarch realised that he was being pursued by a determined and armed Scottish party, under the command of Sir James Douglas. The now panic-stricken Englishmen had to ride desperately for forty more miles before they reached the safety of the castle of Dunbar, held by the Earl of March, a sympathiser with the English cause. Edward skulked behind the castle walls for a couple of days before he escaped to safety in a fishing vessel. As a result of their defeat at Bannockburn, the English were forced to recognise Scottish independence.

All over the world some leaders continued to flee from the enemy simply because they were frightened. One of these was Philip, the

Duke of Orléans and brother of King John II of France. Philip joined his brother against the English at the Battle of Poitiers in 1356, but lost his nerve at a crucial moment and fled with his army without having struck a blow, leaving havoc in his wake and a gaping hole in King John's defences.

A large-scale desertion without even engaging the foe, and led by such a prominent figure, caused a great deal of comment. It was to figure in the plans of other ambitious would-be leaders and led to considerable scrutiny of what Philip had actually done on the battlefield.

Edward, the Black Prince, the son of Edward II, had invaded France and advanced inland, slaughtering and looting. King John II of France hurried to meet the invader and intercepted the English close to Poitiers. The French were superior numerically but attacked on a very narrow front between thick hedges and marshland, thus nullifying their advantage.

English archers staved off several French cavalry charges, causing John II to order many of his horsemen to dismount and charge in an infantry onslaught. Their initial assault was led by the Dauphin, the 19-year-old son of the king. There was some fierce fighting, but the French could not penetrate the English line and withdrew.

Meanwhile, the Duke of Orléans had been waiting with his force to make the second thrust. When Orléans saw the Dauphin retiring to regroup, he assumed that the battle had been lost. In sheer panic he turned and fled, his men following. The contingent had not struck a blow or lost a man. Greatly encouraged, the English charged. John II fought bravely but was forced to surrender with his other son, Philip. More than 2,000 Frenchmen were killed.

While starting an uprising could be a relatively straightforward affair, maintaining its impetus was much more complicated, as the English rebel Jack Cade discovered. In 1450, he entered London in triumph at the head of a band of followers, protesting about the loss of English possessions in France and the general corruption of the administration of King Henry VI. Cade's men captured James Fiennes the Lord High Treasurer and executed him.

Thinking on their feet, King Henry's officials persuaded Cade's retinue to abandon their leader, promising the rebels a royal pardon and a sympathetic hearing for their grievances. The men promptly deserted their leader in droves, leaving Cade almost alone. He was declared an outlaw: 'The said Captain was tried and proclaimed a traitor by the name of Jack Cade, in divers places of London, and also in Southwark, with many more, that what man might or would bring the same Jack Cade quick or dead, should have 1,000 marks.'

Cade was arrested in Lewes and a skirmish ensued in which he was mortally wounded.

An ambitious deserter during the Wars of the Roses was a Kentish squire named Henry Lovelace. He fought for the Yorkists at the Battle of Wakefield but was taken prisoner. After a time he was released and rejoined the Yorkist force. However, it seems probable that he came to an agreement with his Lancastrian captors during his period of imprisonment to defect.

During the Second Battle of St Albans in 1461, Lovelace was as good as his word. He suddenly took his men over to Queen Margaret's side, leaving a vital gap in the defences of the Earl of Warwick, who was commanding the Yorkist army. Warwick was forced to withdraw from the field. The deserter Lovelace was well rewarded by the Lancastrians for his treachery although his ambition to become the Earl of Kent was not fulfilled.

Other leaders who put self-interest first were Lord Thomas Stanley and his brother, Sir William Stanley. In August 1485, Henry Tudor, supported by France, landed in Wales with 2,000 French mercenaries and a few Lancastrian noblemen. He marched into England, gathering support en route. Richard III marched to greet him. They met close to Market Bosworth at Ambion Hill and the ensuing battle lasted for two hours. The Duke of Norfolk, leading Richard's vanguard, was killed early on, but Richard fought bravely, while Henry Tudor stood off a little way from the heat of the combat.

Richard III was depending on the Stanleys, whose combined force was estimated at about 6,000 men. Both noblemen had promised to support the king but he suspected, with some justification, that the brothers had also been in secret negotiations with Henry.

As the battle raged, William and Thomas Stanley took up positions a short way from the action. No one could be certain which side the thus far inactive brothers were supporting. In one desperate last foray, Richard galloped down from the high ground, trying to engage Henry Tudor in personal combat. The small group accompanying him even succeeded in killing the challenger's standard-bearer.

For a moment it looked as if Richard's brave intervention was going to turn the course of the battle. It was then that William Stanley made his move. He ordered his waiting men to attack the monarch. The ferocity of their charge drove back the king's forces. Richard III was killed and Henry was triumphant.

Henry VII showed his gratitude to William Stanley by making him Lord Chamberlain and a Knight of the Garter. Lord Thomas Stanley was created Earl of Derby. However, it seems as if treachery clung to each brother like a cloak. Ten years later William Stanley was executed for supporting the uprising led by the youth Perkin Warbeck.

In Elizabethan England, it was relatively easy to raise a company of soldiers. The trick lay in keeping the unit together once the troops had received their signing-on bounties. In 1592, it was reported: 'Many soldiers of a company levied in Hertfordshire have deserted their captain without leave ... These men now lurk in very riotous and disordered sort in the remote places in the county.'

The Earl of Essex also had difficulty in keeping his troops together, partly because he spent too much time away from them pleasure-bound. The handsome and charismatic Robert Devereux,

Earl of Essex, was a favourite of Queen Elizabeth I, but this was to change dramatically

He was born in Herefordshire and educated at Cambridge University. As a young man Devereux fought with distinction against Spain in the Low Countries but lost favour with Elizabeth when, without royal leave, he accompanied Francis Drake on an expedition to Portugal and then, also without the Queen's knowledge, married the widow of poet and soldier Sir Philip Sidney. However, he soon re-entered the monarch's good graces when he commanded the English forces fighting against the Spanish in 1591.

But even here Devereux proved too restless to be a good commander and was constantly getting bored and riding off, causing the exasperated Queen Elizabeth to issue her captain a public reprimand:

> The Council very sharply rebuke the Earl of Essex, for the Queen greatly dislikes that he left his army without any head except a Sergeant-Major and journeyed to the king [of France], especially since she understands by letters from the French king that this journey was made voluntarily without any request from him. She therefore condemns him of rashness, reminding him that the purpose of his voyage was the recovery of Rouen and Newhaven.

Devereux did his volatile best to keep in his monarch's graces, writing in one of his ingratiating letters:

> The two windows in the office of Your Majesty will be the poles of my hemisphere, where, until Your Majesty decides that I am unworthy of his paradise, I will not fall like a star, but I will be absorbed as vapour the sun, which elevates me to a vertex.

Six years later, Devereux lost more ground when he failed to destroy the Spanish fleet on an expedition to the Azores. By this time Elizabeth was beginning to think that her favourite was growing too arrogant. In 1599 she sent him to Ireland as Lord Lieutenant upon the outbreak of the Roman Catholic Irish Rebellion there.

He landed in Ireland with a force thousands of men strong, but found himself constantly outwitted by Hugh O'Neill, Earl of Tyrone and the leader of the Irish rebellion, and his officers, who continually retreated before the cumbersome English advance and then launched lightning raids against the invaders. The outmanoeuvred Devereux was forced to deplete his force by leaving English garrisons all along the way.

Devereux was infuriated by the attacks of the 'rogues and naked beggars', as he termed the Irish irregulars, and soon was tormented almost beyond endurance by his inability to get to grips with them. He was also upset at being so far from the centre of matters at Queen Elizabeth's court and unable to exert any influence there. In addition, he knew that he was being laughed at in London by his enemies for his lack of success against the Irish.

After being defeated in battle south of Arklow on the River Clonnough, Devereux hastily concluded an unsatisfactory truce with the Irish, without consulting Queen Elizabeth. An hour before he left Ireland, in a fit of pique, Devereux handed over command of the army to the Earl of Ormond. Accompanied by his personal household and a number of officers and troops, he took a ship back to London, abandoning his army.

At first Devereux was greeted kindly by the monarch but then suddenly he was arrested and tried on charges of contempt and disobedience. He was deprived of his estates and public offices and placed under house arrest.

This was all too much for someone of Devereux's fiery temperament. He tried to raise a rebellion in the streets of London, hoping to force Queen Elizabeth to dismiss some of his adversaries from her council. He was arrested, tried for high treason and condemned to death. On 25 February 1601, Robert Devereux, Earl of Essex, was executed at the Tower of London.

The tried and tested pretext of desertion was now, and had been for some time, an established method of gaining information about the enemy, or even a prelude to launching an attack. During the Battle of Kosovo in 1389, the armies of the Ottoman Empire, led by Sultan Murad I, invaded Serbian-ruled Kosovo and fought an alliance of Serbia, Bosnia, Bulgaria and other nations, commanded by Prince Lazar.

A Serb, Miloš Obilich (or Obilić), believed that if he could get to Sultan Murad before the battle started and kill him, the Turks might be dismayed enough to retreat. He rode to the Turkish camp and said that he was a leading knight in the Serb Army and that he was willing to desert and fight for the Turks.

Obilich was taken to the tent of Sultan Murad. He threw himself at the feet of the Turkish leader, as if to kiss them. Then, from beneath his robes he produced a knife and stabbed Murad in the stomach, killing him at once. The Sultan's guards hacked the Serb to death on the spot.

Other versions of the story claimed that Obilich had been lying wounded on the ground when the Sultan passed and launched his attack from there, or that he had taken part in a raid on the Turkish camp and, heedless of his own safety, had hacked his way to Murad's camp and then slain Murad.

Whichever version was true, the Turks still engaged the Serbs and their allies. For a time it looked as if the Serbs might drive the Ottomans back. But the Turks were fighting under the command of Murad's son, Bayezit, who rallied his troops and defeated the Serbs with great slaughter. Bayezit ordered the killing of the Serb leader, Prince Lazar, to avenge the death of his father. He left so many Serb corpses on the battlefield that hundreds of blackbirds came to devour them. Today the battle area is known as the Field of the Blackbirds. This defeat ended the power of the Serbs, who were forced to accept the overlordship of the Turks and came under Ottoman rule.

There were so many desertions in seventeenth-century England that the death penalty was often used as a deterrent for straying troops; any soldier arrested three times for desertion was almost certain to be condemned to death. Many deserters caught in the London area were shot in Hyde Park. Often the firing squads, designed to be a public deterrent to deserters, were also made up of men who had deserted, to impress upon them the likely penalty if they left their posts again. Such warnings were not very effective. More and more, reluctant soldiers were being conscripted on both sides during the English Civil War and few were averse to leaving if the opportunity presented itself. Almost a third of foot soldiers on both the Royalist and Puritan sides left without permission.

Sometimes the best that a deserter could hope for was to be captured by the other side. Most forces were so short of men that they would accept stray trained soldiers, no matter what their backgrounds or previous allegiances. Sometimes, too, the punishment of death was only decreed reluctantly and selectively. In August 1600, a report stated:

> At the late Assizes in Essex six soldiers that were levied for the service in Ireland and did run away were condemned. Although the least offender deserveth to suffer death, and her Majesty desireth rather the reformation of the abuse than the severe punishment of the delinquents, nevertheless that some example may be made it is thought meet that the sheriff shall take two of the most lewd disposition of those six whose offence is most notorious and least show repentance, whereof one shall be executed in some principal town in the county, and the other to be sent unto Stratford the bow, to be executed near unto the bridge.

The death penalty was seldom used in the case of aristocrats, which proved to be lucky for the Earl of Newcastle during the English Civil War. An extremely wealthy landowner, horseman and patron of the arts, who had written books on riding and swordsmanship, William Cavendish, Earl of Newcastle, once spent £20,000 entertaining King Charles I, and on another occasion lent his monarch £10,000. It was said that altogether he had spent some £700,000 in support of the Royalist cause. During the Civil War he was appointed commander of the Royalist forces in the north. In 1643, he defeated the Parliamentary Army at the Battle of Adwalton Moor. A chivalrous if temperamental man, Newcastle released the captured wife of the Roundhead Army commander Sir Thomas Fairfax and sent her back safely to her husband.

Newcastle then had to contend with an invading Scottish army of 20,000 men and retreated to York, where he was besieged until Prince Rupert came to his rescue. Rupert and Newcastle engaged the Parliamentary force at Marston Moor on 2 July 1644. By this time Newcastle, who was against engaging three armies of the Parliamentarians in open conflict, had fallen out with Rupert and arrived late for the battle, although he fought bravely when he arrived with his regiment, known as the 'Whitecoats', most of whom were wiped out.

Seeing that the engagement was lost, Newcastle and his second-in-command, Lord Eythin, fled from the battlefield to Scarborough. There he announced his intention of abandoning King Charles and leaving for the Continent. Both Rupert and the king begged Newcastle not to desert the Royalist cause, but the humiliated former commander declared, 'I will go to Holland. I will not endure the laughter of the court!' Newcastle sailed for the Continent with a considerable entourage, including his two sons and his brother. Other lesser Royalists followed his example and defected to the Continent in his wake. Charles I surrendered to Parliament, was tried and executed.

For some years the Earl of Newcastle wandered around Europe, living at different times in Hamburg, Paris and Rotterdam, before settling in Antwerp. In 1660, he returned to England at the Restoration, at the same time as Charles II, who created him first Duke of Newcastle. However, his estates and much of his fortune were never restored to him fully, perhaps because of his defection after Marston Moor. He lived thereafter as a semi-recluse.

Throughout his exile, Newcastle's second wife, Margaret Lucas, had stood by her husband; in times of trouble true friends and lovers can often show their true colours. Newcastle certainly appreciated that at least his desertion had revealed the strength of his marriage. When she died in 1673, he had engraved upon her tomb in Westminster Abbey:

> She was most virtuous and a loving and careful wife and was with her lord all the time of his banishment and miseries, and when he came home never parted from him in his solitary retirement.

The spate of desertions during the Civil War was rooted in a number of things. Most troops and many of their commanders were completely untrained and had no idea what to expect of military life. Men fled after they had been defeated in battle or because they had not been paid or properly equipped. Some left because they had heard that their own homes were being threatened by troops on the other side. Most units were formed locally; the men in them knew each other well and could be persuaded to leave their posts in groups. By 1643–44, the Royalists had been forced to conscript troops, leading to much disgruntlement in the ranks. Administration on both sides was chaotic; often the numbers of deserters could only be guessed at, although by the end of the Civil War it was estimated that most units were at only 50 per cent of their full strength due to casualties, disease and desertion.

5

'FOLLOW THE FLAGSHIP!'

Sir, hang half a dozen of them and throw them into the sea!
– Martín Alonso Pinzón advises Christopher Columbus on what to
do with incipient mutineers and deserters. Later, Pinzón deserted as
well, abandoning Columbus to sail in search of gold.

Soldiers had been deserting in large numbers since the beginning
of recorded time. As seafarers began making voyages to uncharted
lands, the number of seamen taking to desertion increased in similar proportion.

By the fifteenth and sixteenth centuries the Age of Discovery was
well under way. The Bristol-based Venetians John and Sebastian
Cabot discovered Labrador, Columbus made his voyage to the
West Indies, Cabral attempted to enter the Indian Ocean and was
blown by storms as far as the coast of Brazil. Cortés conquered
the Aztec Empire and led the way to the discovery of Mexico,
while Vasco da Gama rounded the Cape of Good Hope on his way
to India.

These voyages in tiny ships were eventful, dangerous and
extremely uncomfortable. While the admirals achieved glory
and, oftentimes, wealth, ordinary seamen and junior officers,
lured initially by thoughts of riches and adventure, were less well
rewarded, living in cramped conditions and existing on rotting
food, with the ever-present danger of sudden injury or death. They
followed obsessed commanders and explorers like Vasco de Balboa,
whose only instructions to the captains of his tiny fleet were 'Follow
the flagship and ask no questions!' Sometimes the thoughts of these
seamen strayed longingly to the prospect of turning their smaller

craft around or striking out on their own for the safety of the nearest available shore. It was small wonder that all the pioneers of exploration by sea and land had their problems with deserters.

Marco Polo was only seventeen in 1271 when he set out on foot for China with his two uncles but he was soon to have his first encounter with desertion. Two teaching friars from the Dominican order who accompanied them, Niccolo de Vincenze and Guillaume de Tripoli, grew discouraged and left the expedition before it had even reached the extreme borders of Armenia. Their decampment was, as Marco Polo succinctly put it, 'through fear'.

Hernán Cortés, leader of the Spanish expedition to the Aztec Empire in Mexico in 1519, was so well aware of the dangers of desertion among his 600 men that he had the four boats of his expedition drawn up onto the sand and burnt, thus adding a new phrase to the language, 'burning boats', for making sure that there could be no retreat on the part of his apprehensive followers.

A few years later, in 1526, another Spanish explorer, Francisco Pizarro, found himself on a beach off an island off Panama with the starving remnants of his crew. In an act seldom heard of in his time he gave them the choice of whether to desert him or not. He had heard of a great unknown land to the south full of gold and silver. The captain's men begged him to take them home in their battered vessel. Pizarro drew a line in the sand with his sword. 'There lies Peru and its riches,' he told his followers. 'Here, Panama and its poverty. Decide, each man, what most becomes a valiant Castilian.' Thirteen men opted to follow their leader. The rest opted to try to make their way back to Spain. Pizarro established friendly relations with the inhabitants of the coast of Peru and returned five years later with a properly equipped expedition.

There were no such choices for the Arctic explorer Henry Hudson. After a very hard voyage aboard the ship *Discovery* in his search for the Northwest Passage to China in 1611, his crew mutinied under the leadership of Robert Juet and set Hudson, his son and several seamen adrift in a small boat, never to be seen again. The *Discovery* got home, but Juet and other ringleaders of the desertion died on the voyage back. The surviving crew members were arrested but their contradictory evidence so obfuscated events that they were later released.

Ambitious underlings were responsible for many desertions during this period. On a voyage hundreds of miles from home it was eminently possible to seize a vessel from the master, desert a cause and sail off on a completely different expedition.

The most famous of all the great voyages of discovery, that of Christopher Columbus in 1492, set the tone for much that was to follow, by providing its own defector, even if he did later deny the charge. Martín Alonso Pinzón, a wealthy Spaniard, captained one of the three ships in the 1492 expedition led by Christopher Columbus, which discovered the West Indies. Pinzón, a good seaman and brave fighter but idiosyncratic and stubborn, was an experienced seaman and pilot when he was selected to captain the *Pinta* to accompany the *Niña* and Columbus's *Santa María* on the voyage to the New World. The *Pinta* was a small, three-masted vessel of 70 tons, 17 metres long and 5 metres across the beam. It had a crew of twenty-six. Her name means 'the painted one', a reference to seafront whores.

The fleet, backed by King Ferdinand and Queen Isabella, left Spain on 3 August 1492 looking for a westerly route to Cathay, or China. The obdurate Pinzón began to annoy Columbus almost from the start. The admiral respected his captain as a navigator but knew that Pinzón was far too much of an individualist to work in a team. Two months after they had set sail, Pinzón persuaded Columbus to change course and sail in a more south-westerly direction. If the fleet had adhered to the admiral's original setting, the three ships would probably have landed on the mainland of North America, not the islands of the West Indies.

Nevertheless, it was Martin Pinzón who first sighted land and claimed the pension promised for life by Ferdinand and Isabella to the initial member of the expedition to see an unknown coastline. The explorers landed and named their discovery San Salvador.

The three ships spent several weeks sailing among the islands of the West Indies. Then, off the coast of Cuba, to the great fury of Christopher Columbus, without permission Martin Pinzón in the *Pinta* suddenly sailed away from the other two vessels. Pinzón had been complaining about the state of one of the masts on his vessel, causing Columbus to grumble in his journal:

If Pinzón had exerted himself as much to provide himself with a new masthead in the Indies, where there are so many fine trees, as he had in running away in the hope of loading up his vessel with gold, they would not have laboured under that inconvenience.

There was no doubt in the admiral's mind that his Spanish captain had been seduced by tales from the islanders of great deposits of gold to be discovered on some of the islands in the group. There was nothing to be done about the abrupt desertion, so he continued on the voyage with the *Santa María* and the *Niña*, finally anchoring off the coast of what is today Haiti. A sudden storm wrecked the *Santa María*, and Columbus and his crew had to transfer to the *Niña*.

There were now too many men for the one vessel, so Columbus left a number of volunteers ashore until he could return for them on a future voyage. On 14 January 1493, the *Niña* sailed for home. Two days later Columbus encountered the wayward *Pinta* and her captain.

The admiral ignored the feeble excuses presented by the recalcitrant Pinzón, realising that the chances of the expedition getting safely home would be much greater if both vessels sailed together. The *Niña* and the *Pinta* travelled in convoy for almost a month and then were separated again in storm off the Azores. Columbus's 'Journal' recounts: 'Then the *Pinta*, of which Martín Alonso Pinzón was captain, began to drift also, but she disappeared very soon, although all through the night the Admiral made signals with lights to her.'

The suspicious Columbus could not be sure whether the *Pinta* had foundered in the bad weather or whether Martin Pinzón, knowing that his vessel was the faster of the two, had sped on for Spain to bring home first the news of their discoveries. Columbus and the *Niña* reached Spain on 15 March 1493. Pinzón and the *Pinta* arrived at the same anchorage only a few hours later.

Columbus, now famous, made three more trips back to the new continent. Martín Alonso Pinzón died in 1493, the year in which he arrived back from the epic voyage of discovery.

Some excursions were not as successful as others and Pinzón was not the only captain of a vessel to abandon his admiral. Another was an Englishman, John Winter. Winter was one of the sea captains who set out from Plymouth on 15 November 1577 with Francis Drake on the voyage which was to end with the first circumnavigation of the world.

The purpose of the voyage had been to harry Spanish settlements along the Pacific seaboard. Drake sailed in the *Pelican*, later renamed the *Golden Hind*, while Winter was in command of the smaller 80-ton *Elizabeth*. There were also three even smaller vessels. The voyage was hard and it was September 1578 before Drake finally entered the Pacific.

In October, the vessels were battered by a great storm. Drake ordered the remaining vessels to anchor in an inlet to the north of the Straits of Magellan, before a powerful gust of wind snapped the *Golden Hind*'s cable, sending his flagship careering helplessly to the south.

When dawn broke the following day, Winter saw that the *Elizabeth* was alone in the inlet. He sailed back into the Magellan Straits and anchored in a large bay there. For two days his men kept large fires burning in the hope that Drake's ship might see the signal.

Greatly disheartened, Winter sailed farther back along the straits. He waited there for three weeks and then, believing Drake to have perished with his men, he headed back for England. It was later a matter of speculation whether the captain had been forced by his men to return, or if he had instigated the idea. The return voyage was almost as perilous as the outward trip but eventually the *Elizabeth* limped back into Ilfracombe.

John Winter faced considerable criticism for abandoning his admiral, even though he had not unreasonably assumed his leader to be dead. Drake achieved glory with his voyage round the world, arriving back at Plymouth in 1580. In the following year he was knighted on board the *Golden Hind* by Queen Elizabeth I. Winter's claim on immortality was less dramatic. He returned to the West Country with a hold full of slender evergreen trees he had found in the rain forests of South America. The local inhabitants had informed him correctly that the plants of the tree could be used for stomach problems and as a cure and a preventative for scurvy. As a result Captain Winter had the *Drimys winteri* named after him.

By now even soldiers were beginning to desert during their overseas voyages and in the sixteenth century the authorities were concerned by the number of men being transported across the English Channel and deserting on landing in considerable numbers.

> It is credibly reported that, notwithstanding the Council's orders for the restraint of such soldiers as without passport draw themselves from the service of the French king in Normandy, above 200 men of strong and able bodies are landed at Dover and the places near without passport.

Such deserters almost invariably hurried inland to avoid being trapped by press gangs and forced to serve on vessels setting out on the increasing number of voyages of exploration being conducted. Some soldiers, however, were serving too far from home to risk deserting. Some bided their time until they found a more hospitable environment in which to take their leave.

Because of the range of the sea voyages being undertaken and the consequent colonisation and garrisoning of discovered lands, soldiers in the sixteenth century were being conveyed over ever further distances, with the concomitant problem of a lengthy journey home should they wish to desert while overseas.

One of the first soldiers to solve this problem in his own epic manner was Fernando Lopez, an officer in the Portuguese Army. Lopez deserted at Goa while in action against the Indian force commanded by Rasul Khan, in 1512. Eventually, the Portuguese force, under Alfonso de Albuquerque, defeated the Indian Army and Rasul Khan sued for peace. As one of the conditions, he handed Lopez back to the Portuguese along with several other deserters.

De Albuquerque had promised that he would not execute the deserters, but still he exacted a heavy recompense. Each absconder had his right hand, the thumb of the left hand, his nose and his ears severed. Still uncertain as to whether he might eventually face the death penalty, in 1515 Lopez stowed away on a ship bound for Europe. He was discovered but allowed to work his passage home. The longer the voyage took, the more worried Lopez became. With his horrendous disfigurements he would easily be recognised as a deserter when he reached Portugal, and might yet face further punishment.

Accordingly, when the ship put in at St Helena, an island ten miles long and seven miles across and over a thousand miles from the coast of West Africa, Lopez went ashore with a party of seamen, ran away and hid. The sailors searched in vain for him but, understanding the reason for Lopez's second desertion, they left the ex-soldier a barrel of biscuits out of the kindness of their hearts, some salted beef, dried fish and a few items of clothing. Before they sailed away they even lit a fire for Lopez, which he could keep replenished on his lonely vigil.

St Helena, a volcanic island, rose almost sheer from the water. Lopez lived there on his own in a cave for a year before another vessel put in. Afraid recapture, he secreted himself until the ship had left. When he returned he saw that the crew, having noticed signs of habitation, had left him some food and a live cockerel.

It became a custom over the decade that Fernando Lopez lived on St Helena for visiting vessels to leave food for the hermit – although no one ever saw him. His cave became something of a tourist attraction for visiting sailors, who would travel in groups from their ships to see signs of the castaway's life.

Eventually the fame of the recluse of St Helena spread. King
John III had a letter dropped off at the island, promising Lopez
sanctuary if he would agree to return to Portugal. In the end the
Portuguese deserter was betrayed by the second inhabitant to settle
at St Helena. This was a Javanese youth who had also escaped from
a ship putting in at the island. When the next ship arrived, in 1525,
the boy gave himself up and also showed the captain where the
famous hermit was hiding.

The captain of the vessel tried to persuade Lopez to end his ten-
year tenure in the wilderness. Lopez promised to think the matter
over and eventually agreed to leave St Helena and return to Portugal.

Soon Lopez found that he hated living in the busy metropolis
of Lisbon and begged to be sent back to his island castle. King
John agreed to his request and Lopez was once more transported
into exile. On his second sojourn there he was no longer a recluse.
He showed himself willingly to visiting vessels and engaged in
conversations with their crews. In return they presented him with
stores, plants and a supply of domestic animals, including ducks,
hens, pigs and goats. One visitor said that the former deserter had
succeeded in turning a few acres of ground into a model of Noah's
Ark. Fernando Lopez lived contentedly on the island until his
death in 1545.

It was not long before European vessels were sailing even further
than India, not always with the complete approval of their crews.
The first European deserter of whom there is any record leaving
his ship in the distant Pacific was Gonzalo de Vigo, a seaman on
Magellan's epic voyage round the world.

De Vigo served as a cabin boy on board the *Trinidad*, Magellan's
110-ton flagship, as it sailed into the Pacific in 1520, on an expedition charged by the Spanish king to circumnavigate the world.
The trip was hazardous and before de Vigo deserted, Magellan had
already put down a mutiny and suffered the desertion of one ship
and the wreck of another. On the terrible voyage the surviving
crew members were reduced to eating rats and the broiled hides of
animals slaughtered earlier for food.

At the beginning of 1521, the *Trinidad* sighted and landed at one of the southern-most islands of the Mariana group, where the islanders stole a skiff, a small boat propelled by one oarsman, and Magellan burnt fifty of their houses in retaliation, before sailing on to Guam in the Philippine archipelago. Here Magellan was killed in a skirmish on shore.

Despite his commander's death, de Vigo was so determined not to continue with the hardships of the voyage that he stayed on shore with two other deserters and took his chances. He was surprisingly well treated by the islanders and allowed to remain. The other two seamen soon died but de Vigo settled in to island life.

He accompanied some islanders on one canoe voyage of some 450 miles. De Vigo was even given a canoe and allowed to paddle from island to island, as the fancy took him. He was picked up in 1526, five years after his desertion, when he paddled out to the *Santa Maria de la Victoria* when it put in to Guam, and was taken on board. The ship's log announced 'He came on board and was of great use to us, as he knew the language of the islands.'

Gonzalo de Vigo was then brought back to Spain, where he vanished into obscurity.

By the end of the sixteenth century, more and more adventurous souls were establishing colonies in remote parts of the world as developments in seamanship and navigation encouraged vessels to travel farther. They were not always well treated by those in charge of their well-being. One example of this was Pedro Sarmiento de Gamboa, a renowned Spanish navigator and explorer, who was placed in charge of a fortress in the Straits of Magellan.

In 1581, the Spanish had decided to build a small fortress to guard the entrance to the South Seas at the foot of South America. Two years later, 430 men, women and children arrived from Spain to colonise the outpost.

The commander of the new colony was Sarmiento, a proud, quick-tempered but courageous man. The colonists soon discovered that their new home was a storm-tossed, inhospitable place, already occupied by native Indians. Their first fortress was soon deemed poorly located, so Sarmiento led a 300-mile march to a new site, while the remaining colonists travelled by ship.

Sarmiento named the new colony Rey Don Felipe and set to work to build a fort and houses there. It was little better than their first landfall. The Indians continued to attack, the soil was poor and the winters freezing. Sarmiento had to put down an uprising and execute the ringleader.

The circumstances surrounding the leader's consequent desertion are unclear. He sailed in the colony's only ship, the *María*, saying that he was going to visit the people who had been left behind at the initial settlement. A storm caught the *María* and the next that is heard of Pedro Sarmiento is him sailing into the harbour at Rio de Janeiro in July 1584.

It is possible that the Spaniard was driven off course. However, many of his contemporaries felt that a seaman of his skill and experience should have been able to ride it out and remain with his colonists, instead of sailing thousands of miles to the north in search of safety.

It may be significant that Sarmiento made no effort to return to his colony. He sent a number of supply ships to the straits, but none of them got through to their destination. Most of the colonists died miserably of disease and starvation. One of them, Tomé Hernandez, was picked up on the coast by a British privateer under the command of Thomas Cavendish. Hernandez said that inland there were some colonists still alive. Years later he swore a declaration before a notary public, giving an account of Cavendish's actions that day: 'The General then desired this witness to tell the other two soldiers to go to the rest of their people and that for his part he would come to embark them all and that he would wait for them.'

However, Cavendish hastened to catch a fair wind that had sprung up and sailed away before the survivors could be brought down to the shore. Hernandez managed to scramble on board and sail with the pirates. Cavendish never returned but perhaps appropriately renamed the settlement Port Famine (now Puerto del Hambre).

Sarmiento's adventures were not yet over. He was captured at sea by a fleet headed by Sir Walter Raleigh but released on the orders of Queen Elizabeth I. On his way home he was then taken by French Huguenots and imprisoned for a time. After a period of writing and reflection he was made admiral of a Spanish expedition to the Indies, but died at sea.

In 1595, when a Spanish fleet invaded Cornwall and razed Mousehole, it was guided by a renegade English deserter, a mysterious Captain Richard Burley said to have come from Weymouth. He sold his services as a guide to his former home area to the Spaniards and took a full part in the attack, but distinguished himself when the Spaniards were about to burn a Protestant church. The deserter assured the soldiers that to his certain knowledge Mass had been celebrated in the building in the past and for that reason it deserved to be saved. The Spaniards concurred and sailed back to France, leaving the church untouched. They took with them Captain Burley, who disappeared from recorded history as rapidly as he had appeared.

The history of desertions at sea followed the same general pattern as those on land. Their causes varied from disillusionment with one's lot to a desire to escape danger. But many maritime desertions also introduced the concept of loyalty as a factor to be taken into account by stressed and bewildered seamen called upon to make decisions about their actions. Should they follow their leaders blindly into the unknown or go back?

On Pizarro's expedition, thirteen men remained with him on his quest for Peru, while the remainder sailed home. Pinzón, on the other hand, had no scruples about leaving Christopher Columbus and making his own bid for glory and gold. John Winter probably genuinely believed that his commander, Francis Drake, was dead before he headed back to England. The reasons for Pedro Sarmiento abandoning his settlement in the Straits of Magellan have never been ascertained.

In each of these cases, opinions were divided among some of the seamen on the voyages as to which course of action they should take. Edward Cliffe, serving on John Winter's vessel *Elizabeth*, summed up the feelings of many after their captain had told them that they were returning home because he feared that the admiral of the expedition, Francis Drake, was dead and that the prevailing winds were too strong for them to continue. Cliffe made it clear that most of the men on board were 'abandoning our voyage by compulsion of Mr Winter, sore against the will of the mariners'.

6

VAGRANT SOLDIERS

Did you ever hear told of that hero
Bold Nevison it was his name?
And he rode about like a brave hero,
And by that he gained great fame.
– 'Bold Nevison', ballad, Anon.

Throughout the seventeenth and eighteenth centuries, as armies continued to expand and grow more professional in their organisation and administration of discipline, so did resentful ordinary soldiers carry on deserting in an increasing torrent of bloody-minded departures. Most of these foot soldiers were never named and have left no mark outside yellowing regimental records. Others, however, later achieved fame in other walks of life and their earlier flights may the more easily be traced.

For example, in 1685 the 25-year-old Daniel Defoe, later to become famous as the author of *Robinson Crusoe* and *A Journal of the Plague Year* and sometimes regarded as the father of the English novel, fled from the Battle of Sedgemoor after the Duke of Monmouth's army had invaded the West Country in an attempt to depose King James II. The rebellion was put down with great slaughter, Monmouth was caught and executed and Defoe was fortunate to escape with his life. He left no written account of his part in the rebellion, although local legend has it that while the writer was hiding in a cemetery close to the battlefield he found himself sheltering behind a gravestone bearing the inscription 'Robinson Crusoe', a name he noted and later used for his book.

It was certainly not difficult to join the army or navy during the run-up to the numerous Continental wars pursued by Britain, when soldiers and sailors were needed urgently. Recruiting bands scoured the country, offering cash inducements to anyone who would enlist for twenty-one years in the infantry. The lure of this money even saw the birth of professional deserters who would join up in one part of the country, take the fee and promptly desert, and then volunteer again hundreds of miles away. It was a high-risk strategy but lucrative. Any deserter who was caught had the letter D tattooed in his armpit as a brand of his previous flight.

There were no job relocation schemes for deserters. Former sailors and soldiers who had abruptly and permanently severed relationships with their former military employers had to live by their wits, and this often meant resorting to crime.

By 1591, this problem of deserters turning to crime had reached such proportions that the authorities were forced to issue a public announcement:

> A proclamation is published against vagrant soldiers, declaring that there is a common wandering abroad of a great multitude of whom the most part pretend that they have served in wars on the other side of the seas, though it is known that very many of them neither served at all, or else ran away from their service…

Fortunately for many deserters their previous military training and familiarity with horses and firearms had equipped them for at least one civilian occupation, that of a highwayman, as a member of the ironically dubbed Knights of the Road. A considerable number of deserters drifted into this perilous and usually short-lived vocation.

One of the most notorious of these was William, sometimes called John, Nevison. Before he became a renowned highwayman, Nevison had been a common thief, seducer and army deserter.

At the age of fourteen, the Pontefract-born Nevison stole a silver spoon, ten pounds in cash and a horse from his father, a steward at a local hall, and set out for the wide world. Arriving at the outskirts of London he slit the throat of his horse and buried it, in case it should be found and identified, and went to work for a brewer, before robbing his master of several hundred pounds and escaping to Holland.

Here the well-built and personable Nevison persuaded the daughter of a wealthy merchant to rob her father of a considerable sum in money and jewels, and run off with him. They were caught, the loot retrieved and Nevison was thrown into prison. Being a resourceful sort he decided to hide himself among thousands of other troops by joining the English Army in Flanders, and became a soldier in the English force under the command of the Duke of York, who was fighting the Spanish at Dunkirk.

Nevison seems to have acquitted himself well enough as a fighting man but found the discipline irksome. During the course of a few skirmishes he had accumulated a certain amount of booty, which would tide him over until he entered a new line of business. In 1659, he deserted by the simple resort of riding away from the battle-lines as fast as he could. Nevison returned to England and became a highwayman, where he soon achieved a considerable reputation for daring and even gallantry, it being claimed that he never harmed his victims. Over the course of the next few years he made a great deal of money from his thefts, so much so that a price was placed on his head and a number of bounty hunters inevitably began to search for him.

Nevison's most remarkable exploit was his almost incredible ride from Rochester to York. At about four in the morning, the highwayman believed that he had been recognised after committing a robbery at Gad's Hill near Rochester. In an effort to divert suspicion he rode over 200 miles to York, by way of Chelmsford, Cambridge and the Great North Road. Reaching York by 8 p.m., Nevison dismounted and strode into a game of bowls in which the mayor of York was partaking. Engaging the dignitary in conversation, Nevison impressed himself on the mayor's mind by laying a substantial bet on the result of the game before leaving.

When the highwayman was arrested for the Gad's Hill crime he was acquitted, because no one believed that he could have

ridden from Kent to Yorkshire in such a short time. Unfortunately
Nevison never received full credit for his feat of horsemanship. Fifty
years later, in his novel *Rookwood*, the writer Harrison Ainsworth
attributed the feat to another, lesser, highwayman, Dick Turpin.
Eventually, William Nevison was arrested at The Magpie public
house in Sandal, Wakefield. He was tried and hanged at York Castle
on 4 May 1684.

There were so many deserters on the run engaged in nefarious
activities that public warnings against sheltering them were issued
all over London:

> The Lord Mayor is required to cause verbal proclamation to be
> made throughout the City and suburbs that all victuallers, innkeep-
> ers, alehouse keepers and other having in their houses any soldier
> that has been levied shall upon severe penalties bring him forth to
> receive punishment according to the laws. Likewise, if any soldier
> hath run away from his captain or sold or pawned his armour and
> furniture, it shall be seized and the party with whom it is found
> committed to prison.

Such announcements had little effect and the deserters-cum-
highwaymen continued to do business. Like Nevison, Jack Bird, a
contemporary, also served in the army in the Low Countries. Bird
deserted from the Duke of Monmouth's forces and became a highwayman with a comparatively highly developed sense of justice and
fair play.

He was born in Stainford in Lincolnshire in 1648. Bird was
apprenticed to a baker when he left school but ran away to Lincoln
where he enlisted in the Foot Guards. He took part in the siege of
Maastricht during the Anglo-Dutch War, but considered the going
rate for a foot soldier of five pence (one groat) a day insufficient
recompense for risking his life.

Bird hid in Amsterdam with a number of other deserters of
different nationalities but was apprehended stealing a piece of silk
from a market stall. He was sentenced to a year's hard labour. Bird's

definition of hard labour was not that of his gaolers, so in order to teach him a lesson they chained him to a cistern in a cellar and turned on several taps. In order to prevent the water rising above his head, the prisoner had to pump for his life.

The deserter returned to England after his prison sentence and set himself up as a highwayman in the Kent region, achieving a great deal of publicity when he held up an eccentric aristocrat and his entourage. The earl offered to fight Bird for the sum of money he had about him. The highwayman accepted the offer but the aristocrat's chaplain intervened. His master was too old for fisticuffs, he argued. Instead he, the man of God, would take the old man's place, if Bird agreed.

By now slightly bemused by the course events were taking, but still game for anything, Bird accepted the challenge and took on the chaplain, while the earl and his servants settled down to enjoy the resultant scrap. The highwayman triumphed within fifteen minutes, and the delighted nobleman handed over his purse, which contained a meagre twenty guineas, and declared that he had received splendid value for the money.

In character to the end, Bird met his end in quixotic fashion. One night on the London Strand, the highwayman and a female companion knocked down a passer-by and stole his money. The woman was soon caught and subsequently sent to Newgate Prison. Instead of thanking his good fortune, Bird boldly went to Newgate to negotiate or bribe his accomplice out of prison. Unfortunately he encountered an honest turnkey and was arrested himself. Brought to trial, Bird denied that the woman had helped him. She was released while Bird was condemned to death. He was hanged at Tyburn on 12 March 1690, at the age of forty-two.

Soon the profession of highwayman became almost overcrowded. The cessation of the second English Civil War in 1649 saw a large number of now unemployed Royalist soldiers taking to the broad highway for traveller prey. Nevertheless, a goodly number of deserters doggedly still continued to take up the footpad's trade.

One such was Patrick O'Bryan, but he differed from most of

his contemporaries in that he started as a knight of the road by moonlighting while he was still in the Coldstream Guards, until he deserted in order to devote all his energies to his true vocation of robbing people.

Irishman O'Bryan left Galway as a youth to enlist in the Guards in London. With his profligate lifestyle he soon ran up large bills in local taverns and shops, and he was dunned for repayment on all sides by creditors, who threatened to report him to his superiors. In an effort to supplement his income he started to leave the barracks at night and rob passers-by.

O'Bryan's extracurricular activities were so successful that one night he did not bother to return to his barracks. Before long the former guardsman achieved great fame in the public prints when on the Winchester road he held up a stagecoach bearing Nell Gwyn, the king's mistress. *The Lives and Exploits of the Most Noted Highwaymen* by Charles White, published in 1836, describes O'Bryan's opening remarks to the courtesan: 'Madam, I am a gentleman; I have done a great many signal services to the fair sex. Now, as I know, you are a charitable woman. I make bold to ask you for a little money, though I have never had the honour of serving you in particular.' Admiring his straightforward approach, Nell Gwyn presented the highwayman with a purse of ten guineas, and the pair parted with an exchange of pleasantries and compliments.

O'Bryan achieved even more notoriety when he was apprehended at Gloucester, sentenced to death and hanged. When his body was cut down and carried away by friends, faint signs of life were detected in the highwayman's body. A surgeon was quickly called and what had apparently been a corpse was restored fully to life. Within a short time he was back as a highwayman again. On several occasions he was recognised, causing a rumour to spread that the ghost of Patrick O'Bryan was haunting the open road.

He was caught for the second time when one of his accomplices was arrested and betrayed O'Bryan's hiding place. The Irishman was seized at his lodgings near the Haymarket in London and taken to Newgate. He was tried at the Salisbury assizes and confessed to his robberies and killings. He was hanged on 30 April 1689. To make sure that it would not be revived again, this time O'Bryan's body was hung in chains.

Most highwaymen were former soldiers but George Seager took to the highway after a stint as a sailor as well as a trooper. As a seaman Seager was dismissed from his ship, joined the army and deserted from his regiment before taking up the office of professional robber. Born in Portsmouth, Seager undertook a number of labouring jobs in the port as a young man before becoming a sneak thief. He was then taken by a press gang and forced into service before the mast on the man-of-war *Ruby*.

Taking Seager on board proved to be one of the worst decisions the captain ever made. Within days the new recruit was industriously robbing his companions and taking any valuable object from the ship that wasn't nailed down. He was caught rifling his companions' possessions on a number of occasions and whipped before the mast. As this punishment seemed to have no effect on the incorrigible rogue, finally the captain ordered that Seager be keelhauled. This involved a trussed culprit being dragged under the keel of a vessel and a gun being fired over his head when he finally came to the surface on the far side.

Even this did not deter Seager from pilfering, so the captain dismissed him the next time that the *Ruby* put in at Plymouth. The discharged seaman begged his way back to Portsmouth and, based on his maritime experiences, decided that there were lucrative takings for a cunning thief in a barracks room, so he joined the army, enlisting in Gibson's Regiment.

Seager was as much trouble in the army as he had been at sea. On one occasion when he was on night sentry duty, he bruised the officer of the watch by hurling a fusillade of stones at him. When asked why he had assaulted his superior in this fashion, Seager evaded punishment by replying innocently that as a soldier new to the regiment he considered it his duty to repel anyone approaching his post.

Seager's fellow troopers were not so easily bluffed. On a number of occasions, when he was discovered stealing in the barracks room, he was forced to run the gauntlet, being whipped with the soldiers' heavy belts as he ran between their ranks.

In order to get rid of him, Private Seager's superiors posted him to Flanders, where he lasted only a short time. One day he wandered into a Brussels church, where he noticed an English priest taking the confession of a wealthy woman. As was the custom, the penitent handed the priest some coins.

Noticing this, Seager entered the confessional as soon as it was vacated, held a pistol to the priest's chest and ordered the astonished man to hand over the money. The priest gave Seager the two gold pieces. Seager then bound the father and left him lying on the floor. Deciding that the authorities would soon be after him, Seager did not return to his barracks but deserted and set off on the long journey back to England.

When he reached his homeland, George Seager started out as a highwayman and robber. For a time he did well enough at the trade in and around London but, as was his wont, he overreached himself. One night he broke into the house of a certain Lord Cutts and stole valuables worth £240. He was soon apprehended, tried and hanged at Tyburn on 27 January 1697.

Another deserter-cum-highwayman of the time with a ready tongue and complete absence of morals was Jack Withers. Withers was a glib and audacious thief who transformed himself into a particularly unpleasant murderer after he had deserted his regiment in Flanders.

He was born in Lichfield in Staffordshire and became a thief in London after abandoning his Lichfield apprenticeship. Soon caught, the magistrates gave their prisoner the choice of a prison or the army. Withers selected the latter, thinking it the better of two evils. He was sent to serve near Ghent.

It was here that the soldier proved himself to be a resourceful thief. Slipping into a church after a particularly well-attended mass ceremony, Withers forced the lock of a donation box with a crooked nail and fled with the contents. However, he had stuffed his pockets too full of coins and some of them fell onto the marble floor of the church, making a great deal of noise.

Withers was caught and brought before a cardinal. Thinking on his feet, the soldier declared that he was a wretched Protestant heretic who had visited the church in a state of great distress and religious uncertainty. He had, Withers declared, maintaining a straight face, sworn to the Virgin Mary that if only she would give him a sign, he would become a Catholic himself. At that moment, Withers went on in tones of awe and wonderment, the donations box under the image of the Virgin Mary had sprung open and the grateful soldier had taken this as a sign to help himself.

Whether the cardinal actually believed this incredible story or whether he saw in it a chance for a great public relations exercise is not known, but at the conclusion of the story the prelate cried out, 'A miracle! A miracle!' Withers was conducted with great pomp and ceremony back to the church, and welcomed as a convert to Catholicism before being allowed to go amid great applause from the congregation.

His unexpected success in Ghent prompted the venal soldier to push his luck. Not long after his escape, he entered a church in Antwerp and stole a silver crucifix, secreting the icon in his breeches and shuffling out among the milling crowd of worshippers. Withers was suspected of the crime and decided that it was time that he left the Low Countries and returned home before the avenging military, civil and ecclesiastical authorities all closed in on him.

He deserted and fled back to England where he became a highwayman, linking up with a like-minded but less vicious robber called William Edwards. On the road near Beaconsfield in Buckinghamshire, the pair attacked a member of the aristocracy travelling with his footman. The latter proved a doughty opponent. In his master's defence he shot Withers's horse, forcing both highwaymen to flee on Edwards's mount.

Hiding close to Uxbridge, the two robbers next held up a postman and robbed him of eight shillings. Then, to the horror of Edwards,

Jack Withers stabbed the courier to death, disembowelled him and, in order to hide his carcass, filled the corpse's body with stones to weigh it down and threw it into a pond.

The body was found within twenty-four hours and a great hue and cry was roused to apprehend the perpetrators of the vicious attack. Several months later the two men were caught trying to carry out another robbery. Both men were condemned to death at Norfolk assizes. On 16 April 1703, on the scaffold shared by the two men at Thetford, William Edwards accused Withers of the murder of the postal carrier. Both were executed.

Many other deserter-highwaymen died on the gallows. In 1715, Henry Powell, who had defected twice from his regiment in Flanders, was hanged for a highway robbery at South Mimms in Hertfordshire. On the gallows, among his last words were: 'I account this ignominious death as a just judgment for my sins against the Divine Majesty and my neighbour.'

The history of deserters at this time is predominantly the story of male fugitives but there was also a handful of women who went on the run, sometimes in odd circumstances, in the seventeenth and eighteenth centuries. The first recorded female deserter appears to have been Mary Frith, who became one of London's best-known seventeenth-century pickpockets, famed for her ability to cut dangling purses free from the clothing of her victims, thus earning her the sobriquet of Moll Cutpurse.

She was born in London in 1584 and from an early age displayed masculine tendencies, preferring to play boys' games, fighting and beating her male peers, and wearing masculine garb. An uncle persuaded the credulous girl that her aggressive instincts would be best fulfilled by serving as a male crew member on a merchant vessel from Gravesend bound for New England.

However, when her sex was discovered and her new shipmates tried to take advantage of her, Mary Frith, who definitely was not interested in that sort of thing, deserted by diving over the side and returning to her old haunts.

After this false start, Mary took to her new life with enthusiasm, becoming an adept 'diver', as pickpockets were known, and always wearing men's clothing. For a time she took to the open road as a highwayman. A highlight of her career occurred when she waylaid and robbed General Fairfax, one of Oliver Cromwell's leading commanders, on Hounslow Heath. She was apprehended for this crime and sent to Newgate Prison, but was able to bribe her way out of trouble.

Disconcerted by her brush with the law, Mary next bought a house near The Globe tavern in Fleet Street and set up as a very successful fence of stolen goods, buying in goods from local thieves and pickpockets. She specialised in selling valuables back to their true owners and many respectable members of the gentry made their way to her abode to seek what had originally been taken from them. In the proceedings of the Star Chamber in February 1621, one Henry Killigrew, gentleman, reported that he had been in congress with a prostitute when his purse had been taken from him. He had gone at once to Mary Frith because, by doing so, 'many that had had their purses cut, or goods stolen had been helped to their goods again'. Before her death at the age of seventy-four, Mary Frith, as Moll Cutpurse, had gained a reputation as one of the leading villains on London's criminal scene.

Hannah Snell was much more law-abiding but probably rather more adventurous than Mary Frith had been. Her celebrity in the eighteenth century stemmed from serving as a man in both the army and the navy, deserting from the one in order to join the other.

In 1743, upon the death of her parents, 20-year-old Hannah Snell moved to London to live with her sister and her husband. Within a year she took up with a Dutch sailor, who stole from her and left her with a young baby, who died within a few months.

Hannah decided to join the army as a man. She borrowed some of her brother-in-law's clothing and enlisted at Coventry, under his name, James Gray, in the 6th Regiment of Foot, which was preparing to take part in the operation against the Jacobites under Prince Charles. Some biographies of Hannah speculated that she had joined the army in search of the errant father of her child, but why she would be looking for a seaman in the 6th Foot has never been explained satisfactorily. It is more likely that a desire for adventure impelled her.

Some time later the regiment was sent to Carlisle and Hannah Snell deserted. As she explained to her anonymous biographer in *The Female Soldier*, published in London in 1750, she fell out with a vindictive sergeant:

> When she first entered the service at Coventry, she marched to Carlisle where she was whipped for neglect of duty. The method she used to prevent the discovery of her sex was this, according to her own declaration her breasts were then not so big by much as they are at present.

She made her way to Portsmouth and enlisted in the marines, sailing on the sloop *Swallow* to India. Here she took part in the siege of Pondicherry, where she was wounded; to avoid her sex being discovered, she even treated her own wounds. In 1749, she sailed back to England on HMS *Eltham*. She then travelled with some of her shipmates where, at last, she told them that she was really a woman.

Her sister confirmed her story to the other marines and seamen and when they had recovered from their shock they urged Hannah to cash in on her amazing story. This she did by approaching the Duke of Cumberland as he travelled in an open carriage through St James's Park and thrusting a petition upon him, telling her story and begging for financial recompense for her wounds sustained in battle in India.

The Duke actually read the petition and was so impressed by it that he recommended a pension of thirty pounds a year for the 27-year-old female marine, although there is some doubt as to whether Hannah Snell actually received any of the money. Instead, she took advantage of the publicity engendered by a hastily written biography, cheap portraits of her on sale at street corners and a number of newspaper accounts of Hannah's military exploits, by appearing on the stage. She performed at London theatres and then on tours of the provinces with an act which consisted of singing patriotic songs and giving a display of military drill.

In her book, Hannah emphasised her femininity: 'I am as much a woman as my mother ever was, and my real name is Hannah Snell.' She married and had two children but fell on hard times and ended her days ill, violent and rambling in Bedlam asylum, where she died at the age of sixty-eight.

Mary Anne Talbot was one of sixteen illegitimate children. She claimed that her natural father had been a peer of the realm, and it is a fact that someone paid for her education at a boarding school. By 1792, she was in London and the mistress of a Captain Bowen of the 82nd Regiment of Foot. Mary either cared for her lover very much, or her lover exercised a Svengali-like influence on her because, when Bowen's company was posted to the West Indies, she went with him in the guise of a boy as her lover's servant, adopting the name of John Carter.

Almost at once the regiment was posted back to Europe to take part in the siege of Valenciennes in Flanders. Determined to stay with Bowen, Mary Talbot enlisted with him as a drummer boy. She was wounded twice in action and in each case insisted on treating her own injuries, in case her true sex should be revealed.

Bowen was killed during the siege and Mary was distraught. She deserted and, still dressed as a boy, signed on as a crew member of a French privateer. The vessel was captured by a British ship and the resourceful Mary persuaded her captors that she had been pressed on board the enemy craft against her will.

Still not assuaging her desire for adventure, the girl deserter served as a powder monkey and then a cabin boy on several other vessels, before being recaptured by the French and condemned to a period in a Dunkirk prison.

Released after an exchange of prisoners with Great Britain, Mary, still not twenty years old, sailed for America as a steward on a merchant vessel and vanished from history.

In the violent era represented by the seventeenth and eighteenth centuries many men and a few women who served in the armed forces were given opportunities to become skilled in the martial arts. They were taught to shoot and ride, and to become disciplined and accustomed to danger. When they were discharged or deserted, some of them put their military skills to use as thieves and robbers. Specifically some of them became highwaymen because they could use a pistol and sword and could easily buy or steal a horse. A contributing factor to the success of these trained riders was the poor state of the roads. The best coachman could not outrun a trained horseman on those rough and pitted surfaces.

Patrick O'Bryan and his colleagues were only following in a long tradition. As long ago as 205 AD, one Bulla the Lucky deserted from the Roman Army and took to the roads of Italy. For several years before his capture and death, being thrown to the lions in the arena, he became a feared highwayman. At one time he had 600 men following him in his company. Like many of the gentlemen of the road who were to follow him, Bulla was well aware of one of the main contributory causes for his men taking to crime. After he had committed a robbery he would send his victims on their way with this dictum ringing in their ears: 'Carry this message back to your masters ... Let them feed their slaves so that they might not be compelled to turn to a life of banditry!'

7

LOST LEADERS

I have not brought you victory; I found it here among you!
– Skanderbeg (George Kastrioti) rallies his Albanian rebels, 1443

Leaders have used desertions for different purposes. Some have utilised them in order to gain high position, while others have been forced to flee. An example of the former is the Albanian patriot and freedom fighter known as Skanderbeg, although his real name was George Kastrioti. In 1443, Skanderbeg deliberately left one battle in order to fight in another one, for a totally different cause. Skanderbeg was serving the sultan of Turkey as a mercenary when he suddenly deserted on the battlefield and rode off to lead an Albanian uprising against their Turkish masters.

Brought up in a noble Albanian family, he was taken as hostage to the Turkish court while still a youth and became a soldier in the sultan's army, assuming the name of Skender (Alexander). He fought so well that he was promoted to the title of *bey*. In time his name was corrupted to Skanderbeg, and he was known as this for the rest of his life. Although he was serving far from home he remained a fierce nationalist and was determined one day to lead his country to freedom from the Turks.

In 1443, Skanderbeg was fighting with the Turkish Army against the Hungarians at Nish in Serbia, when news was brought to him on the battlefield that an Albanian uprising against Turkish rule was taking place at home.

Skanderbeg and other Albanians serving in the Turkish Army had been expecting such an event for some time and had laid plans accordingly. At a signal from their leader, Skanderbeg, his nephew

Hamza and several hundred Albanians in the Turkish Army, to the amazement of the Turks and Hungarians alike, turned and galloped off the field.

Skanderbeg and his compatriots reached Albania and threw their weight behind the successful rebellion. Skanderbeg himself captured Kruja, his father's old estate. The Albanian League was formed by the local princes with Skanderbeg at its head and this later became an independent state. He led an Albanian army against the Turks, forcing them back, and formed shrewd alliances with European countries against the threat of the Ottoman Empire.

Known as 'Lord of Albania', Skanderbeg repelled the Turkish Army for twenty-five years and became an international hero, the subject of plays, poems and even an opera.

King James II was also defeated in battle – at the Battle of the Boyne in Ireland, in 1689 – but made no further attempts to defend his crown. James ascended to the throne of Great Britain in 1685, but his increasingly Catholic policies so upset many of the people and Members of Parliament that three years later they invited the Protestant William of Orange to invade the country, which he did, with an army of 25,000. King James averred that he would never desert his people, but still fled.

When William landed at Brixham and started to advance, the royal army at Salisbury retreated at once. In London, James repeated that he would stay and face the usurper. In fact he had already sent his wife and child abroad.

Some of the king's supporters fell on their knees and begged the monarch to remain at Whitehall. However, James had heard that Catholic churches all over London had been torched and that the homes of prominent Catholics were being ransacked. Still he reassured his adherents that he would not leave them. He went to bed, taking to his chamber the Great Seal of England, for which he had plans.

At 3 a.m. on 11 December 1688, King James II rose from his bed, dressed in the plain clothes of a country gentleman, and put on a black wig. Then taking the seal with him, the king left the palace by way of a secret passage, accompanied by Sir Edward Hale.

James and his companion then crossed the Privy Gardens and entered an undistinguished hackney coach, driven by his groom, Richard Smith. He was joined by his equerry Captain Ralph Sheldon. A small rowing boat known as a wherry was waiting for them at Millbank to carry them across the Thames. As they passed Lambeth the king hurled the Great Seal into the river, to hamper the efforts of any succeeding administration. James was next conducted in a carriage to Emley Ferry near Sheerness with the hope of boarding a fishing vessel which would take him across the English Channel to the safety of France. The fishermen whose boat it was had not been informed of the identity of their passenger but, by the time the fleeing monarch boarded the vessel, rumours of the king's flight had already reached them. They were reluctant to risk the punishments that would be meted out to anyone assisting James and sent him ashore again.

Here the king was roughly handled by a crowd which had gathered on the coast, and he was robbed of his jewellery, watch and money, before a number of local Catholic gentlemen came to his assistance. He was given shelter in an adjacent house, where his retainers remained on guard against possible attacks from the crowd, which was swelling rapidly. Word of the arrest was sent to William of Orange, who had reached Windsor with his entourage. Bishop Burnet, who was also present, described the reaction to the news from the coast:

> I went immediately to Bentinck [William's friend and envoy] and wakened him, and got him to go to the prince, and let him know what had happened, that some order might be presently given for the security of the king's person, and for taking him out of the hands of the rude multitude who said they would obey no orders but such as came from the prince.

James was allowed by William of Orange to escape to Dublin, where he established a government in exile, before moving on to France, where he died in 1701. The Great Seal of England was retrieved from the Thames by a fisherman, who returned it to Whitehall.

Peter I of Russia was acknowledged as one of Russia's most influential statesmen and reformers and a great general, but early in his reign Tsar Peter the Great amazed his followers when, on one occasion, he deserted his troops and fled for safety.

Coming to the throne in 1682 as a child, it was not long before Peter was making great efforts to modernise his country and draw it closer to Europe. He spent a year touring the Continent, even working with his hands in dockyards the better to understand naval technology.

In 1698, Peter allied himself with Frederick Augustus, elector of Saxony and King of Poland, and went to war with King Charles XII of Sweden. As a result Peter hoped to increase Russia's land holdings in the Baltic area. The Swedish monarch was only sixteen at the time but he proved himself to be a clever and resourceful fighter.

Peter advanced with 40,000 men to meet the Swedes. He laid siege to the town of Narva but was surprised when Charles XII made a brilliant counter-march and, in November 1700, took the Russians from the rear at Lagena, nine miles from Narva.

Peter the Great, for all his experience and courage, panicked. Stopping only to hand over control of the army to the stupefied Prince de Croÿ, the emperor of Russia rode off to safety as fast as his horse could take him.

Charles took advantage of the confusion among the enemy ranks and charged at the Russians through a snowstorm. In less than an hour, the surviving defeated Russians were riding from the battlefield as quickly as their Tsar had done earlier.

But, returning to winter quarters and then diverted into a successful attack on Poland, which ended with complete victory over the combined Saxon and Polish armies, he could not pursue his advantage against the Russians. He announced his contempt for the behaviour of his enemies: 'There is no pleasure in fighting the Russians for they will not stand like other men but run away at once.'

Peter the Great soon recovered his nerve and renewed his campaign against the Swedes. He expressed his determination to learn from his mistakes: 'I know very well that these Swedes will have the advantage of us for a time, but they will at length teach us to beat them.'

The Great Northern War, as it was known, dragged on from 1700 until 1721. After his initial losses Peter I regrouped and defeated Charles XII at the Battle of Poltava in 1709. In 1718, Charles was killed in battle and his successors sued for peace. As a result, Russia took the place of Sweden as the pre-eminent Baltic power and, under Peter the Great, also became a major European force.

As a young prince, the future Frederick the Great, King of Prussia, later an outstanding general who guided his small kingdom until it took its place at the head of a united Germany, tried to escape from his coarse father's influence. His early years were unhappy ones and his disastrous attempt to flee almost led to an international incident.

Frederick's father, Frederick I, regarded his sickly son with contempt, considering him effeminate because of an early and prolonged interest in art and literature. Determined that the boy would grow up to be a soldier, Frederick I subjected him to a Spartan upbringing, putting him in charge of a contingent of 100 cadets when he was only nine, and promoting him to the rank of major when he was fifteen.

Nothing could persuade Frederick to take to the rough barracks life he was being asked to accept. His father, furious at the youth's indifference, often humiliated him by admonishing him in public. Finally, when he was eighteen, Frederick decided that he could take no more. He was the grandson of King George I of England, so he conspired with two friends, Lieutenant Katte and Lieutenant Keith, to escape across the channel to the more relaxed atmosphere of the London court.

The plot was betrayed. Frederick and Katte were both arrested, although Keith was warned in advance and was able to make his escape. Frederick I was infuriated by the efforts of his son and his associate to desert and had both men detained in the same prison. The news that the crown prince had been gaoled for desertion rocked Europe, especially when Lieutenant Katte was court-martialled and sentenced to death for his part in the plot.

Prince Frederick was forced to watch the beheading of his friend, having first asked Katte's forgiveness for involving him in the tragic affair. He then fainted at the sight of the lieutenant's death. He was deprived of his rank and put on trial himself. For fifteen months he was kept in Küstrin Prison, until finally the diplomatic efforts of the scandalised major European powers secured his release.

Frederick apologised humbly to his father and promised to do his best to become the sort of soldier that the monarch wanted him to be. The prince resumed his military career but lived relatively quietly until the death of his father, when he inherited the crown. His troubles were not yet over though. The new King Frederick II assumed command of the Prussian Army and invaded Silesia, hoping to take the province from Austria. On the snow-capped fields of Mollwitz, the Austrian cavalry acquitted itself so well that Frederick galloped from the field in fear, leaving one of his generals to redeem the situation and win the battle for the Prussians. Later, the shame-faced monarch admitted, 'Mollwitz was my school!'

To the surprise of many, Frederick II later proved to be one of the great military geniuses. He was a great tactician during the War of the Austrian Succession (1740–48) and the Seven Years War (1756–63), making Prussia Europe's leading military power. He spent much time and care on the maintenance and training of the army.

Frederick continued his interest in the arts and, for all his later reputation as a cold, calculating man, he retained memories of his dreadful period under arrest for desertion. It was said that after a day's battle had gone badly, a certain deserter was brought before him. The fugitive grenadier said that he had fled because things had gone badly for his regiment that day. Onlookers expected the king to order the man's execution, but Frederick had been in the other man's shoes.

'Come,' he had said softly, before sending the man back to his unit. 'Let us fight another battle today; if I am beaten we will desert together tomorrow!'

Emperors and kings also were not averse to deserting if they considered the action expedient or life preserving. Both Napoleon Bonaparte and his brother Joseph fled for different reasons within a few years of one another. The charismatic and gifted Napoleon, who could do little wrong in the eyes of his followers, once stood accused of deserting his troops and leaving them to starve without him.

By 1798, Napoleon Bonaparte was a rising French general. He had marched against the Austrians and forced them to sue for peace. Then the French ruling assembly, the Directorate, sent him with 35,000 troops to Egypt. His mission was to destroy British influence in the Red Sea area.

Things went wrong almost from the start. Nelson destroyed the French fleet at the Battle of the Nile, cutting off the French supply routes. Napoleon managed to win the Battle of the Pyramids against the defending Egyptian troops and enter Cairo, but after that he and his men were bogged down in a virtual stalemate, deprived of supplies in an inhospitable climate on barren terrain. Although he marched into Palestine, at one stage his exhausted troops were on the point of mutiny.

When an alliance of Britain, Turkey, Austria and France was formed to oppose France, Napoleon realised that he could do little of value to enhance his career in Egypt and that he would do better to cut his losses.

Napoleon left Egypt under great secrecy with the frigates *La Murion* and *La Carrière*. With him he took some of his senior advisers, three generals, his personal attendants and several hundred men. Napoleon embarked at the port of Bulaq at 3 a.m. and sailed on to Alexandria. He handed over a proclamation to his troops, promising that he would return soon. He then left Egypt for ever.

It took the flotilla of two frigates and two courier vessels forty-seven days to reach France, arriving at the beginning of October. Such was Napoleon's personal popularity that he was greeted with acclamation upon his return to Europe. His failures in Egypt were ignored by the public. He was offered any command he wanted by the Directorate. Napoleon refused the offer, citing the need to rest and recuperate from his experiences in the Middle East. He bided his time in considered fashion and within two years launched a successful coup to topple the Directorate, assuming total command in France. In the *Memoirs of Napoleon Bonaparte* by his private secretary Louis Antoine Fauvelet de Bourrienne, the writer recounted a first-hand account of the disembarkation on 22 August 1799, as told to him by Ganteaume, one of the officers accompanying Napoleon: 'The General-in-chief and his companions got into the dinghies that took them to the ship. They cast off that very night to ensure that by daylight they were out of sight of the English cruisers moored at Aboukir.'

Bonaparte's former army of the Nile, now under the command of the hapless General Kléber and thoroughly demoralised, was left to rot in the desert for three years, starved of supplies and reinforcements. Kléber always considered that Napoleon had deserted him. By the time the survivors surrendered to the British in 1801, one in three of the original French land expedition had died.

Napoleon's older brother Joseph fared little better. He was raised to high estate by Napoleon but did not share his sibling's military genius, and at the Battle of Vitoria in 1813, he fled from the field.

Joseph studied law at the University of Pisa and subsequently achieved prominence at home in Corsican political circles. He followed in Napoleon's wake when his brother began to rise swiftly. In turn he was made King of Naples and then of Spain. He was a well-meaning administrator but was very unhappy in his second post, hated by the Spanish and treated with contempt by his French military advisers. He begged to be relieved of his crown but Napoleon would not hear of it.

In 1813, Joseph Bonaparte was driven from Madrid by the

advancing British forces. He made an ill-judged stand close to the village of Vitoria, where his force was first pushed back and then overwhelmed. Wellington's victory would have been even more decisive if many of his troops had not abandoned their advance to loot the French treasure wagons; dozens of ordinary soldiers became wealthy men as a result of their treasure hunting exploits at Vitoria. In a letter to the Spanish Minister of War, Wellington admitted that it was impossible for his officers to restrain the drunken looting of the thousands of British troops now roaming the countryside. He estimated that some 12,000 of his troops had deserted in order to rape and pillage. The looting was exacerbated by the headlong flight of many wealthy aristocrats from the town. As the pursuing forces of Wellington drew nearer, many of the wealthy lightened their loads by discarding from their coaches gold and silver plates and jewellery boxes. Many of the troops in pursuit stopped to collect the plunder. Heartened by the results, they abandoned thoughts of battle and went off in search of more loot. As a result some became rich men.

The duke particularly censured the conduct of the British 18th Light Dragoons. Their debauched behaviour and desertion figures caused their commander-in-chief to thunder that they were: '...a disgrace to the name of soldiery in action as well as elsewhere and I intend to draft their horses from them and send the men to England if I cannot get the better of them'.

Giving the order to retreat, Joseph drove from the field, leaving behind his crown, his sceptre and most of the royal treasure. He was taken from the scene in a carriage marked with the royal arms of Spain, accompanied by a hastily assembled mounted escort, recruited to assist him in his desertion.

His vehicle made extremely slow progress through the press of retreating soldiers and refugees and before Joseph could get far the carriage was overhauled by a mounted British officer, a Captain Wyndham of the 14th Light Dragoons. Wyndham levelled his pistol and fired a shot through the rear window of the carriage. In a panic, Joseph hurled himself out of the door on to the road on the far side and raced on foot after his escort. Without ceremony he was hoisted on to a riderless horse and towed away at a great pace. He reached Bayonne in an abject condition, scorned by his fellow countrymen for deserting his post.

Joseph remained in Paris while Napoleon fought and lost at Waterloo. For a time the former king lived in Switzerland. Then he went to the USA where he purchased an estate and lived in considerable style.

Captain Wyndham, who had fired the speculative shot at the King of Spain in his carriage, emerged from their brief encounter with a souvenir he found in the general looting after Joseph's flight. It was Joseph Bonaparte's personal silver chamber pot. The captain donated it to his mess and it became a tradition for the 14th Light Dragoons to drink champagne toasts from it at ceremonial dinners, earning them the nickname of 'the Emperor's Chambermaids'.

Antonio López de Santa Anna was altogether more flexible. Before achieving notoriety as the leader of the Mexican Army that wiped out the Texan defenders of the fort at the Alamo, he pursued a cunning political and military career which saw him change sides on several occasions.

He was born in Jalapa, Veracruz in 1794, the son of a colonial official, and became a military cadet at the age of sixteen. He fought with courage against the Indians and was once wounded by an arrow.

During the Mexican War of Independence, Santa Anna at first fought with some success for the royalist Spanish force. However, when the insurgent Agustín de Iturbide approached with a large army, Santa Anna deserted the royalist cause for that of the rebels. Before his defection he had just been promoted to the rank of lieutenant colonel. Santa Anna made Iturbide promise that the deserter would retain this rank in the rebel army.

Agustín de Iturbide overthrew the Spaniards and became emperor of Mexico. At first, Santa Anna served his new master, but soon fell out with the emperor and helped instigate an uprising against him, forcing Iturbide to abdicate. Santa Anna then supported Vicente Guerrero for the presidency but, true to form, deserted his cause and helped to depose Guerrero, finally becoming president himself. Finding the day-to-day administrative tasks of office irksome, he delegated them to others and devoted himself to a hedonistic lifestyle.

United States settlers in Texas then rebelled against Mexican rule and declared an independent republic. Santa Anna, having repelled an inefficient Spanish invasion of his country by a yellow-fever-plagued army, bestirred himself sufficiently again to lead an army of thousands against a Texan force of less than 200 besieged in the old Franciscan mission of the Alamo. After a twelve-day siege, every fighting man in the old compound had been killed, including such semi-legendary frontier luminaries as Jim Bowie and Davy Crockett.

Sam Houston, leader of the Texans, gathered a large force and six weeks later attacked Santa Anna's Mexican Army. The overconfident general had neglected to post guards. His force was defeated and Santa Anna surrendered at the Battle of San Jacinto.

The president signed a treaty promising Texan independence and then was forced into temporary retirement. He bounced back, however, and took part in an engagement against a brief French naval siege of Veracruz. The enemy vessels were sailing away as Santa Anna arrived, but in a final skirmish he had part of his leg blown away. He had the limb buried with full military honours. Later, at ceremonial parades, Santa Anna would ride at the fore, brandishing his wooden leg above his head as a sign of his military valour.

This military exploit helped Santa Anna to regain some of his lost prestige. He returned to politics and seized power after a revolt, but was then defeated and exiled in 1845. He then took part in his final act of chicanery. Mexico entered into an ill-advised war with the USA. The glib Santa Anna persuaded President James Polk to send him home in a US warship, promising to work for peace there. As soon as Santa Anna landed on Mexican soil, he reneged on his promises to Polk, changed sides again and led a Mexican army unsuccessfully against the Americans using his troops as pawns in his game of desertion and counter-desertion. The victorious invaders exiled Santa Anna once again and he spent ten years plotting to return to power, even offering to serve Emperor Maximilian, who had been placed on the throne of Mexico by the French. His efforts came to nothing. When he was finally allowed home, blind and impoverished, his plotting days were over.

Charles Edward Stewart was assuredly not in the same class as Frederick as a military tactician and was accused by some of abandoning his men in the face of the enemy.

Charles had invaded England from Scotland with his Highlanders, in an attempt to take the throne from George I, but had turned back at Derby after recruiting few English volunteers to his cause. He halted his retreat north to meet the Duke of Cumberland, George I's son, at Culloden, near Inverness. He attempted to surprise the English with an abortive night attack, but succeeded only in exhausting his depleted force. He then marched his men back to his headquarters at Culloden and prepared for a daytime assault.

The next day the English attacked. Cumberland's gunners poured grapeshot at the Scots, who launched a spontaneous counter-attack, without the orders of their officers. They were pushed back. The Highlanders then turned and ran.

Prince Charles watched his troops retreat. He made as if to move forward to rally them, but the bridle of his horse was seized by General O'Sullivan, who led the prince from the field. Some of his retinue went with Charles, but others stood their ground and expressed forcefully their opinion that a leader's place was with his men. Lord Elcho, in particular, was heard to call the retreating prince 'a damned cowardly Italian!', a reference to Charles Stewart's birthplace.

Captain O'Neille, one of Prince Charles's aides, later wrote in his journal for 16 April, as quoted in *The Jacobite Rebellions* by James Pringle Thompson (1914):

That night the prince retired six miles from the field of battle and went next day as far, and in three days more arrived at Fort Augustus, where he remained a whole day in expectation his troops would have joined him. But seeing no appearance of it, he went to the house of Invergarry and ordered me to remain there to direct such as passed that day the road he took. I remained there two days and announced the prince's orders to such as I met, but to no effect, every one of them taking his own road.

Charles was hunted across the Highlands but received loyalty and shelter from the clans. He made his way back to France and then Italy. He married and drank heavily for the rest of his life. It was rumoured that to the end of his life he kept under his bed a strong-box full of gold coins, in case he was ever called upon to invade England again.

8

'A TORRENT OF MUTINY!'

They Might fly if they pleased to Omiah King Ottou or to the Most distant Country known to these people. His authority would bring them back and Dead or Alive he'd have them.
– Captain Cook addresses incipient deserters on his third voyage to the Pacific

As vessels began to travel to more and more exotic and attractive parts of the world, so the temptation to dive over the side of a ship and abscond to an island paradise grew ever stronger. At the same time captains began to devise stronger punishments for their deserters. These did not always act as a deterrent. Even under the rigour of the discipline of the Royal Navy, seamen continued endeavours to achieve their release. There were some particularly notable efforts by complete crews, as well as individual sailors, to defy the remote power of the Admiralty in Whitehall.

One of the best-known mass desertions at sea was the mutiny on HMS *Bounty* in the South Pacific in 1789, but this had already been preceded by a number of individual attempts to take leave of the vessel, especially by Charles Churchill, a marine corporal master-at-arms, responsible for maintaining discipline on board ship. He took part in the notorious South Seas mutiny against the ship's captain, Bligh.

The *Bounty* sailed from Great Britain in 1787 under the command of Lieutenant William Bligh, a fine seaman and strict disciplinarian. The intention of the voyage was to collect breadfruit plants from Tahiti in the South Pacific and transport them to the Caribbean, where they would be planted as a source of food for plantation slaves.

The crew members had a long and idyllic sojourn on Tahiti, selecting and loading the cargo. When the vessel finally sailed, a number of seamen reacted adversely to Bligh's harsh regime and, led by master's mate Fletcher Christian, mutinied off the Friendly Islands (now Tonga).

On 5 January 1789, seduced by the attractions of the island, the burly, bullying Churchill deserted on Tahiti with two other men and went to live among the islanders. The three men were recaptured on 22 January. The two other deserters received twenty-four lashes. Churchill, the man who normally administered such punishments, was sentenced to twelve lashes.

Churchill's second desertion came as a result of the mutiny, in which he played a prominent part, resentful of Bligh for having ordered his punishment after his initial absence and desirous of returning to the pleasures of Tahiti. Just before dawn on 28 April, Christian, Churchill and some other mutineers broke into Bligh's cabin armed with bayonets. They pinioned his arms, while Churchill growled, 'Make a sound, Mr Bligh, and you will be a dead man!'

Clad only in his nightshirt, Bligh was hustled up on deck and placed near the mizzen-mast, under armed guard. After some debate the ship's captain and eighteen loyal crew members were set adrift in an open boat with one sail, while the mutineers and a number of loyal seamen, making a total of twenty-five, sailed back to Tahiti.

Fletcher Christian, some of the mutineers and a few Tahitian men and women sailed off in the *Bounty* again, eventually settling on the remote Pitcairn Island. Churchill and a number of others had had enough of life at sea and remained on Tahiti.

When the chief with whom he had taken shelter died, Churchill emerged as the new leader of the tribe, the first white Tahitian chief. This was partly through the blood-ties of the woman with whom he was living, but also because of his strength and size and musketeering prowess. His triumph was short-lived. He fell out with his right-hand man, Thompson, who had raped a local girl,

killed several islanders on the other side of the island and consequently been forced to flee.

Suspecting that the other man would challenge his leadership, Churchill had some of his men steal Thompson's arms as
he slept. Thompson discovered another weapon and shot and
killed Churchill. In turn Thompson was stoned to death by
Churchill's followers.

Eventually a British warship arrived at Tahiti and arrested the
surviving fourteen deserters, taking them back to face trial in
England. One of the witnesses at the trial was the newly promoted
Captain Bligh. In an epic feat of seamanship, he had navigated his
23-foot launch from the Friendly Islands on a 3,168 mile, 49-day
journey to Timor in the Western Pacific, before being brought back
to England with the other loyal members of the crew.

Four of the accused seamen drowned in a storm on the voyage
home. The ten survivors were court-martialled, and three of them
were hanged.

By the end of the eighteenth century word was spreading among
seafarers and frequenters of waterfront taverns that far away in the
South Seas lay beautiful islands with magnificent climates, eager,
acquiescent women and a lifestyle in which the hardest daily activity any man had to undertake was to throw a stone at a palm tree
to bring down a coconut. Captain Cook's three great voyages of
discovery to the Pacific between 1768 and 1776 did much to put an
official imprimatur on such wide-eyed gossip, a prospect not even
blighted by their captain's untimely and savage death in a skirmish
at the hands of the Hawaiian islanders.

One of the first seamen to propagate this idyllic gospel and do
his best to sample the delights of the South Seas was John Marra,
a cheerful, quick-witted, irresponsible seaman on James Cook's
second voyage to the Pacific between 1772 and 1775. On this
voyage the Irishman Marra plagued his captain with constant
attempts at desertion.

Cook's first voyage of discovery had been so successful that the
Admiralty sent him out again with two vessels and a commission to

circumnavigate the globe as far south as possible and look for the
location of the rumoured southern continent. Cook was successful
once again, landing in New Zealand and in Tahiti and Tonga.

The commander had a number of problems on the voyage, one
of them being the antics of John Marra. Of a nomadic nature,
the Irishman had served on many ships, leaving them whenever the
fancy took him. On the voyage out, when he was refitting in Batavia,
Cook was approached by representatives of the Dutch Navy, who
wished to arrest the Irishman for various offences he had committed while serving on one of their ships, including desertion.

The gregarious Marra was a good seaman and cheerful company,
so Cook refused to let him go, although later he might have
concluded that he would have had a more peaceful time if he had
left the rogue to his fate at Batavia.

To start with, Marra made two attempts to desert at Tahiti. On
each occasion he dived overboard to a canoe provided by friends
he had made easily from among the islanders. He was rounded up
each time and brought back to the *Endeavour*. His captain seemed
to sympathise with the free-spirited seaman, writing almost longingly in his log, 'where can a man spend his days better than at one
of these isles where he can enjoy all the necessaries and some of the
luxuries of life in ease and plenty?'

Marra showed his empathy with Cook's remarks when they
reached New Zealand. Here he made another escape-bid, this time
swimming ashore when the vessel dropped anchor. He was hunted
down and caught. This time he was given twelve lashes, although
the Irishman declared indignantly that he had only gone ashore
to seek women! He continued to be punished regularly. A typical example, recorded in the ship's log, announced that William
Harvey, midshipman, had 'punished John Marra with twelve lashes
for desertion and also for insubordination'.

Upon his return to Great Britain, Marra showed another example
of resourcefulness by putting his name to a book about the voyage,
entitled *Journal of the Resolution's Voyage in 1772, 1773, 1774 and 1775,
on discovery of the southern hemisphere by which the non-existence of*

an undiscovered continent between the equator and the 50ᵗʰ degree of
southern latitude is demonstratively proved.

The book, probably written by the editor under Marra's name,
has been described as a rag-bag of diary entries, comments and
plagiarisms from Cook's account of his first voyage to the Pacific,
but in addition to publicising the hedonistic pleasures of the South
Seas it is to be hoped that the good-natured and independent
seaman made at least some money from it. Despite the floggings
ordered by Captain Cook, the former gunner's mate had nothing
but praise for his former commander and his powers of leadership
to the end:

> He never suffered any of his men to be idle, but constantly employed
> the armourers, the carpenters, the caulkers, the sailmakers, rope-
> makers, the other tradesmen on board, as well as the foremastmen,
> and professed navigators in doing something, each in his own way,
> which though not immediately wanted, he knew there would be a
> call for before the voyage was completed.

In 1797, a particularly violent uprising occurred aboard, HMS
Hermione, a frigate of the British Navy. The crew mutinied
and sailed their vessel to the Spanish, handing it over to them and
pleading for sanctuary.

The *Hermione* had been patrolling the Mona Channel off Puerto
Rico. It was under the command of a sadistic 28-year-old, Captain
Hugh Pigot, whose savage conduct had driven his men to the brink
of rebellion.

He had had a midshipman whipped for refusing to kneel before
him and admit a mistake, and had threatened to flog the last man
to descend from work on the mizzen-mast. In their haste to get
down two of the seamen had fallen to their death. The callous Pigot
had ordered their bodies to be thrown over the side. The next day
he proceeded to order the whipping of another dozen men.

His seamen had had enough. On the night of 21–22 September,
more than twenty of them stole a supply of rum and drank it to

build up their courage. Then they took cutlasses and stormed their captain's cabin, thrashing and stabbing him and throwing his body over the side. A lieutenant and a midshipman were also attacked and killed. Midshipman David Casey, whose life was spared, later gave evidence at the trial of the mutineers as to what he had witnessed:

> I perceived Mr Douglas, Second Lieutenant, run past my hammock, calling out for mercy, and on getting abreast of the Midshipman's Berth, saw him seized by several of the crew. Those men fell on him and left him apparently dead on the gratings of the after hold. I then saw Mr Smith, the Midshipman, put to death in the like manner in the same place.

The mutineers then took a rest from their slaughter and repaired to the thousand gallons of rum stored on board. A surgeon's mate called Laurence Cronin emerged as the leader of the uprising, although so far he had taken little part in the mutiny. On his instructions another nine officers were murdered and their bodies disposed of over the sides of the ship.

Cronin then proposed that the surviving crew members sail the *Hermione* to La Guaira on the coast of Venezuela and ask for shelter from the Spanish authorities there. The Spanish accepted the surrender of the deserters, albeit reluctantly, fearful of an international incident, but showed little pleasure in the company of the fugitive English deserters, who mainly had to fend for themselves in the inhospitable port. Some signed on with visiting French and American merchant vessels, the rest dispersed and fended for themselves as best they could in South America.

In Whitehall, the Admiralty was furious about the incident and set out to hunt down as many of the deserters as they could, no matter how long it took. In this they were remarkably successful. More than forty of the *Hermione*'s former crew-members eventually were rounded up and tried; many of them being hanged. One of the ringleaders, David Forrester, had even re-enlisted in the navy and served for three years before he suffered the misfortune of being recognised in the street in Portsmouth and arrested and executed for murder. Another of those apprehended and hanged was 14-year-old John Hayes. His muttered excuse for taking part in the uprising was that he had been the victim of 'a torrent of mutiny'.

Not all deserters, like Hayes and his companions, went ashore by choice. Sometimes they were marooned by their captains for insubordination or mutinous acts; others were cast ashore, only to find all attempts at discipline breaking down in their new surroundings.

For over 100 years the sea-lanes of the world were haunted by those plundering nautical highwaymen who went under many titles – buccaneers, privateers, corsairs, freebooters, gentlemen on the account – but are now better known by the generic term of pirates. If they were caught they were usually hanged, suffering the caress of the hempen halter.

A privateer was a semi-official armed vessel, owned by an individual or individuals, with a commission from the government to attack vessels, especially merchant ships, belonging to hostile nations.

The crews of privateers were usually men with chequered pasts, not disinclined to take advantage of any promising situations. If this meant deserting or even attacking their captains, it was regarded as all part of a day's work.

Many of these scoundrels were deserters from navies of the world, so most pirates thought little of deserting from one another if the price should be deemed right. In fact their actions gave a new word to the language – marooners.

It became a pirate practice to deposit recaptured would-be escapees on the first isolated island encountered. Eventually the term was used for anyone stranded or marooned.

A great example of business acumen and ruthlessness was displayed on one occasion by a leading buccaneer, Henry Morgan, who later attained respectability as deputy governor of Jamaica and a prosperous merchant. One of his privateering expeditions gained notoriety for the manner in which he cruelly abandoned most of his men and sailed off with the loot.

The son of a Welsh farmer, Henry Morgan went to sea and ended up in Jamaica where he became a buccaneer captain. The buccaneers, who got their name from the strips of smoked, preserved meat known as *boucan*, a staple diet of the original inhabitants of the West Indies, were little more than pirates who had the permission of the Council of Jamaica, the ruling body, to attack Spanish ships in the Caribbean. With Spain and England at war, the navy could not afford ships to guard the coasts of the West Indian islands.

In 1671, after a number of earlier successful raids, Morgan, then thirty-four years old, organised a secret expedition to raid and loot the wealthy Spanish settlement of Panama. He sailed with a fleet of thirty-six vessels, eleven of them French, carrying almost 2,000 men. On the last stage of the attack, to reach the city, Morgan and his men had to make an exhausting trek across the Isthmus of Panama. They ran out of food and water and existed on rats and the leather of their powder-carriers. Many of the buccaneers died in the heat.

The remainder reached Panama on 18 January. Ten thousand fresh and well-armed Spanish troops came out to do battle with Morgan's depleted force. After a conflict lasting hours the Spanish turned and fled. Morgan and his pirates entered Panama and looted it. Loading up every mule he could find, Morgan then led a journey back across the isthmus with an enormous treasure.

It might have been expected that after two incredible journeys on foot and a victory against vastly superior odds, leader and men might have bonded considerably. The reverse was the truth. The buccaneers, with some reason as it turned out, distrusted Morgan. For his part, Morgan decided that the booty was far too good to be distributed among so many men, so he laid plans to ensure that most of it came to him and a few lieutenants. While the pirates raped and caroused, Morgan had the guns of a defensive position on the coast carried out to his ship. At the same time he made sure that most of the plunder was also battened down in the holds of three or four selected vessels.

Suddenly Morgan turned his reinforced artillery on the shore, demolishing most of the remaining fortifications. Then, with his small fleet and loot worth about 6 million crowns, he sailed for Jamaica.

The deserted buccaneers raced down to the shore. They found that Morgan had taken most of the available cannon, powder and food with him, leaving them powerless. One of their number, Alexandre Olivier Exquemelin, complained sententiously, 'We were left in such miserable condition as might serve for a live representation of what reward attends wickedness at the latter end of life.'

Shortly after this cold act of desertion, Henry Morgan was recalled to England by King Charles II. He travelled with some trepidation, wondering if he was going to be punished for his many transgressions. His fears were heightened when he was forced to wait for three years before being granted an audience with his monarch.

However, to the buccaneer's great relief, he discovered that Charles had been so impressed by his reputation as a doughty man of action that he wanted Morgan to return to the West Indies and clean up the area for him. He knighted Morgan, made him deputy governor of Jamaica, and sent him back to catch and hang every pirate he could. Morgan attended to his new brief with gusto and considerable success before retiring to the pleasant life of a wealthy local landowner.

Sometimes the crews of vessels turned on their leaders, or even on one another. This happened in 1720 on a voyage of the vessel *Speedwell*. The *Speedwell* deserters were a bunch of malicious and incompetent seamen who abandoned their captain when they were shipwrecked on a remote island. Their ship was a 24-gun privateer under the command of Captain George Shelvocke. Even before the shipwreck he had upset his crew to such an extent that he had been forced to put down two mutinies. One of these uprisings had been subdued with the aid of a passing French vessel. The grateful Shelvocke had dined on board the French ship little

realising that it had a cargo of 3 million dollars in gold, which could
have been his for the taking.

The ill-starred voyage encountered a traditionally unlucky bird,
described in Shelvocke's *A Voyage round the World by way of the
Great South Sea*, published in 1726:

> We all observed that we had not had the sight of one fish of any kind
> since we came into the southward of the straits of le Maire, not one
> sea-bird, except a disconsolate black Albatross, who accompanied
> us for several days, hovering about us as if he had lost himself, till
> Hatley, my second Captain, observing in one of his melancholy
> fits, that the bird was always hovering near us, imagined from his
> colour that this might be some ill-omen … he, after some fruitless
> attempts, at length shot the Albatross, not doubting (perhaps) that
> we should have a fair wind after it…

This episode preceded the ship's subsequent dire misfortunes and
incidentally provided Samuel Taylor Coleridge with the inspiration
for the inciting incident in his poem 'The Rime of the Ancient
Mariner'.

On 25 May 1720, the privateer was wrecked off the Juan Fernandez
Islands in the South Pacific Ocean, some 400 miles off the coast of
Chile. All the crew made it ashore but Captain Shelvocke promptly
lost control of his men. As soon as they reached the safety of the
shore, the men split up into groups, wandering aimlessly over
the island. They ignored their captain's pleas to return to the shore
and help salvage material from their foundering vessel. Next, the
ship's carpenter insisted on a cash payment before he would build
a small craft in which they could escape.

The jeering seamen then took away Shelvocke's sword and pistol
and fed him only on scraps of food they left on their plates. One
officer went mad, and another was beaten up when he tried to stand
by his captain. A seaman called Morphew became the temporary
leader of the dissidents, but soon fell out with the others.

Twelve of the men decided to desert on a permanent basis and spend the rest of their lives on island. They stole everything they could lay their hands on. With an uncharacteristic display of firmness, Shelvocke led a party against them. At the sight of an armed party bearing down on them, led by a suddenly unexpectedly resolute captain, the deserters surrendered without putting up a fight.

When the escape craft was completed forty of the sixty-four survivors piled in and put to sea in it. Soon they were living on nothing but conger eels. They became so desperate that they rowed furiously at a passing French privateer, hoping to capture it but were easily beaten off.

Eventually the crew of the *Speedwell* reached England. Captain Shelvocke was accused by the backers of the expedition, the Gentlemen Adventurers, of embezzling more than $15,000 belonging to them. He was arrested but bribed his way out of prison and fled to the Continent.

Occasionally, however, a privateer would go too far and suffer the consequences. A case in point was that of Captain William Kidd. He was a successful privateer and merchant, a former officer in the Royal Navy. He was commissioned to hunt down pirates and French vessels in the seas off Madagascar. However, after he had killed a man, he 'went native', deserted with his crew and became a pirate himself.

Kidd was born in Greenock, Scotland, in 1645. He had fought bravely for his country in the war with France and then had accrued a considerable fortune as a privateer, commissioned by his government to attack enemy vessels. He owned considerable estates in the area of New York.

So highly was he thought of as a navigator that Kidd was recalled to England and asked to command a new galley, the *Adventure*, a vessel of thirty-four guns and with a crew of eighty, to put down pirates off the seas of Madagascar and take any French ships encountered in the area.

Because of the ongoing war with France, the Admiralty was unable to spare ships for this venture but were glad to condone a private expedition, which would include harassing the French.

Kidd's expedition was backed by the Earl of Belmont, an Irish peer. The approval of King William III was secured, His Majesty graciously agreeing to take 10 per cent of the profits and granting a commission to 'our trusty and well-beloved Captain William Kidd'.

Kidd recruited most of his crew in New York but was hard put to find good seamen for the voyage and had to be content with taking on board the scourings of the dock area before he could at last leave for Madagascar. At first the desultory expedition went relatively well, Kidd scrupulously engaging only pirates and French vessels. However, when the *Adventure* put in at Madagascar he lost many crew members to less honest vessels, the absconders reckoning that there were higher profits in outright piracy.

When he left Madagascar with a depleted crew, Kidd was approached by the remaining seamen with a request that the *Adventure* turn to piracy and sail off 'on the account'.

The captain refused and had an altercation with the ship's gunner William Moore as a result. For some reason the captain called Moore a lousy dog. The gunner replied bitterly, 'If I am a lousy dog, you have made me so, you have brought me to ruin and many more!' The infuriated Kidd picked up a bucket and brought it down with all his force upon the head of the other man, killing him.

This traumatic experience seemed to affect Kidd greatly. Soon afterwards he changed his mind and embarked with his men upon a voyage of blatant piracy, attacking and plundering all the ships he came across. He was immediately labelled a deserter by the Admiralty.

For a time the *Adventure* was spectacularly successful. The pirates took vessel after vessel, including the wealthy treasure ship the *Quedagh Merchant*. Unfortunately for Kidd he was too successful. When he sailed back to New York laden with booty and claiming that it all came from privateers and French vessels, he was not believed.

Among the ships he and his crew had taken were a number belonging to the influential East India Company. Its officials were instrumental in having Captain Kidd arrested and clapped in chains when he went ashore in New York. He was taken back to England and had to wait in Newgate Prison for almost two years before he was brought to trial. His crime was judged a particularly heinous one as he had once held the king's commission to track down privateers and by going over to the other side could be pegged as a deserter. Captain William Kidd was found guilty of piracy among other charges and condemned to be hanged, to which he replied: 'My Lord, it is a very hard sentence. For my part I am the most innocent person of them all, only I have been sworn against by perjured persons.'

The sentence was carried out at the appropriately named Execution Dock in 1701. The *Newgate Calendar*'s censorious epitaph for Kidd ran in part: 'of the haunts of the pirates rendered him one of the most proper men in the world to have extirpated this nest of villains, but his own avarice defeated the generous views of the greatest'.

Despite all efforts to deter and punish deserters, some individuals showed great perseverance in their efforts to achieve freedom and encourage others to do the same.

Herman Melville wrote several books about life in the South Seas. Parts of them were based on his experiences after deserting from a whaling vessel among the islands of the Marquesas. They inspired many would-be adventurers.

The son of middle-class parents, Melville worked as a bank clerk and a schoolteacher before deciding to see the world. In his early twenties he signed on as a member of the crew of the *Acushnet*, bound for the coast of South America.

When, in June 1842, the vessel put in for fresh food at one of the Marquesas Islands in the South Pacific, Melville, impressed by the beauty of the area, decided to desert and explore the island. He did not return from a shore party and spent about a month living with the islanders in one of the lush valleys. He was picked up by another ship calling in at the Marquesas and travelled on to Hawaii, where he spent some time before returning to the USA.

Melville wrote two books based on his time in the South Seas,

Typee and *Omoo*. They presented highly idealised accounts of an idyllic paradise where 'all was mirth, fun and high good humour'. At first they were believed to be accurate accounts of long sojourns in the area by the writer. In fact they were amalgams of Melville's brief encounter with the islanders, his imagination and the results of a great deal of reading about the area. In his writing, especially in *Typee*, he did much to confirm the generally held opinion of the South Seas as a remote tropical paradise: 'There seemed to be no cares, griefs, troubles or vexations. The hours tripped along as gaily as the laughing couple doing a country dance.'

Melville spent some time as a merchant seaman, using his experiences for other books, including his masterpiece *Moby-Dick*. He was not particularly successful as a writer during his lifetime and by 1866 he was working as a customs official in New York. He was not fully appreciated as a great writer until thirty years after his death.

A more prolonged desertion in the Pacific than those of Marra and Melville was undertaken by Samuel Jervis, who deserted from a sailing vessel in Tasmania and lived for many years with a tribe of aborigines before returning to civilisation.

He was born at Shenstone Park near Lichfield in 1773. His father, a squire, was killed in a hunting accident when the boy was only ten. His uncle, Captain John Jervis, took responsibility for him and Jervis sailed for several years on the South Seas trading vessel, known either as the *Royal Fox* or the *Regent Fox*.

On what was to become his last trip to Australia, Jervis fell out with the ship's boatswain. In an effort to frighten the youngster the boatswain told him that Captain Jervis wanted to take over Shenstone Park and intended marooning Sammy on a desert island before sailing home to claim the estate.

The gullible youth believed the story. When the vessel put in at Tamar Heads in Tasmania, he went ashore in a boat with others to fetch water. Reaching the shore he ran off and hid until the other seamen stopped looking for him and rowed back to the ship.

Jervis watched the ship sail away. Almost at once he was captured by a tribe of aborigines. They treated the white boy kindly and for about twenty-six years Jervis lived with them, adopting their wandering, hunting lives and customs in the Quamby region of Tasmania.

Eventually, perhaps in about 1815, Jervis encountered an isolated settler called Cox and his family, the first whites he had seen in a quarter of a century. He left the tribe and was taken in by the family. He lived with them for some years, even assuming their name.

Jervis, or Sammy Cox as he was now known, spent the rest of his long life in Tasmania, working as a gardener and odd-job man. He spent his last years at the Launceston Home for Invalids in Tasmania. According to their records he died in 1891, when he must have been 118 years old!

Another South Pacific deserter who led a life as hazardous though much shorter than Jervis's was John Renton, who deserted from his vessel in the South Pacific and was captured in the Solomon Islands where he spent eight years living among the islanders.

An 18-year-old native of the Orkney Islands, Renton was shanghaied in San Francisco in 1858, forced to work as a seaman onboard a vessel leaving to collect a load of guano from the South Pacific. He hated life onboard the ship and with four companions stole a boat and deserted. Tides and winds carried the small craft over 1,000 miles to the north coast of Malaita in the Solomon Islands, where it ran on to a reef.

Islanders rescued the five exhausted deserters, but three of them died shortly thereafter. The resilient Renton made a quick recovery and endeared himself to the islanders with his youthful high spirits and keenness to please. His companion did not mend as quickly. Tired of looking after him, the Malaitans took him out to sea and clubbed him to death, throwing his weighted body over the side of their canoe.

Eventually Renton took up residence on Sulufou, one of the incredible artificial islands of the lagoon, constructed laboriously, stone by stone by islanders wishing to escape the attentions of mosquitoes and marauding bushmen on the main island.

Renton spent eight years in the Solomons, working as a canoe builder and net mender. Slowly the rumour began to spread among visiting vessels that a white man was stranded somewhere in the lagoon. Some captains began to make active but unsuccessful efforts to find the castaway. One of them actually managed to get a letter to Renton, which after his rescue he showed to the *Melbourne Argus* of 28 December 1875:

To a White Man
It has been reported to me that there have been white men on this shore. I have searched all over but can find no traces at all. If any white man should chance to get this, he should try to get across to Isabelle where vessels frequently call, in two months I shall return to Buccotta Island and if a white man could make his way there by that time I will give him a passage to Sydney.
Captain Macfarlane

Renton took part in two war-party raids on other villages before being rescued in 1875 by a labour-recruiting vessel, the *Bobtail Nag*. One day the marooned seaman saw the visiting vessel from the top of a palm tree. He found a section of plank and a charred stick and scrawled a message on the plank. He threw the plank into a canoe going out to trade with the labour-recruiting vessel

The odds against the message being seen by anyone on the *Bobtail Nag* must have been enormous. By sheer chance, however, it was spotted and a ship's boat was sent ashore to investigate. Renton was found and purchased from his captors for a number of planes, blades and axes. He was taken to Queensland, where he wrote a book about his experiences on the artificial island and became a government agent on labour recruiting vessels travelling to islands of the South Pacific, seeking hands for work in the sugar fields of northern Australia.

Renton's task was to supervise the return of time-expired islanders from the plantations to their homes, and to ensure that any other islanders recruited were treated humanely. In 1878, three years after he had been rescued from Malaita, Renton was sailing among the islands of the New Hebrides on a vessel called the *Mystery*, supervising a number of islanders being taken home from Queensland. The ship visited the island of Aoba, and Renton and one other member of the crew went ashore to fetch fresh water. Unfortunately, their visit coincided with the holding of a feast in the area in which by tradition human flesh was supposed to be eaten. John Renton, who was not yet thirty, and his companion, were attacked, clubbed to death and eaten.

The defection of John Renton was originally prompted by harsh conditions on board the guano vessel to which he had been forcibly recruited. The same could be said of many other deserters who believed that any sort of life would be preferable to the one they were presently suffering. Many of them were also buoyed by the innate confidence that with their skills and experience they would be capable of surviving in any new worlds they encountered. Something would always turn up. This display of arrogance was evident as early as the reign in Egypt of Psamtik I (656–609 BC). Having not been relieved for three years, the troops of one of his garrisons deserted and started to march towards Libya to offer their services there. The emperor pursued and caught up with them, begging them to stay and not to desert their wives and children. One of the deserters made a coarse gesture to the emperor and said confidently, 'Wherever we go, we are sure of finding wives and children!'

9

'THE GLORIOUS EMBLEM OF NATIVE RIGHTS'

It was the glorious emblem of native rights, that bring the banner that should have floated over our native land so many years ago. It was St Patrick, the harp of Erin, the shamrock upon a green field.
– John Riley describes his pride in fighting under the Irish flag for Mexico

During the English Civil War, desertions on both sides were rife and over a third of foot soldiers on both the Royalist and Parliamentary sides left their posts. This applied to officers as well as men, although members of the commissioned ranks tended to transfer their allegiance to the other side, while ordinary soldiers went home.

Hope of promotion, increased pay, disenchantment with the current cause or poor conditions, as well as a genuine conversion to another way of thinking, were all reasons for a soldier's desertion. A particular thorn in the side of the Royalists in all these respects was the opposing Earl of Essex. The earl's army was renowned for its success in battle, high pay and rapid promotion prospects for those who caught his eye. Other officers were utterly pragmatic about their reasons for fighting and thought nothing of switching their allegiances. Such an attitude was exemplified by a Captain Carlo Phantom, a Croatian who made no secret of his reason for espousing the Royalist cause: 'I come to fight for your half crown and your handsome women.'

John Hurry, or Urry, was a serial turncoat during the Civil War. Upon the outbreak of hostilities he joined the Earl of Essex's army, attracted by the money on offer. He fought bravely, but was annoyed because he was only promoted to major. In 1643, he went over to Prince Rupert and his Royalists, taking with him a cache of secret information about the Parliamentary side's military intentions. Hurry fought bravely for his new allies and was knighted after the Battle of Chalgrove. He then made a serious miscalculation and returned to King Charles's ranks, believing that the Royalists were about to triumph. In 1648 he was captured by Cromwell's troops. By this time his capricious inclinations had attracted too much attention and condemnation. Sir John Hurry was executed.

Group and individual desertions in the English Civil War were an annoyance to authorities on both sides, but a far more pressing problem was the defection of large numbers at the same time. At the Battle of Nantwich in Cheshire in 1644, Nantwich, loyal to Cromwell's cause, had been besieged by Lord Byron, the Royalist general, for six weeks. General Fairfax, with a force of 3,000 troops, marched across the Pennines to the relief of the town.

King Charles I had recently made peace in Ireland. He ordered his army fighting there was to return to England and join Byron at Nantwich. The army landed at Chester and at once marched to the aid of the Royalists. However, most of the troops in the new force were disgruntled with their lot and had no great affinity with the king's cause. The average pay of a foot-soldier was six shillings a week, with the occasional bonus of another six shillings if a particularly suicidal charge had to be made. Such wages did not encourage an over-abundance of loyalty.

Byron and his reinforcements prepared to meet the advancing Roundhead newcomers on a hill at Acton, a mile to the west of Nantwich. He ordered his infantry and artillery to cross the River Weaver and take up new positions. A sudden thaw made the frozen river flood, washing away the only bridge in the area. Byron's forces were suddenly split by the raging torrent.

Byron set his remaining force off on a six-mile march to find a suitable place to ford the river. Meanwhile, Fairfax arrived with his army and attacked the Royalist infantry on the hill. Because of the local preponderance of thick hedgerows, Byron's cavalry could not be utilised effectively to aid the hard-pressed infantry.

To add to the troubles of the Royalists, William Brereton, the Parliamentarian defender of Nantwich, suddenly sallied out of the town with a large detachment, and attacked Byron's forces from the other side. After some confused fighting the Royalist infantry suddenly surrendered and 1,500 members of Charles's Irish Army promptly went over to the side of the Parliamentarians. The English Civil War continued for another few years, until Charles surrendered to the Scottish army in 1646. He was handed over to Parliament and was tried in 1649 before being beheaded on 30 January.

The best way to attract advantageous offers of desertion was to develop a striking reputation as a fighting body. By the eighteenth century, some military units had reached such an advanced state of military efficiency that other generals offered their members all sorts of inducements to come across. One unit comprised almost entirely of such sought-after deserters was the Husaren Regiment.

Several Prussian monarchs made efforts to persuade Hungarian deserters to join their army in the eighteenth century, resulting in the formation of this elite if motley corps. At the time many Hungarians were serving Austria far from home throughout the vast Habsburg Empire. Their courage and fighting abilities were widely recognised. Both Frederick I of Prussia and his son Frederick William backed recruiting drives to persuade these Hussars to desert and join Prussia. Agents were sent to convince officers and men to leave the Austrian force by offering money and other bribes.

So many Hungarians succumbed and came over to Prussia that two regiments of Hussars were formed. Their members wore traditional Hungarian uniforms and were used in battle for scouting duties and surprise attacks. So highly were these Hungarians prized that in 1759 a royal edict was published forbidding Prussian officers from insulting their new allies. In a further effort to persuade the Hussars to stay, troops were exempted from the usual physical punishments meted out to ordinary soldiers.

National pride and a deep-seated distrust of one's neighbours also led to a number of large-scale defections. Between 1743 and 1783, there were several mass desertions from Scottish regiments in Great Britain. Then an isolated country, most Scots lived in small villages and primitive farms, often separated from one another by bad weather, moors and rugged mountains. The clan system still existed but as a result of the abortive uprising of 1745, the English government began slowly but systematically to render the country impotent by dismantling its social structure, disarming the clans, forbidding the wearing of the tartan and replacing Gaelic with English in Scottish schools.

There were still Scottish regiments loyal to the crown but they were distrusted – and well aware of the fact, which made the Scottish troops discontented and suspicious.

The first Scottish mass desertion was instigated by a gifted and unusual soldier called Farquhar Shaw, the son of a Strathspey laird. He caused great national alarm when he refused to remain with his regiment in England and hot-headedly led a march back to Scotland, for which he was executed.

Shaw was renowned for his prowess as a shot and swordsman and for his size and strength. When the regiment known variously as the 42nd, the Royal Highlanders and the Black Watch was formed for the purpose of guarding Scotland from the raids of the wild clans, Shaw was one of many wellborn young men to join. Some of his noble companions in the ranks even brought their own body servants with them to enlist. These were gentlemen rankers, men of independent means and minds, accustomed to thinking for themselves.

Shaw soon made his mark in the regiment. News of his skill with the musket, pistol and broadsword reached as far south as London. King George II asked that three of the regiment's best swordsmen be sent to the capital to give an exhibition of their athletic prowess. Shaw and two other privates were selected and performed for the king and members of his court with the sword in the great gallery of St James's Palace.

King George was so impressed with the exhibition that he rewarded Shaw and his Black Watch companions with a bag of guineas. The Scots received the gift politely, but on their way out gave the money to a doorman, explaining that gentlemen did not accept tips. Shaw and the others returned to Perth, only to hear that the Black Watch had been ordered to march to London before embarking for Flanders as reinforcements for the English force supporting Austria against France and Bavaria.

Many of its troops were reluctant to leave Scotland, believing that they had been recruited to serve only in the Highlands. However, their march south in full Highland garb in 1743 caused so much awe and wonder that bountiful hospitality was bestowed on the soldiers as they passed through different communities.

When they reached the capital, expecting to be reviewed by the monarch, the troops were disappointed to hear that he had sailed for Hanover on the day of their arrival. Then rumours began to spread among the ranks that the government was fearful of Stewart sympathies in the regiment. Charles Edward Stewart, the representative of the exiled House of Stewart, was lurking on the Continent, planning to restore a state of absolute monarchy to Scotland, a scheme he attempted to put into practice only two years later in the uprising of 1745. The men of the Black Watch feared that they were destined to be transported to the American plantations, there to spend their lives as field slaves.

The men of the Black Watch deserted en masse in May. Shaw and two brothers, both corporals, Malcolm and Samuel M'Pherson, emerged as leaders of the company. The disgruntled Scots gathered on Highgate Common and began to march northwards, keeping as far as possible to woodland, where it would be difficult for would-be observers to keep track of their progress. Each man carried his arms and fourteen pounds of ball ammunition. An admiring contemporary report declared that the forced march 'exhibited considerable military skill and strategy'.

The alarmed Secretary of State for War issued an edict urging all commanding officers of units between London and Scotland to

keep a watch for the deserters. On Thursday 19 May they were seen
near Northampton. A regiment of horses was sent out to establish
the location of the Scots. They were discovered in Ladywood, some
four miles from Oundle. More English troops were despatched to
surround the woodland.

A certain Captain Ball, who knew the country, was sent to negotiate with the deserters. The Scots demanded a free pardon and
the right to keep their arms before they would emerge from their
hiding place. The doughty Ball refused the terms and informed the
recalcitrant Scots that the wood was surrounded by troops and that
the absconders would be cut to pieces if they did not surrender.

About thirty of the Scots then yielded and returned to the main
body of troops with Captain Ball. They were allowed to keep their
arms but the priming powder was blown from the firing pans of
their muskets, rendering them harmless.

After much discussion the remainder of the deserters under Shaw
and Corporal M'Pherson also yielded. They were marched back
to London, incarcerated and then put on trial. The deserters were
found guilty and all sentenced to be shot. In the event only three
were executed: the M'Pherson brothers and Farquhar Shaw.

The executions took place on the parade ground of the Tower of
London at 6 a.m. on 12 June 1743. All the Highland deserters were
drawn up to see the three soldiers killed.

Afterwards the survivors were split up and sent to serve in such
areas as the West Indies, North America and Gibraltar. In 1887,
in a gesture of rehabilitation, a monument was raised of Private
Farquhar Shaw in full Highland garb at Aberfeldy.

Just four years after the Black Watch mutiny came another great
Scottish desertion. This time it occurred among the men of the
Seaforth Highlanders. In September 1787 they were stationed in
Edinburgh in a state of some discontent. They believed that their
officers were unnecessarily harsh in the execution of their duties and
that in addition they were owed considerable payment in arrears.

When it was announced that the regiment was to be shipped
to Guernsey in the Channel Islands to repel a threatened French

invasion, the troops rebelled. They assembled not far from Edinburgh Castle and refused to march to their disembarkation point. Their cause was taken up by many passers-by, who pelted their officers with stones and encouraged the soldiers to stay put. After much persuasion the officers of the regiment were able to urge the troops to march towards the waiting transports. About 500 of the men boarded the ships, but the rest dug in their heels and refused.

Those troops still on shore shouldered their arms and marched away from the quayside with their bagpipes playing. They stopped at Arthur's Seat, where they took up residence. In the eighteenth century the hill was surrounded by marshy fields and the roads were little more than sheep-tracks. Anyone approaching the Seat could be seen at a distance. The camp was a well-organised one. The soldiers appointed their own leaders and stationed sentries at strategic intervals. The mutineers were supplied with food and drink by many sympathetic residents of the city. To the alarm of the authorities the deserters began to assemble fresh supplies of ammunition.

The authorities brought in large supplies of troops, including the 11th Dragoons, the Buccleuch Fencibles and the Glasgow Volunteers. However, every effort was made to end the dispute by peaceable means. General Skene, second-in-command of the Scottish forces, visited the deserters' camp and promised that their grievances would be investigated if only they would return to their barracks. He was followed by the Duke of Buccleuch, the Earl of Dunmore, Lord Macdonald and many other members of the Scottish establishment.

After much hard negotiating the deserters were offered a free pardon and the payment of all arrears of money due to them. The authorities, however, refused to dismiss some of the officers named by the troops. The deserters agreed to the terms. They headed down the hill back towards Edinburgh, where they were met by General Skene and greeted him with three cheers. The soldiers then returned to their duties and received their back pay. It was an encouraging if rare example of how, with give and take on both sides, agreements could sometimes be reached between rankers and senior officers.

Another mass defection from one army to another occurred during the US–Mexican war of 1846–48. Throughout this period an entire battalion of the Mexican Army was made up largely of Irish deserters from the United States Army. It was known as the St Patrick's Battalion, or the *San Patricios*.

The leader of the *San Patricios* was a Galwayman called John Riley, who was born in 1817. In 1845, he was serving in the US Army on the US–Mexican border, possibly as a gunnery sergeant. Many Irish émigrés joined the American Army, because work was difficult to come by in their new land. In the 1840s there were more than 5,000 Irish troops serving with the Americans. Conditions for new recruits were not good. They were disparaged as foreigners first and scorned second because most of them were Roman Catholics. At the time there were no Catholic chaplains in the United States Army.

One Sunday, Riley was granted permission to cross the border to attend Mass on the Mexican side. Once there he promptly deserted and joined the Mexican Army. He was granted a commission as a lieutenant and his monthly pay rose from $7 to $57. With the blessing of the Mexican high command Riley set out to raise an Irish battalion to fight the Americans in the war that was looming. In this he was aided by Patrick Dalton, a deserter originating from County Mayo.

Riley and a few others crossed the border surreptitiously and set out on a campaign to recruit dissatisfied Irish soldiers serving in the US Army. They gave out handbills and called secret meetings, promising their listeners better pay and grants of land in their new home. They met with great success, persuading a large number of men to desert in the first few weeks. Some of the defectors even swam across a river to enlist with the Mexicans.

Soon the Irish desertions became a major problem to the US military hierarchy, as more and more troops left. As well as the Irish soldiers, some Americans defected too; Irish civilians working in Mexico also joined the *San Patricios*.

When war broke out between Mexico and the United States, the St Patrick's Battalion, well led by John Riley, fought bravely in a number of battles between 1846 and 1847, at Matamoros, Monterey, Buena Vista, Cerro Gordo and Churubusco. The Mexicans were no match for the better-armed and equipped Americans and were driven back. The *San Patricios* continued to fight fiercely, perhaps because they suspected that they would be executed as deserters if they were caught.

Finally the Irish contingent was defeated at the Battle of Churubusco in 1847 and the survivors, John Riley among them, surrendered. They were tried for desertion by the Americans. Sixty-eight were sentenced to death by hanging. John Riley and fourteen others evaded the death sentence because they had deserted before the outbreak of war. Instead they were given fifty lashes and each man was branded with a D for deserter. In addition, those who were not condemned to die had to dig graves under the gallows of their former colleagues-in-arms who were being executed.

As a result of the outcome of the war, the United States took control of over half a million square miles of Mexican territory; Mexico was allowed to retain its army. It recalled John Riley after his punishment and he managed to attain the rank of brevet colonel.

A more spontaneous mass desertion took place in 1824 in Peru. The Battle of Ayacucho saw the final defeat of Spanish colonial rule in Peru and the emergence of a burgeoning Peruvian independence. The success of the insurgents at the battle was partly due to the fact that many South American Indians deserted the Spanish Army and came over to the rebel side.

The Spanish had ruled Peru through a series of viceroys ever since they had taken the land from the Incas in 1532. Over the years they imposed a rigid caste structure in the country. The ruling class consisted of those of pure Spanish blood. Then came the *mestizo*, people of mixed Spanish and Indian descent. Very much at the bottom of the pile, condemned to menial tasks and an abysmal standard of living were the Indians, descendants of the original inhabitants of Peru.

It was a situation ripe for insurrection, especially as by the nineteenth century neighbouring South American countries were beginning to assert their independence. Two of the greatest freedom fighters soon combined to plot Peru's freedom. In 1822, Simón Bolívar, who had freed Venezuela, Columbia and Ecuador, met José de San Martín, leader of the liberation struggles in Argentina and Chile. They decided that Bolivar would be entrusted with leading the campaign for the independence of Peru.

At the Battle of Ayacucho, Bolivar's deputy, the Venezuelan José de Sucre, was in command. He led a force of some 6,000 men, including Peruvians, Chileans, Colombians, Venezuelans and Argentines. The battle took place on a high plateau near the town of Ayacucho. The Spanish Army consisted of 9,000 men and was heavily armed with artillery pieces.

When the two forces lined up opposite each other on the plain there was suddenly an exodus of South American Indians from a number of neighbouring countries who had either been pressed into the Spanish force or who were serving as reluctant mercenaries. Many of them saw friends, neighbours and even relatives in the insurgent army. Before the Spanish officers could stop them or even fire more than a few token shots at the deserters, hundreds of their troops were now embracing members of the rebel army and preparing to serve at their sides.

The rebels opened the battle with a brilliant cavalry charge of such ferocity that the Spaniards, already shaken by their unexpected defections, turned and ran. Some 2,000 of them were hacked down. The Spanish viceroy and his generals surrendered. The show of solidarity between Bolivar's forces and the deserting Indians reinforcing his ranks had done much to cast off the Spanish yoke.

Many of the desertions in armies of pressed conscripts were caused by the sheer resentment of those pressed into service at having to leave their homes and normal lives, some of whom attempted to leave the military environment as soon as possible.

It was ever thus. Conscription dates back to the armies of Ancient

Egypt, starting in about 2700 BC, when 'military scribes' or recruiting officers toured the provinces seeking out likely candidates for compulsory military service. In China during the reign of Qin Shi Huang (lived 259–210 BC) when the building of the 1,500-mile-long Great Wall of China commenced in order to keep out the barbarians, in addition to half a million labourers 300,000 conscripted soldiers were used for the task. In 1793 after the French Revolution, the Convention of the French Republic raised an army of 300,000 conscripts.

Wherever it was introduced, conscription was unpopular, and constant efforts were made to circumvent it by those caught in its trawl. One of the most unusual of these attempts occurred in a small village near Lavoine in France in the mid-nineteenth century, when it was discovered that the authorities there were registering the birth of most boys as girls to avoid recruitment in later years when they grew up.

With the gradual introduction of universal male conscription in many countries, a significant number of the reluctant pressed soldiers proved to be of superior mental and physical ability compared with the average regular professional soldier. As a result, the quality of defection in the armed forces rose markedly as many conscripts began to outwit the non-commissioned officers placed in charge of them. Some attempts at desertion were decidedly ingenious; one recruit arranged to be smuggled out of his unit wrapped in a carpet.

10

SNOWBIRDS AND WOODLAND

Whereas by my proclamation dated the tenth day of last month, a Pardon was offered to all deserters from the army dispersed in different parts of the States, who should join their respective corps by the first of May next.

– Proclamation issued by George Washington, 22 April 1777

The American Revolutionary War, or War of Independence, was fought between 1775 and 1783, when the American colonists made their spirited bid for independence. In the spring of 1776, the Continental Army of the colonists drove the British out of Boston, but later were made to evacuate New York.

Over a period of time, the Americans were joined by forces from France, Spain and the Netherlands. Among ordinary soldiers, there were many thousands of deserters during the Revolutionary War. It was estimated that almost 25 per cent of the soldiers involved deserted.

In an effort to redress the balance, the Americans made a conscious effort between 1776 and 1784 to encourage and award defectors from among the better trained British soldiers and their allies, in an effort to lure them over.

Almost from the start of the war King George III of Britain hired many German soldiers from the German princes who normally employed them. The soldiers themselves received little more than their food for risking their lives so far from home. More than 20,000 Hessians – so called because the majority of the mercenaries came from Hesse-Cassel – were recruited in all from the 300 principalities that made up Germany.

The Hessians were not treated well by their employers. J. G. Seume, one of their number, described in his diary the initial voyage of his unit from Portsmouth to New York in 1776. He complained of:

> ...biscuits (which had to be) broken by cannon balls, water barrels full of worms. What can be said of the British Quartermaster's Department which sent these people to sea without proper food or drink? What of the Duke of Brunswick who sent his subjects to Canada without durable boots or stockings and without overcoats?

They soon became even further discontented with their lot on the American continent. The Hessians soon believed that they were being given too much of the fighting to do and that they were regarded with disdain by the British. A particular bone of contention was that when officers were taken prisoner, the British were exchanged for their American counterparts, while the Germans often had to remain incarcerated.

The American revolutionaries soon capitalised on this resentment. They began to make official overtures encouraging the Hessians to change sides. There was even a tariff offered for potential deserters. Any German officer who brought over with him forty men was offered 800 acres of woodland, four oxen, one bull, two cows and four sows. Individual soldiers would each be presented with fifty acres of land. The deserters did not even have to fight but could retire to their new estates. Any officers who did volunteer to serve the American cause would be promoted and would serve only in German units.

Surprisingly few officers took advantage of this offer, although in August 1778, two Hessians of commissioned rank did enter Washington's camp to negotiate their futures, but so many soldiers came across that official recruiting stations were set up. Some 7,000 Hessians were killed or died of disease in the North American campaign. About 5,000 deserters stayed on and made permanent homes on the continent.

Thousands of American soldiers continued to desert. Many were fed up with the low pay and alternate boredom and dangers of a soldier's life. Others were homesick; many farmers felt that they had to get home to harvest their crops before their families starved. Desertions were particularly rife when the first winter snows began to fall, so much so that these winter migrants were contemptuously dubbed snowbirds. The sum of $30 was paid for every deserter recaptured, but the Americans did not have the men, or the time, to embark upon large-scale hunting expeditions. When George Washington, the American commander, quartered with his force at Valley Forge in the winter of 1777–78, over 2,000 of his troops deserted, causing one officer to report that 'desertions are astonishingly great'.

In 1781, about 1,500 American troops mutinied at the same time and left their positions in the line. They became known as the Pennsylvania Line deserters. The men were occupying huts at Jockey Hollow during a winter break in the fighting. They were particularly dissatisfied because they believed they had been cheated into serving longer than was necessary. The period for which they had volunteered had been 'three years or longer'. The men considered that this meant they should serve the shorter of these two alternatives. As the war had been in progress for more than three years they argued that they should be allowed to go home. Two sergeants, William Bowzar and Daniel Connell, were particularly vociferous in their complaints and came to be regarded as the ringleaders of the uprising.

At about 10 p.m. on 1 January 1781, armed soldiers suddenly rushed out of the huts, captured a supply of guns and ammunition, and prepared to leave the camp. Officers tried to persuade the men to stay and a number of shots were fired, causing fatalities. The mutineers ran from hut to hut, trying to drum up volunteers to join them. Then the deserters lined up and marched off to Vealtown, four miles away. They spent the night there, hoping to be joined by other absentees, before going on to Philadelphia.

General Anthony Wayne, in charge of the troops, followed the deserters at a discreet distance, begging the men not to go over to the British. The mutineers moved off again and, on the evening of 3 January, took over the village of Princeton, pitching their tents there. Wayne still tried to negotiate, imploring the troops to appoint spokesmen and promising that there would be no victimisation if they returned to the line. The deserters appointed a board of sergeants as their representatives, but would not allow General Wayne to address them.

Congress assembled hastily and tried to decide what to do. When the British forces heard what was happening, their leader Sir Henry Clinton smuggled agents across the lines, promising pardons to deserters who came over and granting them immunity from serving with the British. Two of these agents were captured and hanged by the colonists.

Anthony Wayne, however, approached the board of sergeants and negotiated with them, causing George Washington to fear that his general would be kidnapped and held as a hostage. At the end of protracted negotiations, one of Washington's representatives wrote to his commander-in-chief:

> We are happy to inform your Excellency, that the terms offered to the Pennsylvania troops are at length finally, and, as we believe, cordially and satisfactorily agreed on, and, tomorrow, we expect the Pennsylvania line will be arranged in its former order.

It was decided that over 1,000 of the longest-serving troops would be discharged and that most of the remainder would be sent on leave. Many of the discharged men later re-enlisted.

A Scottish seaman who became a hero of the US Navy during the Revolutionary War only reached the USA in the first place because he had deserted from his ship. His name was John Paul, although he later changed it to John Paul Jones. Jones was born in 1747. The son of a gardener, he was apprenticed to a ship-owner at the age of twelve and made a number of cross-Atlantic voyages. His advancement was rapid and he first assumed command of a vessel when the captain and first mate died. Jones brought the ship and its cargo safely home and for this act he was made a captain by the shipping line which employed him.

On one of his voyages, he had a member of his crew flogged for neglect of duty. The man subsequently died and Jones was arrested, although he was cleared of the charge of manslaughter. In 1773, he delivered a cargo to the Caribbean island of Tobago. He decided to invest the money he had received in a cargo for the return journey, instead of paying his crew for their shore leave. This infuriated the seamen of his vessel, *Betsy*, and one of them attacked Jones. Years later, on 6 March 1779, Jones gave a written account of the incident to his friend Benjamin Franklin in Paris, published in *The Life and Letters of John Paul Jones* by Mrs Reginald De Koven. Jones used the third person to describe the attack, saying that his assailant:

> …armed himself with a bludgeon with which he returned to the quarter-deck and attacked the Master [Jones]. The Master was thunder-struck with surprise, for he considered the man's ravages as the natural effect of disappointed rage which would soon subside of itself. But now his sole expedient was to prevent bad consequences by returning again to the cabin. Unhappily at that instant, the assailant's arm being high raised, he threw his body forward, to reach the Master's head with the descending blow. The fatal and unavoidable consequence of which was his rushing upon the sword-point.

Jones went ashore to give himself up. There he found himself the object of much local resentment on Tobago because of this second death under his command. Friends of Jones advised him to flee to Virginia on the mainland of North America to avoid trouble on the island. Jones did so, hastily abandoning his command without notice.

He had a hard time of it at first, existing off the charity of friends. To preserve his anonymity, during this period he changed his name from John Paul to John Paul Jones. Eventually, thanks to the effort of a congressman who wanted to see a fair share of commissions in the new continental navy go to his southern constituents, Jones, now technically a Virginian, was made a lieutenant, and then a year later in 1776, he was given his own command.

Under his new name of John Paul Jones, the captain became the greatest of contemporary naval commanders. In a series of daring actions he sank a number of English ships during the Revolutionary War. This culminated in 1779 when Jones, commanding a combined American–French squadron, defeated the British Baltic merchant fleet, guarded by a number of warships. When challenged at one stage to surrender, Jones answered in the immortal phrase, 'I have not yet begun to fight!'

The majority of the Revolution's leaders were American born and bred, although several of them deserted their cause for different reasons. One of these was Robert Rogers. Rogers, a charismatic New Hampshire leader and brave fighter, displayed shifting allegiances and served under a number of flags in his lifetime, but took umbrage when George Washington, mistrusting his motives, refused his offer of help during the American Revolution. As a result, Rogers fought for the British instead.

Rogers, who had always been a keen hunter and trapper, left his farm in 1755 to fight for the British against the French during the Indian Wars, mainly to escape from a charge of counterfeiting. He showed great aptitude and was placed in command of a company of Rangers, a tough, irregular fighting force. Travelling light and fast, he and his men were so successful that the English placed him in command of all the colonial Ranger companies, forerunners of commando units of later generations. He wrote several books about his exploits, which cemented his fame. One of these was *The Journal of Robert Rogers, the Ranger, on his Expedition to Receive the Surrender of the Western French Forts, Oct. 20, 1760–Feb. 14, 1762.* One of the typical triumphal entries ran:

> We rowed eight miles, and at half a mile short of the fort and front-
> ing it, I drew up my detachment on a field of grass, from hence I sent
> Lieut. Kesleys and McCormick with seventeen 36 Royal Americans

to take possession of the fort. The French garrison laid down their arms, English colours were hoisted and the enemy's taken down.

Rogers cemented his reputation when he led a company of 200 Rangers in a march to destroy the village of the Abenaki St Francis tribe in Canada. He then went on to fight with General Wolfe at Quebec and later participated at the Battle of Bloody Ridge.

After the war, with possible charges of illegal trading with Native Americans and other financial irregularities in the offing, Rogers escaped to England when he could secure no advancement at home. He failed to persuade King George III to back his proposal for an expedition from the Mississippi River to the Pacific. King George III did place Rogers in charge of the fortress of Michilimackinac, and he and his wife lived there for two years. He was then accused of embezzlement and treasonable dealings with the French, but neither could be proved. All the same, Rogers deemed it prudent in 1769 to return to England. Here he accumulated vast debts and was thrown into prison, until his brother paid off some of the money.

In 1775, Robert Rogers returned to North America and offered his services as a soldier to George Washington. The American leader suspected that at the same time Rogers was negotiating with the British and volunteering to command one of their forces, if the price should be right.

Washington had Rogers thrown into prison, but the former Ranger escaped by claiming that he wished to appear before the rebel Continental Congress. Escorted there, he escaped and made his way to the English lines. Here he fought in the New York area and was placed in command of a company called the King's Rangers, but he was proving such a rogue that it was taken away from him. He ended his military days as a recruiting officer, trading on his previous Rangers' reputation. By 1780, Rogers had returned to England, existing miserably for fifteen years on his half-pay before dying in a cheap London lodging house in 1795.

Even more of a turncoat than Rogers was Benedict Arnold, a hero of the American Revolution who later became disillusioned with his lot and entered into secret negotiations with the British to deliver the fortress of West Point to them. Subsequently he had to flee for his life when his plot was discovered.

The son of wealthy parents, Arnold was born in 1741 and grew up to be an impulsive, restless youth. When he was about fourteen he ran away from home on several occasions to join the New York militia to fight the French in the Indian War. On each occasion he became homesick and deserted. Because of his age no action was taken against him.

He became a prosperous businessman, married and had three children. Upon the outbreak of the American War of Independence in 1775 he volunteered for active service and was made a captain in the state militia. He distinguished himself in a number of military engagements, both on land and on the lakes, was badly wounded twice, and secured the admiration of George Washington himself.

However, Arnold was always a discontented man, quick to respond to what he imagined to be personal and professional slights. When he married for the second time he began to live beyond his means and took part in several dubious business ventures. He was even court-martialled and reprimanded for requisitioning govern-ment wagons for his own commercial needs. He petitioned often for the return of money he claimed to have spent in equipping his forces. When, amid all this, he was passed over for promotion Arnold began to consider going over to the British side.

At that time there was strong support among American Tories, who were also known as Loyalists or the King's Men, for a return to British rule. It was estimated that almost half a million colonists, or 20 per cent of the total, were content to remain under Britain's wing. Arnold began to cherish thoughts of leading this movement, especially as the British authorities were promising to redress the grievances of the Americans and to accede to most of their requests, except for the granting of independence. Disillusioned and impoverished, Benedict Arnold started to enter into treasonable correspondence with Sir Henry Clinton, leader of the British forces stationed in New York City. In 1779, Arnold had been placed in command of the strategically important American fortress of West Point and its considerable stock of supplies. He offered to hand it over to the British. In return Arnold wanted the sum of £20,000 and preferment in the British Army.

On 20 September 1780, a British agent, Major John André, was landed from the sloop *Vulture* at Haverstraw on the River Hudson, not far from West Point. He was accompanied by Joshua Smith, an American of Loyalist Tory sympathies. At midnight on 21 September, André met Benedict Arnold by moonlight on the bank of the river. There Arnold handed over six pages of documents, including plans of the fortress, which André secreted in his boot. Arnold also promised to weaken a link in the chain placed across the river by the Americans to keep back British vessels. Ships of the British fleet would be able to break through the barrier and sail upon West Point, which Arnold promised to surrender, along with its 3,000 men.

André then returned to West Point. The English officer and Smith spent the night at the latter's farmhouse, meaning to rejoin the *Vulture* at daybreak. However, an American shore battery spotted the British ship and opened up its guns on it. Hastily the vessel weighed anchor and sailed for safety, leaving André and Smith on the shore.

The two men decided to walk back to New York City. Unfortunately for them they were captured by a small party of American militiamen. The documents, letters and maps were discovered in André's boot and Arnold's plot was revealed.

On Monday 25 September, Arnold was at breakfast with some aides at Robinson House, an American military headquarters building, just across the Hudson from West Point, awaiting the arrival of George Washington for a meeting. A messenger delivered a despatch to Arnold from Lieutenant Colonel John Jameson, a commander of the American troops in the region. The message reported the news of the capture of the British spy, Major André.

Calmly, Arnold excused himself from the table and went upstairs to inform his wife Peggy that his capture was surely imminent.

Bidding his beloved a hasty farewell, Arnold ordered a horse to be brought round and galloped off as fast as he could.

Peggy Arnold went downstairs and appeared to have some sort of a fit, accusing Richard Varick, one of Arnold's young aides and a close family friend, of ordering the killing of her child. She then collapsed and had to be supported in a state of agitation to her room. Whether she had been genuinely unhinged by the news of André's arrest or whether Peggy Arnold was trying to distract the attention of the others from the unexplained disappearance of her husband has been a matter of dispute.

In the meantime, Benedict Arnold, abandoning his command and the American cause, galloped to his barge and had himself rowed out to the still-hovering *Vulture*. Swiftly he was transported to New York City and safety.

Major John André was hanged as a spy. Joshua Smith was acquitted on a charge of espionage but later on was imprisoned for being a Loyalist. He escaped and was given a small pension by the British.

Benedict Arnold was reunited with his wife Peggy. He was made a general and provided with a pension by the British and given lands in Canada. He was never fully trusted by his new allies and moved in vain to London in the hope of securing some sort of employment, living in apprehension of being captured by the Americans. Captain Johann von Ewald, who served under Arnold in 1781, wrote that the renegade:

> …consistently displayed his former resolution, which, however, was mixed with a cautious concern due to his fear of the gallows if he fell into the hands of his countrymen. He always carried a small pair of pistols in his pocket, as a last recourse to escape being hung.

He died in obscurity in 1801; Peggy died three years later.

In 1781, the British surrendered at Yorktown and the American nation went on to achieve its independence. Not unnaturally, relations with Great Britain continued to be poor.

In 1807 an international incident was sparked over the matter of British deserters taking refuge on American vessels. Britain and France were at war and some of the naval actions took place in the waters of the Caribbean. Both British and French ships were appearing off the shores of the USA in increasing numbers. Many of them put in to American ports for supplies and repairs.

Four sailors, William Ware, Daniel Martin, John Strachan and Jenkins Ratford were deserters from the British Navy. Ware, Martin and Strachan were Americans who had been taken aboard British vessels by press gangs and forced to serve before the mast. Ratford was a discontented British seaman. All four men deserted from the British vessels *Melampus* and *Halifax* and made their way to Portsmouth in New Hampshire. Here they all signed articles on the American frigate *Chesapeake*, about to sail for the Mediterranean.

The British suspected that there were deserters serving on the *Chesapeake* and complained to the American authorities. As a result, Robert Smith, Secretary of State for the US Navy wrote cautiously to the captain of the *Chesapeake* in a letter quoted in 'Yankee Ships and Yankee Sailors-Tales of 1812', by James Barnes:

> It has been represented to me that William Ware, Daniel Martin, John Strachan, John Little and others, deserters from a British ship of war at Norfolk, have been entered by the recruiting office. You will be pleased to make full inquiry regarding to these men (especially if they are American citizens), and inform me of the result. You will immediately direct the recruiting officer in no case to enter deserters from British ships of war.

The commander of the American vessel, Captain James Barron, investigated and satisfied himself that Ware, Martin and Strachan were citizens of the United States, and ignored all requests to deliver the deserters up to the British. Because Ratford had enlisted under an assumed name he was not at first discovered.

Vice Admiral Berkeley, in charge of the British North American station at Halifax, was annoyed by Captain Barron's response to his request. He issued orders to all vessels under his command that,

should the *Chesapeake* be encountered at sea, it should be stopped
and the deserters recovered.

The British warship which encountered the *Chesapeake* soon after
the American vessel had left Portsmouth on 22 June 1807, was the
Leopard, captained by Salisbury Humphries. The American vessel
was in such a state of unpreparedness that much of its cargo still
littered its decks as the crew tried to stow the casks and crates away
to restore some semblance of order on board. Humphries ordered
the *Chesapeake* to hove to, and sent over a small boat containing
copies of his orders from Admiral Berkeley. He ordered Captain
Barron to send over the deserters on board his ship.

Barron refused to do so. The *Leopard* thereupon fired seven
rapid broadsides into the helpless American cargo ship, practically
from point-blank range. Three American sailors were killed and
eighteen wounded. Captain Barron struck his colours. The British
commander sent over a boarding party and dragged the four deserters back to the *Leopard*. Ratford was found hiding in a coal-hole.

Salisbury Humphries took his prisoners back to Halifax to be
tried for desertion. The *Chesapeake* limped back to Portsmouth,
bearing its dead and injured and news of the attack, which was to
scandalise all the citizens of the USA.

President Jeffries expressed the outrage of his fellow countrymen.
He ordered British vessels out of American waters and refused to
allow American ports to offer repair facilities to British ships. He
made various other threatening noises, but he knew that at that
moment his fledgling nation was in no state to go to war with
Great Britain.

The British made a grudging apology for the attack on the
Chesapeake and made some financial restitution, but continued to
stop and search American vessels for deserters from the British Navy.
William Ware, Daniel Martin and John Strachan were sentenced to
death and then reprieved on condition that they re-enlisted in the
Royal Navy. The Briton, Jenkins Ratford, was hanged.

The fallout from the *Chesapeake* incident was not quite over.
Captain Barron was suspended from duty for five years for his part

in surrendering the deserters. As a result, he fell out with another officer and former friend, Stephen Decatur, sitting on the board of enquiry. Some years later Decatur, a rising star in the US Navy, accused Barron of hiding in England rather than serve in the 1812 war. Barron challenged Decatur to a duel. The two men met with pistols five miles outside Washington. Barron was wounded in the hip, but Decatur was shot in the chest and killed.

The shifting values of patriotism and desertion puzzled many citizens. George Washington appealed to the loyalty of his troops not to desert, while at the same time he attempted to bribe the opposing Hessians to come over to his side. John Paul Jones, after deserting his civilian command, showed great patriotism in fighting for the emerging USA, although it was not even his native country. Robert Rogers displayed a deal of pragmatism by fighting for anyone who would pay him enough. Benedict Arnold achieved high command under the Americans but still betrayed his command.

Some years later a similar dichotomy was still being displayed in the USA in attitudes to the war in Vietnam. At the peak of the war 500,000 US troops were serving in Vietnam and over 15,000 had been killed. The USA was divided between those who believed that the campaign should be continued and those who wanted it stopped. The protest movement grew so strong and well-organised that different groups were publishing pamphlets intended for troops, giving them advice on how to desert rather than be sent to fight in Vietnam. In the USA serving soldiers as well as veterans marched on army barracks in protest against the war.

11

'THE MOST MOTLEY COLLECTION'

No man will be shot who shall voluntarily return to duty.
– Proclamation to deserters from Z. B. Vance, Governor of North
Carolina, 1863

As America grew into a great nation, with a plentiful supply of
heroes and heroines, most of the important events in its history
still managed to produce one or two deserters unimpressed by their
potential places in history. When Meriwether Lewis and William
Clark made their voyage of exploration from the confluence of the
Mississippi and Missouri rivers to the West Coast and back between
1804 and 1806, at least one member of the expedition decamped.
Moses B. Reed stole away under the pretext of looking for a lost
knife, was recaptured and sentenced to run the gauntlet four times,
while his peers flogged him with heavy belts. Such barrack room
punishments, in and out of the armed forces and often devised by
the men themselves, were often used as swift forms of retribution.

The Battle of the Alamo in 1836 is famed for the steadfast behaviour of its defenders, like Davy Crockett and Jim Bowie, who held
out courageously against a vastly superior Mexican force laying
siege to the old mission station. Even here, however, one of the
defending party departed surreptitiously before the walls were
breached. His name was Louis (Moses) Rose and he was a French
soldier of fortune. In later years, when asked for the reason for his
shameful action, he replied, 'By God, I wasn't ready to die!'

The American Civil War was fought twenty-five years after the
siege of the Alamo, between 1861 and 1865, when eleven states
seceded from the Union to form the Confederate States of America

and fight the Union, partly, although not wholly, over the matter
of slavery. In the dreadful war that followed a total of over 560,000
deaths occurred, far more than in any other war fought by the USA
in its history.

It is estimated that as many as 200,000 men deserted from the
Union cause and a great many from the Confederate. Many of
them later returned. Both forces were largely citizen armies and
their members found it difficult to come to terms with military
discipline and organisation. Large numbers of troops on both sides
came back to the fray after they had made what provision they
could for their families, or brought in their crops. Especially in the
South, a predominantly rural area, serving soldiers feared that their
families might starve unless the head of the household returned to
help with the harvests.

Some, of course, decided with shrewd self-assessment that they
were not temperamentally suited for camp life or the battlefield,
and deserted almost as soon as hostilities had commenced. These
pragmatic citizens fervently thanked their Lord that the USA was a
vast and still largely unexplored country and set off with a will for
its wildest parts rather than serve the North or the South. One of
these was a Mississippi riverboat captain called Samuel Langhorne
Clemens. Later, writing under the pseudonym Mark Twain, he
became one of America's most celebrated humorous writers, the
author of *The Adventures of Tom Sawyer* (1876), *Huckleberry Finn*
(1885) and many others. As a soldier he was not quite as successful,
deserting after only a few weeks in uniform.

Though he had authorial aspirations, Clemens had been working
as a riverboat pilot on the Mississippi, but the outbreak of the Civil
War curtailed river traffic so badly that in 1861 he found himself
out of a job.

Vaguely prepared to do his bit in the defence of the South,
Clemens joined an irregular Missouri Confederate company,
the Marion Rangers, a sort of forerunner of the British Home
Guard. The Rangers comprised a light-hearted assembly of young
professional people who met in secret because Union forces were

patrolling neighbouring Illinois. Local farmers supplied the irregulars with mules and horses, and they met frequently with some glee at Bear Creek Hill, outside the river port of Hannibal, providing one another with such a plethora of impressive ranks that in the end there were only three privates in the unit, the rest all being officers. Clemens was appointed second lieutenant and rode to weekend camps on a mule, equipped with a frying pan, blankets and an old Kentucky rifle.

Disillusionment soon set in. The volunteers discovered that military life was not the revelry that they had thought it would be. It rained steadily and the banks of a neighbouring river overflowed. The three privates objected to being allocated all the chores and guard duties, and one of the officers shot his own horse by mistake in the dark.

The Marion Rangers went into voluntary liquidation almost as quickly as they had been formed. This prompted their commander, the self-styled 'General' Tom Harris, reluctantly to leave the comfort of a local farmhouse and order the recalcitrant men to reassemble and re-muster. Clemens and the others refused brusquely and continued on their ways. They were chased from one isolated building by a housewife with Unionist sympathies and inadvertently set fire to a barn at another farm when they tried to cook a meal there. In the panic to get away from the flames, Clemens fell out of an upper storey and sprained an ankle. He decided that soldiering was not for him and abandoned all personal efforts to defend the South.

Like thousands of others, Samuel Clemens wasted no time in leaving the war far behind him and making it impossible for the authorities to catch up with him and assign him to a full-time military unit. He headed for Nevada, worked in the silver mines and then drifted into newspaper writing. He adopted the name of Mark Twain, meaning two fathoms deep in his old riverboat world, and embarked upon his career as a writer, although he never discussed his brief and rather inglorious army career, albeit for one brief mention in *A Private History of a Campaign that Failed*:

> When I retired from the rebel army in '61, I retired in good order,
> at least in good enough order for a person who had not yet learned
> how to retreat according to the rules of war and had to trust to native
> genius ... I knew more about retreating than the man who invented
> retreating.

Some deserters, or men accused of desertion, proved once the
gauntlet was thrown down that they were as capable of fighting
as any man. Much depended upon their leaders. Union Colonel
Joshua Chamberlain, commander of the 20th Maine regiment,
became famous for turning 120 mutineers and deserters into a
force grimly willing to fight to the death to protect the left flank of
the Union line at Gettysburg in 1863, when 150,000 men fought a
three-day battle.

Another courageous display at Gettysburg was put up by Stephen
Flavius Brown – once he was allowed to get going. Brown was a
lieutenant in the 13th Vermont Infantry of the Union Army and
distinguished himself in action while a charge of deserting his post
was hanging over his head.

Brown's unit was hurrying to take its place in formation at the
battlefield and had been double-marching through a heatwave
in order to make up for lost time after a late start. The brigade
commander, General George Stannard, was determined to keep his
force moving and had ordered that no soldier was to fall out for any
reason. Sentries were placed all along the route to stop troops from
leaving their formation.

The 13th Vermont had just passed Frederick in Maryland and its
soldiers were exhausted and dehydrated. Brown thought that they
would be in much better condition to fight if they could at least
slake their thirsts first. He left the column with a few soldiers and
returned with water for the parched men, obtained from a nearby
river. Brown's superior officers saw him leave the ranks and return
and he was arrested for disobeying orders and being absent without leave. As a result his sword, the symbol of his command, was
taken from the young officer. However, with the battle imminent,

there was no time to send Brown to the rear, so he was allowed temporarily to remain with his men. His unit had been stationed in the front line of the Union forces and it was imperative that the line did not break.

Almost at once the section being occupied by the 13th Vermont was attacked by Confederate troops commanded by General Pickett. The Union troops resisted stoutly. They were considerably heartened by the sight of Lieutenant Brown fighting in their vanguard, armed only with a hatchet used for camp chores. Deprived of his sword it was the only weapon that the young officer could find. So fierce was Brown's onslaught that his small unit threw back the Confederates at a time when the battle was undecided. Leading the pursuit, Brown exchanged his hatchet for a sword captured from a surrendering Confederate officer and continued to lead his men until the battle was won.

The news of the officer who had fought with a hatchet when nothing else was available soon spread and was such a morale-booster among the Union troops that the charges against Brown were dropped. He fought on with his unit until he lost an arm at the Battle of the Wilderness in 1864. He then returned to his birthplace, Swanton, Vermont, where he lived until his death at the age of sixty-two.

A less edifying episode, rumours of which did much to harm Union morale at the time, involved General George B. McClellan ('Little Mac'), the Union Commander of the Army of the Potomac at the bloody Seven Days Battle fought against the Confederate forces under Robert E. Lee. After a week's desperate fighting it was alleged that his nerve broke and that for a short time he left the battlefield.

Between 25 June and 1 July 1862, McClellan laid siege to Richmond while the freshly appointed Lee did his best to reinforce the city, drive the Union forces back and cut off McClellan from his supply lines on the Peninsula, the strip of land bounded by the James and York Rivers.

McClellan was popular with his men but frustrated President Abraham Lincoln with his caution and reluctance to follow up apparent successes, often overestimating the size and strength of opposing forces. The sequence of battles fought around Richmond on the Peninsula saw McClellan largely in the ascendant, but he was fighting a series of defensive campaigns which allowed Lee again and again to make progress as the Union Army continued to retreat, giving the Confederates breathing space and breaking the siege of Richmond.

The disheartened troops of McClellan's army began to desert in great numbers; 85,000 men left their units out of several hundred thousand. On the sixth day of the battle, 30 June, McClellan seemed personally to abandon his position and give rise to accusations of deserting his men in the face of the enemy. Without warning he boarded the gunboat *Galena* and in it sailed up the River James, away from the sounds of battle. Later he resumed his command but by that time the Union forces had retreated as far as Harrison's Landing on the James river.

McClellan continued to fight on, but by this time Lincoln had lost all faith in him. On 9 November 1862, General McClellan was ordered to relinquish his command and return to his New Jersey home and await a further posting. He was not sent for again for the duration of the war.

Desertions exasperated some officers so much that they resolved to take punitive action against any who fell into their hands. One officer who took a hard line with deserters and as a result was forced to go into hiding himself was George Edward Pickett, a general in the Confederate Army during the American Civil War. He caused such a furore when he executed captured deserters that at the end of the war he had to flee to Canada and live there for a time under an assumed name to avoid retribution.

Born in 1825, Pickett graduated last in his class at the US Military Academy in 1846 and went on to a number of junior army postings until, upon the outbreak of the Civil War, he resigned to take up a colonelcy in the Confederate force. Later he was promoted to brigadier general and fought bravely but without conspicuous success against the Union Army.

In January 1864, General Pickett led a force of 13,000 Confederate troops against Union positions. After some fighting the Union Commander raised a white flag in surrender. Before he did so, he advised the North Carolinian troops under his command of his intention and urged them to flee before they were taken prisoner. South Carolina had joined with the Confederate cause, but many men from the state had joined the Union side and could technically be classed as deserters

The North Carolinians did as they were bid, but it was too late. On 2 February 1864, fifty-three North Carolinian soldiers wearing the uniform of the Union Army were taken prisoner by Pickett's force. At first they were not recognised, because they were wearing Union uniforms. Later, a number of them were identified by former peacetime neighbours. Eventually a large group of North Carolinians was separated from the other Union prisoners of war.

Pickett, already plagued by desertions from his own unit, had no sympathy for the moral predicament of the Southerners who had fought for the North. He announced that the deserters would be tried in military courts.

In the event twenty-two of the captured North Carolinian troops were found guilty of desertion and sentenced to be hanged. The public executions, held before massed ranks of Confederate troops, were staggered over a period of time, lasting from the 4th to the 15th of February. The episode turned out to be both bizarre and horrific. In some cases the wives of the accused men were informed in order that they could witness the hangings. Some of them even had to transport the bodies of their dead husbands back home for burial. At one of the mass executions the hangman helped himself to his fee from the pockets of the condemned men and then cut off the buttons from their tunics as souvenirs to be sold later.

News of General Pickett's executions caused horror and revulsion in the North. It was announced that for every soldier from the Union Army executed in this fashion, a Confederate prisoner of war would also be killed. Pickett continued to command his force and went on losing his battles. At the Battle of Five Forks he sacrificed almost his whole division and was relieved of his command as a result. The war ended the next day.

With the furore about the North Carolinian executions showing no signs of abating, General Pickett adopted the name of Edwards and fled with his family to Montreal in Canada. There were demands that Pickett be arrested and tried as a war criminal. However, as a former career officer in the US Army, he had many friends among the new military hierarchy. Gradually the matter was allowed to drop and after an interval Pickett returned to the USA. He settled in Norfolk, Virginia, where he entered the insurance business.

Authorities on both sides did their best to gather deserters and packs of reluctant warriors rounded up under armed guards for punishment became a common sight. The poet Walt Whitman remarked upon one disjoined procession that he witnessed:

> Saw a large squad of our own deserters (over 300) surrounded with a cordon of arm'd guards along Pennsylvania Avenue. The most motley collection I ever saw, all sorts of rig, all sorts of hats and caps, many fine-looking young fellows, some of them shame-faced, some sickly, most of them dirty, shirts very dirty and long worn, &c. They tramp'd along without order. A huge huddling mass, not in ranks. I saw some of the spectators laughing, but I felt anything else but laughing.

Many deserters took cognisance of the fact that there was safety in numbers and that they would be in better shape to repel attempts at recapture if they were sufficiently numerous to fight back. Few, however, went as far as Newt Knight, who founded a miniature but effective fugitive empire.

Knight was a Confederate deserter who led a bunch of other lawless absconders in Mississippi. The Confederate Army was in such a poor condition that hundreds of deserters were infesting the rural areas, carrying out raids on local towns and isolated communities. These marauding bands became such a nuisance that a concerted effort was made to wipe them out.

The best known of the renegade leaders was Newt Knight, a former dirt farmer and part-time shoemaker who had been conscripted in 1862 in the 8th Mississippi Regiment. Knight always claimed that he had been sent to work in a military hospital as a medical orderly, but it also seems likely that he was for a time a fighting soldier. He was reduced to the ranks from sergeant for an earlier attempt to go absent without leave.

One of fourteen children and completely illiterate, Knight bitterly resented being dragged from his farm in Jones County. When he discovered, in addition, that any man owning more than twenty slaves could avoid the draft, Knight decided that he was involved in 'a rich man's war and a poor man's fight', and that he should do something about it.

Knight promptly left the military hospital and returned to his farm, making a 200-mile journey on foot. Fearing that a neighbour might betray him to the military authorities, he then made his home amid the almost inaccessible thickly wooded swamps of the area. Soon he was being joined by other deserters. With his cunning and natural authority, Newt Knight emerged as their leader. His headquarters at Leaf River Swamp became known as the Devil's Den. At its peak his band consisted of around 100 fellow Confederate deserters.

There were erroneous reports that during this period Newt Knight seceded from the United States and declared his fiefdom the Free State of Jones, but this never happened. That particular title had been applied jokingly to the area for many years, due to its remoteness and lack of attractiveness.

Occasionally Knight and his men would return home, singly and in groups, and work their farms, but always they returned to the Devil's Den, from which they launched various attacks. It is probable that the deserters did ambush small Union forces, but they also took part in robberies against local citizens, carrying off corn and property, an act which gained them little popularity.

Over a period of three years Newt Knight's men became such nuisances that a number of attempts were made to round them up and return them to their units. One Confederate officer delegated with this task, Major Amos McLemore, got so close to the deserters that Knight decided that he must be got rid of. In a daring attack Knight burst into the house in which McLemore and his aides were staying, and shot and killed the officer, before making his escape.

This led to even greater efforts to destroy Newt Knight's authority in Jones County. Two hundred cavalrymen and a battalion of infantry sharpshooters were despatched to kill or capture the deserters. Their efforts were successful. A number of deserters were caught and hanged; others were sent back to fight in the war again.

With most of his force dispersed Knight's effectiveness was reduced. For the rest of the war he adopted a low profile, especially after his cousin Ben was caught and hanged under the impression that he was Newt. The real Newt Knight lived on in Jones County for the rest of his life. He was over ninety when he died.

As the war entered its closing stages, with the Confederates on the brink of surrender, the problem of deserters continued to plague the Union High Command.

On 11 March 1865, President Abraham Lincoln issued his celebrated 'Proclamation 124 – Offering Pardon to Deserters': '…all deserters who shall, within sixty days from the date of this proclamation, viz., on or before the tenth day of May, 1865, return to service or report themselves to a provost-marshal shall be pardoned.'

On the penultimate day of his life, Friday 14 April 1865, President Abraham Lincoln attended a Cabinet meeting before having his lunch. On returning to his office he went through a pile of papers and happened upon a proposed pardon for a deserter. Lincoln studied the evidence and then signed the pardon, saying, 'Well, I think the boy can do us more good above ground than underground.'

That night President Lincoln was shot by a Southern sympathiser John Wilkes Booth, as he attended a production of the play *Our American Cousin* at Ford's Theatre in Washington. He died the following morning. Nothing is known of the soldier, except that he was a young former member of the Union Army who had been caught, tried and convicted to death for leaving his post.

While thousands of men deserted during the war, very few women are recorded as having done so. One who did was Sarah Emma Edmonds. Born in New Brunswick, Canada, she did not have a happy childhood. Her father had wanted a family of boys to help him on his farm, and although his daughter became a good rider and marksman and even took to wearing a boy's attire, she never secured her father's complete approbation and always in later life spoke of him with bitterness.

Records show that Sarah Edmonds enlisted as Franklin Thompson in Detroit in the 2nd Michigan Infantry in 1861. In her autobiography she expressed her delight in getting away from the bonds of home life and embarking upon a life of adventure denied most contemporary women: 'I could only thank God that I was free and could go forward and work, and was not obliged to stay at home and weep!'

As a rule no medical examinations were carried out at enlistment centres and Sarah Edmonds served as a regimental nurse and a despatch carrier. She fought in the Peninsula Campaign and at the Battles of First Manassas, Fredericksburg and Antietam.

In her occasionally far-fetched autobiography, *Nurse and Spy in the Union Army*, published after the war, Sarah Edmonds also claimed that she served as a spy behind Confederate lines, once masquerading as a black, male field-worker, but these exploits are less well documented and there is some doubt as to their veracity.

Towards the end of the war, Sarah Edmonds was once again serving as a male nurse in a military hospital. There she contracted a severe bout of malaria. She knew that if she reported sick she would be subjected to a medical examination and her true sex revealed.

To avoid this, Sarah Edmonds deserted. She travelled to Cairo in Illinois and booked herself into a private hospital. When she had recovered, she saw in a newspaper that Franklin Thompson had been posted as a deserter from the Union Army. Sarah had intended reporting back to her unit upon her recovery, but this was no longer possible. Instead, she travelled to Washington and worked as a female nurse until the end of the war.

Sarah Edmonds settled down and married Linus Seelye, a Canadian mechanic, and they had three children. Unhappy at being branded an army deserter, Sarah petitioned the War Department for a review of her case. In the 1880s, she was given an honourable discharge and a veterans' pension of $12 a month. She died in 1898.

When General Robert E. Lee surrendered his Confederate Army of North Virginia to the Union forces in April 1865, it was a sign that the Civil War was almost over. Thousands of Southern troops did not wait to be disbanded but abandoned their units and set off, singly and in groups, to make their way home. Some of them caused a great deal of trouble when they were freed from the yoke of military discipline. Texas was plagued by deserters. Although the state was technically still at war, thousands of ragged, half-starved former soldiers poured into the capital Austin, pillaging public buildings and stealing anything that they could get their hands on.

In June, one group of about thirty Confederate deserters, headed by a man known only as Captain Rapp, decided to attempt a much more focused and potentially lucrative robbery than the others to rob the Texan State Treasury just outside Austin.

The deserters made their raid at night. To their surprise they found the building empty. Amid all the confusion the civic authorities had too much on their minds to bother to guard what they regarded as an impregnable building. Hardly able to believe their good fortune, the deserters smashed down the doors and began to try to force open the safes with crowbars and sledgehammers.

After a time, news of the raid reached Austin. Captain George R. Freeman, a law-abiding former Confederate officer, at once assembled a group of twenty volunteers and rode out to the rescue of the state's reserve fund of gold and silver. Seeing the silhouettes of the deserters as they approached the building Freeman and his men at once opened fire.

The raiders fired back. Freeman was wounded in the arm and one of the deserters, a man called Campbell, was mortally injured. After this brief encounter the robbers showed little stomach for the fight and fled at once to the security of a mountain hideout to the west of Austin. They took with them some $5,000 in gold and silver. Captain Rapp and his deserters were never seen again and the money was not recovered.

It was not easy leaving one's unit during and after the American Civil War. In the 1860s, for example, both the fearsome gunslinger Wild Bill Hickok and Buffalo Bill Cody were hired to track down deserters. Hickok was a crack shot who became a gambler, guide, scout, marshal and general adventurer. In 1866, he was appointed a government detective, working out of Fort Riley in Kansas to track down army deserters. For a time the flamboyant Buffalo Bill Cody worked with him, before going on to hunt down deserters during the war between the USA and the Plains Indians. Later both men went on to more lucrative work, Hickok as a saloon gambler and Cody as a master showman.

A number of officers and men who fought with great distinction in the war found it difficult to settle down to peacetime soldiering. George Armstrong Custer was a headstrong, courageous and charismatic American military leader, notorious for his eventual defeat and death at the hands of Sitting Bull at the Battle of the Little Bighorn in 1876. Over the course of his career he had a number of clashes with authority, and on one occasion he was accused of deserting his post.

A vigorous, unconventional and flamboyant man, often attired in bizarre uniforms, Custer had distinguished himself in action on the Union side in the Civil War, where it was claimed that he had had eleven horses shot from beneath him. He was also considered a dangerous glory-hunter by his men and desertion rates among his troops were high. He seldom waited for instructions from superiors and constantly volunteered his men for hazardous duties in the field.

All the same, Custer's successes attracted the patronage of the influential Major General Philip H. Sheridan, the commander of the Army of the Shenandoah. In 1863, at the age of twenty-three, Custer was promoted to the rank of brigadier general.

After the war Custer found soldiering a little on the dull side. He had also made enemies with his attention-seeking ways and obvious ambition and was beginning to smoulder resentfully at his lot.

In 1867, he was placed in command of Fort Wallace in Kansas, with the task of maintaining order among the Plains Indians, notably the Cheyenne and the Arapaho. Angered by the steady encroachment of whites into traditional tribal lands, they had begun to raid isolated settlements and stage stations. In return US forces had started to burn Native American villages.

Custer, already lonely and irate because his wife was not with him, arrived at the fort in the spring of the year, with troops of the 7th Cavalry. He was soon ordered to mount an expedition against marauding tribes along the banks of the Republican River. Before he set out, Custer made arrangements to pick up his wife, Libbie, who was waiting at one of the forts along the route.

Custer was not in a good mood on the expedition and he treated the 350 troops so harshly that some of them started to desert. When the total of absentees had reached thirty-five, Custer sent a party out after one group of nineteen deserters, with orders to bring them back, dead or alive. The search party returned with six of the deserters. Three of the men had been shot while resisting arrest and one of them, Private Charles Johnson, later died. The three wounded men were screaming in agony when they were brought back to Custer's camp. The general rode over to them, waved a pistol at the injured troopers and brusquely threatened personally to shoot them if they did not stop their noise.

After a long hard ride, Custer and his men arrived at Fort Hayes. His troops were exhausted and hungry but Custer was determined to be reunited with his wife. Giving the men only a few hours in which to recover, the general took a detachment of three officers and seventy-five men and set off for Fort Riley, hoping to find Libbie there. Custer absented himself from his command, as one of his court martial specifications later said, 'at a time when his command was expected to be actively engaged against hostile Indians'.

Custer then set off on a weird 200-mile odyssey across the plains in search of his wife. He was so single-minded in his pursuit that when a small detachment he had sent to look for a missing mare did not return, he did not dispatch a larger body of men to search for them. In the event two members of the detached party were killed by Native Americans.

Finally, Custer met up with his wife at Fort Riley. By this time too much damage had been done to his reputation by his meandering journey and his reaction to the deserters under his command.

Custer's apparent flagrant neglect of his duties was what a number of his highly placed enemies, including the influential and very senior military officer General Grant, had been waiting for. Custer was arrested and charged with being absent without leave, forcing tired troops to march with him on a private, non-military mission, sequestering two US Army ambulances and four mules to continue his mission, and failing to take proper steps to protect the two soldiers who had been killed while looking for the missing mare. Custer was also charged with ordering the shooting of the deserters and causing three of them to be severely wounded.

His court martial began on 11 October 1867, two months after his arrest. Custer did not take the stand but had his counsel, Captain Charles C. Parsons, read out a long statement in which he vehemently denied ever being absent without leave:

> Through six years, which I have tried faithfully to devote to my country, and to all, in my judgement, that was honourable and useful … I have never once been absent from my command without leave, as here charged.

Nevertheless, Custer was found guilty on all accounts and was sentenced to be suspended from duty for a year without pay. He heard the news at the head of his regiment of 7th Cavalry, drawn up on the parade ground at Fort Leavenworth. True to type, Custer was mounted on a coal-black horse and was attired in a flamboyant uniform with gold epaulettes, wearing a helmet with an eagle insignia.

He received his sentence impassively and rode off to his home in Michigan. He remained there only for ten months before his mentor, Philip Sheridan, managed to get him reinstated.

Custer served for another eight years, developing a reputation as a fearless Native American fighter, until, on 25 June 1876, he led 266 men of 7ᵗʰ Cavalry against Sitting Bull at the Little Bighorn river in Montana. Custer and his entire command were wiped out. This time there were no deserters.

12

EARLY TWENTIETH-CENTURY BLUES

Legio Patria Nostra! (The Legion is our Fatherland!)
– Maxim adopted by French Foreign Legion, 1880

As the world entered the twentieth century with nothing more than a few local wars to occupy it, most soldiers and sailors settled down to the tedium of garrison and patrol duties. Unfortunately, this boredom only gave some of them increased time to plot even more ingenious methods of getting away.

Peace or no peace, trade continued on the high seas. Conditions on many vessels were harsh, and the less philosophical and tolerant crew members sometimes took it into their own hands to do something about it. In 1902, members of the crew of the British-owned barque *Veronica* mutinied, murdered the officers and then abandoned the vessel in a small boat.

The small trading vessel had been sailing slowly from the Gulf of Mexico on its way to Montevideo. Its master, Alexander Shaw, had a reputation for toughness and had been forced to recruit his reluctant twelve-man crew from the sweepings of the waterfront.

A flash point occurred when the ship's first officer, Alexander McLeod, struck a seaman and antagonised a group of his friends. Two German crewmen, Gustav Rau and Otto Monsson, had revolvers in their kitbags. They enlisted the aid of Dutch seaman Willem Smith and 19-year-old Harry Flohr. Between them they decided to take over the ship.

Their mutiny took place on 8 December 1902. They attacked First Officer McLeod and threw him over the side of the ship. Then they shot and wounded Second Officer Fred Abrahamson.

Two loyal seamen were killed. The fifth man to die in this bloody imbroglio was the captain, Alexander Shaw. He was shot by Rau and his body thrown over the side. Abrahamson and the remaining seamen were also disposed of. The only survivors were the four mutineers and the black cook, Moses Thomas, who had taken no part in the uprising.

Upon Rau, the ringleader's instructions the others changed out of their bloodstained clothing, set fire to the *Veronica* and rowed off in the ship's lifeboat. They took with them a mast and sail, kegs of water, tinned meat and loaves of bread. Piloted by Rau, a former seaman of the German Navy, they sailed on a north-easterly course for five days. When they sighted the coast of Brazil, Rau ordered all the spare food and supplies to be dropped over the side, to add credence to their tale that they had abandoned the *Veronica* after an accidental fire had consumed the vessel and the remainder of the crew.

The deserters landed on the island of Cajueiro on Christmas morning and were soon picked up by a trading vessel, the *Brunswick*, which brought the five men back to England. On the voyage it was noticed that Moses Thomas kept well away from the other four and was most uncomfortable in their company. Eventually, the cook told his rescuers what had really happened on board the *Veronica*.

The deserters were met at Liverpool by the police. Thomas's accusations were backed up by the youth, Harry Flohr, who turned King's Evidence, giving evidence for the prosecution. Rau, Monsson and Smith were arrested and accused of murder, conspiracy, arson, piracy and theft.

When the accused appeared at Liverpool Assizes in May 1903, they faced only the single charge of murdering Captain Shaw, the master of the *Veronica*. They were all found guilty and sentenced to death. The 19-year-old Monsson was recommended for mercy on account of his youth and previous good character. He was reprieved and given a long term of imprisonment instead. Rau and Smith were hanged at Walton Prison.

For those running away from home or seeking adventure, the

French Foreign Legion had always provided a home. Unhappily, its mixture of savage discipline and harsh living conditions also persuaded many legionnaires to go on the run.

In 1908, six deserters from the French Foreign Legion stationed in Casablanca in Morocco, deserted from their unit, secured the assistance of the German consul in the area, responsible for the welfare of German citizens locally, but were arrested by the French as they tried to board a vessel. The event led to an international court case.

It was believed at the time that the men had been encouraged and helped to escape by a group of German citizens living in Casablanca who had aided other desertions of their fellow-countrymen in the past.

Three of the deserters were German, one was French, one was Swiss and one was Austrian. The six men left their camp and managed to reach the German consulate to beg for help. The sympathetic consul felt that he was obliged to assist the Germans, but laid the foundations for all sorts of trouble when he also decided to assist the other three legionnaires.

Casablanca was a French garrison town, with troops in and around it. Many of these soldiers were members of the French Foreign Legion. Discipline was tough in the Legion, its members were paid one *sou* a day and had to enrol for five years. There were many attempts at desertion. In December 1908, an enterprising journalist from the *Daily Express* managed to interview a number of German legionnaires about their lives and was told, 'No man with a vestige of self respect would remain here.'

After giving the deserters shelter and providing them with civilian clothes, the consul arranged for them to be transported back to Germany on a mail-ship, the *Cintra*. On 25 September 1908, a consulate official and a Moroccan soldier employed by the Germans escorted the six fugitives to the docks. The waiting steam ship was anchored some way out in the harbour.

By this time rumours had been spreading around the town and it was generally known what was going to happen. French officials were waiting at the dock, accompanied by police officers. They swooped on the legionnaires in an attempt to arrest them. The consulate official ordered the deserters to board a rowing boat and get themselves out to the *Cintra*. So desperate were the fugitives to get away that in their anxiety they managed to capsize their craft and had to scramble ashore, into the arms of the waiting Frenchmen. The six men put up a terrific fight but were eventually overpowered and led away.

The matter was taken up at the highest levels. Germany lodged an official complaint at the treatment meted out to the deserters under its protection. France replied that Casablanca was under French jurisdiction and that the German consul had no right to interfere. It demanded the instant return of the three German legionnaires involved.

It was agreed that the matter would be taken to the Permanent Court of Arbitration at The Hague. Two German and two French arbiters were appointed under the supervision of a neutral Swedish judge. After grave deliberations some sort of a compromise was reached. It was decreed that the German consul should not have tried to aid the non-German legionnaires, but that the French should have respected the efforts of the local consul, Neudorfer, to disembark the German deserters, for whom he had a responsibility of care.

Rather more to the point as far as the six men were concerned, the French were not required to yield up the deserters. The six men disappeared into the maw of Foreign Legion justice, or retribution.

Perhaps the best-known mass desertion of the first decade of the twentieth century was that of the crew on board the battleship *Potemkin* in 1905. The ringleader of the mutiny was a torpedo quartermaster called Afanasy Matyushenko. He was instrumental in taking over the warship and sailing it away.

It was a time of unrest and riots in Russia. Revolutionaries were planning uprisings and there were constant meetings and secret plots. One group of sailors from a number of ships, infuriated by harsh discipline at sea, had already met ashore and issued a public statement:

We 194 sailors from the Black Sea fleet attending this meeting join our voices to those of the Russian workers represented by their revolutionary wing, the Russian Special Democrat Labour Party. We demand the removal of the autocratic regime and its replacement by a democratic republic.

In June 1905, sailors on board the *Potemkin*, which was patrolling the Black Sea, suddenly protested at being served rotten meat. The captain of the vessel ordered the ringleaders of the mutinous men to be shot but the firing squad refused to fire on their comrades. Matyushenko, a brave and articulate man and a convinced revolutionary, was one of the ringleaders of the uprising. When the firing squad would not kill their fellow seamen, he ordered an attack on the officers; the men obliged and the officers were thrown overboard. Matyushenko then organised the formation of a committee of twelve to direct the running of the warship. They decided to sail to the port of Odessa hoping to link up with other revolutionaries.

When they arrived, flying the red flag, thousands of curious onlookers who had heard of the mutiny greeted them at the harbour. Matyushenko went ashore with a dozen seamen for the burial of one of their comrades, killed in the uprising on board. On their way back from the ceremony the unarmed sailors were fired upon by soldiers. Three were killed or captured. The rest, including Matyushenko, managed to escape to their ship and then, in retaliation, fired several shots at the town from the ship's guns. An uprising followed in the city, which was put down with great slaughter.

By this time, the Black Sea fleet had been ordered to hunt down and recapture the *Potemkin*. Taking a great chance, the *Potemkin* sailed to meet the ships, hoping to gain adherents. To the fury and dismay of the officers, the rails of the other ships of the squadron were lined with cheering sailors. The *George the Conqueror* suddenly raised the red flag and announced that it wished to join the mutineers.

Admiral Krieger, in charge of the squadron, prudently sailed the loyal vessels to Sebastopol while his superiors could consider the situation. For a brief time the *Potemkin* and the *George the Conqueror* sailed side by side as a dissident mini-fleet.

Events began to go badly wrong for the deserters. Loyal petty officers on board the *George the Conqueror* rallied and tried to retake their ship. They managed at least to pile her up on a shoal, rendering the vessel useless and leaving the *Potemkin* virtually alone again. The situation on board was grim, with little food and water. Matyushenko and the others decided to sail to Romania as deserters from the Russian Navy and appeal for sanctuary.

They were met with a subdued response. Romania was unwilling to offend the powerful Russia. Even when Matyushenko hauled down the red flag and offered to buy supplies with money from the ship's strong-box it was only with reluctance that the government agreed to accept delivery of the vessel and allow its sailors ashore. The uprising had lasted barely a week.

The mutineers on the *George the Conqueror* surrendered after their imprisoned officers released themselves and took back control. The 600 disenfranchised seamen from the *Potemkin* tried to scatter to safety. Some found work labouring in factories or on the land. Over a period of time, however, many of them were rounded up by Russian agents and returned to their homeland, where some were executed and others exiled to Siberia. Afanasy Matyushenko managed to get as far as Bucharest and from there on to a British tramp steamer.

In 1907, the Russian government offered an amnesty to revolutionaries. Unwisely the former torpedo quartermaster accepted it. He returned to Russia but was arrested at the border. Later he was hanged.

A much more individual deserter of the period who left military life simply at the behest of his wife was Tom Mix. He became one of Hollywood Westerns' great silent-film stars, the hard-riding idol of millions, but his studio handouts omitted one salient fact about his early career. Tom Mix was a long-term deserter from the US Army.

Born near Driftwood in Pennsylvania, Mix left school after the fifth grade. In 1898, when he was a teenager, he enlisted in the

4th Regiment of the US Army Artillery. For a time he was a guard at the Dupont powder works in Delaware. Although the Spanish–American War occurred during this period, he saw no action but rose to the rank of first sergeant and was honourably discharged in March 1901.

The following month Mix, already bored with civilian life, re-enlisted. But he found the peacetime army equally unexciting. Now married, Tom became pressured by his wife Grace to leave the army and find a better-paid job, presenting him with an ultimatum: life in the forces or her. In November 1902, he deserted by the simple method of not returning from a period of leave. He was posted as being absent without leave.

The US Army of the time made only perfunctory attempts to recover deserters. Mix was a fair rider and he found work touring with a Wild West show. He was next employed on a dude ranch, where Easterners were given a sanitised version of life on the prairie, making it seem much more glamorous and exciting than it really was. Because of his good looks, Mix was used more as a host and greeter than a ranch-hand. His marriage broke up, largely because his father-in-law was disgusted that Mix was a deserter and put pressure on his daughter to leave the itinerant. Mix, who had left the army at his wife's insistence, was bewildered by the latest turn of events.

Mix then drifted on until he found himself in an area where a film entitled *Ranch Life in the Great Southwest* was being shot. Mix managed to get himself on the payroll looking after the horses. He then talked himself into a role before the cameras in a horse-breaking sequence. Tom Mix had found his niche. He appeared in more than 300 movies, many of them one and two-reel efforts. Before long he had attained major stardom and briefly was the highest-paid star in Hollywood.

To help develop his popularity, the studio press departments started issuing descriptions of the new star's glamorous background, accounts taken up eagerly by the fan magazines. It was declared that Mix had charged up San Juan Hill in Cuba with Teddy Roosevelt's

Rough Riders, fought in the Boxer rebellion in China and the Boer War in South Africa, rounded up outlaws as a Texas Ranger and a US Marshal, and that he had broken almost every bone in his body taming wild horses. There was not a word of truth in any of the assertions.

With his film popularity fading by 1935, Mix left Hollywood to become the main attraction of the travelling Sells Floto Circus, at a salary claimed to be anything between $17,500 and $20,000 a week. The *West Seattle Herald* of 6 August 1931 heralded the impending arrival of Mix and the circus by saying: 'Tom Mix, famous movie picture star, is said to receive the highest salary ever paid a circus performer.'

13

ONE IN EVERY TEN

Manacled and blindfolded ... they are tied up to stakes. Over each man's
heart is placed an envelope. At the sign of command the firing parties,
twelve for each, align their rifles on the envelopes.
– Private Albert Rochester witnesses the executions of a number of
deserters during the First World War

During the First World War, over 39,000 British deserters were arrested, many of them in Britain before they had even left for active service overseas. Most of them were sent back to their units for field punishment; a soldier was of more use in the trenches than a prison. However, over 300 Allied soldiers were condemned to death by firing squads for desertion. The total included twenty-five Canadians, twenty-two Irishmen and five New Zealanders. The Australians refused to allow their troops to be executed.

The first British Army volunteer to be executed by a firing squad in the First World War was Joseph Byers, a private in the Royal Scots Fusiliers. He had enlisted at the outbreak of war in 1914, claiming to be nineteen, although in fact he was probably three years younger. He was given some perfunctory basic training and shipped out to France.

When his battalion was ordered to the front, Byers and a friend, Andrew Evans, unable to stand the constant shelling, deserted and fled towards the rear. Both men were soon picked up. Byers pleaded guilty to the charge and accordingly was not represented at his court martial. He assumed that if he admitted to the charges laid against him and was honest and contrite in his manner, he would avoid the death penalty and be sentenced to a long term of imprisonment instead. He was wrong. Byers was not aware that on the trial papers General Sir Horace Smith-Dorrien, Commander of the 2nd Army, had written, 'Discipline in the 1st Battalion of the Royal Scots Fusiliers has been very bad for some time past, and I think a severe example is very much wanted.'

Joseph Byers met his death before a firing squad. Afterwards, rumours persisted that the members of the squad were so reluctant to shoot someone that young that they botched the execution, necessitating three volleys of shots before the youth finally died. His friend Evans was executed soon afterwards.

The fact that Byers had pleaded guilty concerned the High Command, who felt that the young soldier should have been allowed to call witnesses on his behalf. It was decided that from then on in any military cases involving the death penalty the accused would automatically have a claim of not guilty entered.

Like most other executions for desertion, such examples of military justice were invariably hushed up, in case they had a bad effect upon civilian morale. The next of kin of the dead men were often given vague reasons for their deaths. Even the records of the deserters' units were doctored to read 'died in service'. When MPs tried to raise the matter in the House of Commons they, too, were often fobbed off.

Another young victim of the war was Herbert Burden, who was shot for desertion in the First World War. He attained post-war fame when he was commemorated in a sculpture at a memorial site dedicated to the memory of executed deserters.

Born in Lewisham in 1898, Burden was the son of a gardener, a boy soldier who probably lied about his age to join the army – he was only seventeen when he was shot in the second year of the war.

Puny of physique, Private Burden was not highly regarded by his superiors. He had taken part in no major actions at the time of his desertion but had undergone the usual nerve-shattering baptism of shelling in the trenches at Ypres. It all proved too much for the youth.

On 26 June 1915, Burden was ordered to parade that evening as part of a trench working party. He had already been punished more than once for unauthorised absences and had just returned from a spell in a military hospital. Instead of reporting for duty that evening he made his way back to the transport lines of his battalion and from there he went on to the huts of the Royal West Kent Regiment behind the lines. He was picked up after several days and charged.

Private Burden was tried for desertion. It was stated that he was nineteen years old, although in fact he was two years younger – too young to be fighting. He claimed that he had gone to the West Kent lines: 'I went to see a friend of mine in the Royal West Kent Regiment, in which regiment I had served in 1913, and as I had heard that he had lost a brother I wanted to enquire whether it was true or not.' His excuse was not believed. Burden was found guilty and sentenced to death. He was executed on 21 July 1915.

More than seventy-five years later, a sculpture of Private Herbert Burden by the artist Andy DeComyn was selected to represent all those British and Commonwealth soldiers executed for desertion in the First World War. It was placed in the National Memorial Arboretum, near Lichfield in central England, at the head of 306 wooden posts, each bearing the name of an executed soldier.

In contrast to the naive Byers and Burden, the ingenious and quick-thinking William Turpie was a much more calculating deserter and actually managed to bluff his way back to England from France while he was on the run.

A private in the 2nd East Surrey Regiment, Turpie was born in 1891, enlisted in to the army in 1914 and was soon posted to the Ypres salient. When his unit was ordered to the front line, Turpie slipped away to avoid action and walked back to Boulogne. He met a sympathetic sailor who advised the deserter to visit the British Consulate and try to obtain a pass, which would allow him to return unchallenged to England.

In all the confusion of troop movements and refugees clamouring for aid, Turpie actually managed to obtain a pass from the overworked consulate staff and boarded a boat. He then threw his uniform over the side and changed into civilian clothing. When he landed at Dover, the resourceful deserter obtained lodgings at the Seaman's Rest hostel in the town.

However, when he reached the railway station to try to continue his journey inland, he found the police much more vigilant. Challenged for his lack of identification papers, he gave an involved story about having been a fireman on a ship sailing from Leith to Dunkirk, which had been shelled at Dunkirk and forced to put in at Boulogne. Unfortunately, Turpie had given his correct name and address when stopped. The police made enquiries and discovered his true status. William Turpie was handed over to the military authorities, court-martialled, found guilty of desertion and shot on 1 July.

Even more determined and resourceful than Turpie was Ernest Lawrence, a private in the 2nd Battalion of the Devonshire Regiment, who was one of the First World War's most energetic deserters, absconding and being caught on three separate occasions. A poor soldier with a long record of disciplinary offences, Lawrence made his first bid for freedom in March 1917, when he fled from a party designated to bring rations up to the front line. He reached a base camp at Rouen where coolly he claimed that he had been recovering in hospital and now was ready to resume his duties.

A search of the records proved that Lawrence's story was false. He was arrested and sent back to his unit to face punishment for deserting. He was given fatigue duties while awaiting trial and in May promptly escaped again, by simply running away.

This time he made his way to a base camp at Le Havre, asking if he could draw the pay due to him. His pay-book was discovered to be false and Lawrence was arrested once more. He was put on a lorry to take him back to the Devonshire Regiment. Jumping out of the back of the vehicle, Ernest Lawrence ran off again. He made his way to a machine shop of the Royal Flying Corps, gave his name as Private Shakespeare and said that he had been posted there from another unit. Lawrence was given an RFC uniform and an office job while his papers were checked. When they were discovered to be forged the deserter, working away happily, was apprehended yet again.

Private Ernest Lawrence was eventually tried for desertion. In his defence he claimed that he had left his unit because he was anxious to show the military authorities the blueprints of a trench mortar he had invented, because the colonel of his battalion would not allow him leave for this purpose. Lawrence was found guilty and shot on 22 November 1917.

Most First World War deserters were only young but William Alexander, a company quartermaster sergeant in the Canadian Army, was in his mid-thirties when he deserted. In 1917, he was the highest-ranked Canadian non-commissioned officer to be executed.

Born in England, Alexander had served in the British Army before emigrating to Canada. Upon the outbreak of war in 1914, he enlisted in the Canadian Army. As an experienced soldier he was made a sergeant in the 10th (Alberta) Battalion. From 1915 until 1917, Alexander fought in a number of engagements with his unit. On 15 August 1917, his battalion was ordered to attack Hill 70, on the outskirts of Lens on the Western Front, but CQMS Alexander was not present to lead a platoon into action. He had returned to the village of Les Brebis behind the lines, previously used by his battalion as a resting point. After two days of fighting, during which 400 men had been killed or wounded, the 10th Battalion was sent back to the billet to rest. It was here that Alexander was discovered. He claimed that he had left the front line to report sick. When he was medically examined the doctor could discover nothing wrong with the warrant officer. He was arrested as a deserter.

The 37-year-old Alexander was tried and found guilty. He was executed by a firing squad on 18 October 1917.

Few officers were executed for desertion. One of the exceptions was Edwin Dyett, a young sub-lieutenant, the son of a merchant navy officer, who joined the Royal Naval Volunteer Reserve in 1915. Against his will he found himself fighting in France, and was accused of cowardice and desertion. He met his death before a firing squad.

Because there were more reservists than vacancies on ships, some of the volunteers for the navy were formed into the Royal

Naval Division to fight alongside the infantry in France, although remaining under the jurisdiction of the Admiralty. Dyett pleaded not to be sent to serve in the trenches, saying that he was not sure that he would be able to cope. His pleas were ignored and he was posted to the Nelson Battalion.

From the start Dyett was not regarded as a particularly capable officer and even during the thick of the fighting in 1916 he was at first left behind in the reserve trenches at the Somme. Only when his unit started to suffer heavy casualties were Dyett and another officer ordered forward as reinforcements. In the confusion, Dyett and his colleague parted and the former started wandering aimlessly, looking for the unit he was supposed to join at the front.

After some time the hapless Dyett was discovered by another officer, Sub-Lieutenant Fernie. The pair had fallen out earlier on and there was some animosity between the two young officers. Fernie ordered Dyett to accompany him and his unit to the front line. Dyett refused to obey an officer of equal rank and went back to brigade headquarters for fresh orders. After an interval, once again he set out for the front line. He came across a group of stragglers during a particularly intense period of shelling from the German lines and took shelter with them in a dugout.

When matters had settled down and there was a lull in the fighting, Sub-Lieutenant Fernie accused Dyett of refusing to obey orders and accompany him to the trenches. An investigation was launched. Dyett was arrested and court-martialled for desertion. He was found guilty and sentenced to death. On account of his youth and lack of battle experience the sub-lieutenant was recommended for mercy. The recommendation was rejected and the sentence was confirmed.

Edwin Dyett was executed on 5 January 1917, by a firing squad half-hidden in a trench. An eyewitness reported that Dyett's last words were, 'For God's sake put me out of my misery. Well, boys, goodbye! For God's sake shoot straight!'

The last officer to be executed for desertion during the First World War was Second Lieutenant John Paterson. Formerly a trader in

West Africa he had joined the army as a private and arrived in France with the 17ᵗʰ Battalion of the Middlesex Regiment in 1915. Twice wounded in action on the Somme, he was sent home for officer training and commissioned from the ranks. He was posted to the Essex Regiment and sent back to France.

Paterson was waiting to be sent into action from the reserve trenches near Ypres in March 1918, when he went absent without leave. In charge of a working party one evening, he left his men, claiming that he was off to look for a lost pocketbook. He never returned. From a position of safety behind the lines he kept himself in funds by cashing forged cheques. Army detectives were sent to find the culprit.

It seems that Paterson may have been apprehended by chance. On 3 July, two military policemen, Sergeant Harold Collison and a corporal, were on routine duty near Calais when they saw Paterson walking with a French girl he had picked up. Noticing that the officer matched the description of the man passing false cheques they stopped and questioned him.

Paterson gave them a false name and walked away quickly. Their suspicions aroused, the two soldiers followed him to a village where they stopped the officer again. This time Paterson admitted his identity but begged to be allowed to say his goodbyes to the girl in her house before surrendering to the two men.

Rather naively Collison agreed, standing at the back of the house while the corporal was stationed at the front. After about an hour Paterson ran out, making a break for it. Collison alerted the corporal with a shout. Paterson struggled to produce a gun and it went off in his pocket, wounding him. The deserter then tugged the gun free of his pocket and shot the sergeant.

The corporal ran round to the back of the house to tend to Collison and then hurried off to fetch help. By this time Paterson and his girlfriend had both vanished.

The second lieutenant remained at liberty for another two weeks, but Sergeant Collison died of his wounds and an intensive hunt was on for his killer. Finally, the French police picked Paterson up at Saint-Omer. He had abandoned his girlfriend after a just a couple of days. He was charged with murder, desertion and forgery. He was found guilty on the first charge and then pleaded guilty to the other two counts. He was executed by a firing squad on 24 September 1918.

When the need for troops became urgent, a number of deserters were released from prison and allowed to return to the front line. Many of them fought bravely in their second military incarnation and Sergeant Maurice Buckley of the Australian Army actually won the Victoria Cross for gallantry after deserting.

The 22-year-old Buckley, an Irish immigrant living in Australia, joined the 13th Light Horse in December 1914. He was posted to Egypt but contracted a venereal disease and was sent back to his unit. He spent five months there, ashamed of the fact that he was confined with other troops suffering from the same thing and that so far he had not seen action. He walked out of Camp Langwarrin, near Melbourne, and was officially classified as a deserter. Almost at once, still determined to get into the front line somewhere, he re-enlisted under the name of Gerald Sexton.

This time Buckley was posted to France, and served with great courage at Ypres and Passchendaele. He was awarded the Distinguished Conduct Medal for attacking a nest of German machine gun posts. The next month, the last one of the war, he displayed even more courage by charging a series of German positions, putting a number of guns out of action and taking almost 100 prisoners.

When Buckley was awarded the VC for his amazing exploits he realised that his true identity would probably be discovered, so he confessed to his desertion in Egypt. It was generally felt that he had more than made up for his initial desertion by his subsequent feats of heroism. He died in 1921 trying to jump his horse over some railway gates. At his funeral ten holders of the VC acted as his pallbearers, while thousands of people looked on.

The first mass desertion of French troops occurred quite early in the war. The 10th Company of 8 Battalion of the Régiment Mixte de

Tirailleurs Algériens refused an order to regroup and attack while running from a German advance in 1914. They were rounded up, tried and sentenced to the old Roman punishment for desertion: decimation. On 15 December 1915, in Flanders, one in every ten of the troops was shot by firing squads.

By 1917, morale among the French Army serving in the trenches was so low that thousands of men mutinied. Conditions on the front line were almost unbearable. Food was bad and other ranks received little leave, although officers were allowed to go home regularly.

The last straw was a disastrous major attack launched by General Nivelle along the river Aisne on 16 April 1917. He threw a million French soldiers into action. Earlier a French sergeant major carrying plans of the proposed offensive had been captured by the Germans, who consequently had had plenty of time to prepare and ambush for the French attack. Although the French were being slaughtered with every attempted advance, Nivelle persisted with his doomed attack for two weeks; by the second day alone more than 100,000 French troops had died. Morale among the survivors was extremely low. There were many individual and group desertions and then whole units began to rebel.

Over fifty French divisions refused to leave their trenches. Many men abandoned their positions and set out on foot or in stolen vehicles for Paris. At Coeuvres, fifty miles from the French capital, over 1,000 troops revolted, beat up their officers, stole a number of lorries and set off in a long convoy to the railway junction of Soissons. Here they commandeered a train and its driver and forced the railwayman to take them to Paris, where they hoped to persuade the government to put an end to the war.

After only a few miles, however, the train was stopped abruptly by tree trunks laid across the line. Machine guns opened up from concealed positions and the absconders were called upon to surrender by a contingent of loyal troops who had been rushed ahead of the train to detain the deserters. The troops on board the train surrendered without a fight. They were marched the fifteen miles back to Soissons and ordered to return to the front line.

Similar measures were taken all along the French line as the mutiny was quelled. Ringleaders were arrested and over 100,000 troops were put on trial; 23,000 were found guilty, over 400 were sentenced to death but only fifty-four were shot. However, many mutineers and deserters were exiled to the notorious penal colony of Devil's Island, situated a few miles out in the Atlantic off the coast of French Guiana in South America.

Nivelle was replaced with the more conciliatory General Pétain. The quality of the food improved and regular leave rosters implemented. Even so, the French troops let it be known that they would only fight if they were attacked by the Germans. They would take part in no advances. The French High Command accepted the situation, informing their British counterparts that they would have to shoulder the brunt of the fighting until the American troops arrived to bolster the front line.

Another case of mass desertions in action occurred at the Battle of Caporetto in 1917. The initial fighting took place north west of Trieste in northern Italy, between the Austro-Hungarian Army and the Germans on one side and the Italians on the other. The campaign proved to be a disaster for the Italians and led to one of the greatest mass desertions in modern warfare.

On 24 October 1917, after a long stalemate, the German commander, Otto von Below, launched a sudden and unexpected attack on the Italians, concentrating most of his forces along one narrow front. The combined Austro-Hungarian and German force punched a great hole in the Italian line.

Utterly demoralised by the ferocity of the enemy advance, over 270,000 Italian troops surrendered. Thousands more abandoned their positions without firing and fled. They scattered for miles across the countryside. Von Below would have secured an even more significant victory, but he had advanced too far in front of his supply lines and was forced to stop and regroup.

However, the First World War was drawing to a close. The German breakthrough occurred too late to affect the course of the war. Slowly, most of the Italians returned to their units.

In the last months of the conflict, military authorities began to temper justice with mercy. The punishment for mutiny had always been stricter than that for desertion. For this reason, in 1918 a group of Australian soldiers in France had charges of mutiny originally levelled against them reduced to charges of desertion.

On 21 September 1918, 119 troops of the 1st Battalion of the Australian Army in France refused to move back to the front line trenches when they were ordered to return after a spell in the reserve section. They accused their officers of sending them back to retrieve ground lost by British soldiers, as well as having to defend their own section of the line.

The soldiers were arrested and taken back to await trial. The authorities were placed in a quandary. There was no doubt that the Australians were guilty of mutiny while on active service, which was punishable by death, but if so many men, or even a proportion of the whole, were to be executed it would cause an uproar back home in Australia

In the end a compromise was reached. Throughout the war the Australian politicians, alone among the Allies, had set their faces against the death penalty for desertion. This gave General Monash, commander of the Australian forces, a loophole. Except in one instance, he had all the charges reduced from mutiny to desertion.

The subsequent courts martial convicted 118 of the accused men of desertion. They were sentenced to up to ten years' imprisonment, to be served at Dartmoor prison. Soon after the trials the war ended and most of the Australian prisoners were quietly shipped home. As soon as the war ended a number of condemned deserters from other armies had their sentences commuted to various terms of imprisonment, as their deaths were no longer necessary to discourage others.

From 1917 until 1918 over 4 million men served in the US Army. More than 5,000 were accused of desertion during this period, and 2,567 were found guilty. In 1917, the USA was considerably embarrassed by two examples of desertion in army units that had not even left for France. In each case racial discrimination was blamed for the unrest.

In July 1917, troops of the 3rd Battalion of the black US 24th
Infantry were posted to Camp Logan, outside Houston in Texas.
Until this time, the battalion had a remarkably low desertion rate
despite many of the troops, especially those from the northern
states, objecting to the racial discrimination they were subjected to
when they visited the city – they complained that the white police
officers in Houston routinely harassed them.

There were an increasing number of scuffles between black soldiers
and white civilians. A soldier was arrested for sitting in the 'whites
only' section of a streetcar and there were fights between troops and
the white members of the Illinois National Guard. Matters came
to a head on 23 August. A black soldier was arrested, allegedly for
interfering in the arrest of a black woman. A black military policeman who tried to sort matters out peacefully was struck, fired at by
a policeman and then arrested. He was later released.

When the story of the arrest of the military policeman reached
Camp Logan, there was considerable unrest. The white commanding officer of the battalion, Major Kneeland S. Snow, ordered that
all rifles and ammunition be rounded up and guarded by senior
non-commissioned officers. Meanwhile, a soldier burst into the
camp screaming that a white mob was marching on the camp.
The troops at once took back their rifles and ammunition by force
and started firing wildly at the imaginary mob. At this point, with
the white officers unable to control the men, a black sergeant,
Vida Henry of 1st Company, took over, saying, 'If you're going to
do anything, do it!' At 8 p.m. he gathered 100 armed soldiers and
led them into Houston. The deserters fired indiscriminately as
they went.

The first to die were two white citizens who came out on to their
porch to see what the noise was about. They were both shot dead.
The next casualties were white occupants of a stationary car, who
attempted to flee on foot.

The white inhabitants of the city armed themselves and soon
gun battles were taking place all over the Fourth Ward of Houston.
Before they ended, fifteen white men, including four policemen,

had been killed and a dozen injured, one of them later dying of his wounds. Four soldiers were killed.

With the streets cleared, except for the corpses, the soldiers were uncertain what to do next. Henry wanted them to attack the gaol in force, but the soldiers were unwilling to do so and began to split up into aimless groups. Finally, Sergeant Henry advised them to try to slip back into the camp under cover of darkness. He then shot and killed himself.

The Illinois National Guard, which had been attempting to defend the city, was reinforced with 600 soldiers from Fort Sam Houston. Slowly the members of 3rd Battalion were rounded up and marched four abreast under armed guard to Camp Logan.

Within days the entire 3rd Battalion had been moved from Camp Logan to Columbus in New Mexico. A series of courts martial were set up in San Antonio. One hundred and eighteen soldiers were accused of mutiny and riot, and all but eight were found guilty. Nineteen soldiers were hanged and sixty-three received life sentences.

In the same month a number of black soldiers at another camp were accused of deserting from their unit and killing a white citizen.

The soldiers were part of the 1st Battalion of the black 25th United States Infantry, commanded by white officers. Some 167 soldiers had arrived at Camp Brown outside the small town of Brownsville in Houston at the end of July, replacing a white unit. From the start, the enlisted men endured a great deal of racial discrimination when they visited the city. There were frequent scuffles between whites and blacks, as had been the case at Camp Logan.

On 12 August 1917, a white woman reported that she had been attacked by a black soldier. In an effort to defuse the situation the white major in command of the camp imposed a curfew, confining his troops to camp.

At about midnight, shots were fired in the main street of the town. A white bartender was killed and a police lieutenant was so badly wounded in the arm that the limb later had to be amputated. Citizens of Brownsville claimed that soldiers had been seen running away through the night shortly after the shooting and said that they must have been absent without leave from Camp Brown. It was claimed that the men had been firing indiscriminately for about ten minutes; the voices of black men were said to have been heard in the gloom; military rifle cartridges were found scattered about the street.

An investigation was conducted immediately. Major Penrose, in charge of Camp Brown, stated categorically that no soldiers had left the camp that night. Rolls had been called at 10 p.m. and again immediately after the shootings. All rifles were checked and none had been fired recently. In spite of this twelve soldiers were arrested by the Texas Rangers. A Grand Jury did not substantiate charges against them. All the same, feelings against the black soldiers ran so high locally and nationally that President Theodore Roosevelt discharged all 167 black soldiers 'without honour' from the US Army.

The decision caused a furore, but it was not rescinded by the President, despite the efforts of a number of politicians. Not until 1972 did President Nixon award honourable discharges, without back pay, to the 167 Brownsville soldiers.

In the east, desertions among the Russian troops fighting the Germans on the Eastern Front were rife and grew steadily worse, despite Tsar Nicholas personally assuming command of his forces. By February 1917 there had been 195,000 desertions. By August of the same year, after the Bolshevik Revolution had seen Russia withdraw from the war, with many soldiers flocking home from the trenches as a consequence, the estimated figure for deserters was 365,000. Some 626,000 men had been killed in action, while 3.5 million troops were reported as taken prisoner or missing.

Towards the end of the First World War a nationalist regiment was created by the Russians comprising Czech and Slovak prisoners of war and deserters from the Austro-Hungarian Army to fight against their former comrades. It was called the Czech Legion. In 1914, the Czechs were part of the Austro-Hungarian Empire and many of them were conscripted to fight against the Russians. A large number were taken prisoner and assembled in camps. Here they were urged to harness their dislike for their overlords in Austria-Hungary by fighting against them. As an extra lure, the Russians promised Czech independence once the Germans had been defeated.

Encouraged by Tomáš Masaryk, the Czech nationalist leader, thousands of Czechs joined the new unit. At first the Czech Legion fought side by side with the Russians. However, after the Russian Revolution, it became apparent to Masaryk that Lenin wanted to make a separate peace with Germany, which would probably ruin any chances of an independent Czechoslovakia after the war.

In order to dissociate himself from the defeated and discredited Russians, Masaryk ordered the Czech Legion to abandon the Russian front and join up with the remaining Allies fighting in France. The Russians promptly tried to disarm the Czechs. This meant that for a time the Czechs, determined to fight for their own independence one day, joined, rather reluctantly, with the Tsarist White Russians to fight the Communist forces.

Eventually the Czechs managed to disengage and head eastwards to Siberia and then join up with the Allies. By June 1918, many of them had fought their way through to Vladivostok, where they linked up with a Japanese force. After the war, Masaryk became the first leader of an independent Czechoslovakia.

One unusual member of the Czech Legion during this period who became almost a specialist in the art of desertion and displayed a relaxed and pragmatic attitude towards military life was the Czech writer Jaroslav Hašek. In *The Good Soldier Švejk*, Hašek wrote one of the great novels about military ineptitude and the struggles of a humble, reluctant but irrepressible conscript to cope with the awesome idiocies of army life. The author knew of what he wrote, having deserted at least twice and probably three times during his inglorious military career.

An idiosyncratic and irresponsible character, Hašek was born in Prague in 1883, the son of a teacher who died from drink. When he left school he worked for a time as a chemist's assistant and then a bank clerk. Deciding that he preferred the less regimented life of a writer, Hašek gave up full-time employment and lived as a drop-out, scraping a living as a freelance journalist and short-story writer. He became a member of an anarchist group, but was disgraced when he swapped the society's bicycle for a drink.

He then dabbled in stealing dogs and forging their pedigrees, sometimes inventing new breeds, before selling them on. He married but then lived in a brothel for a while, spent time as a patient in a mental hospital and devised an unsuccessful cabaret act. When the First World War broke out, as a Czech he was forced to serve as a private in the army of the Austro-Hungarian Empire and hated every moment of it.

Jaroslav Hašek's first desertion occurred soon after the outbreak of war, when he was serving in the Austrian 91st Regiment. With many other reluctant Czech conscripts, the writer was captured by the Tsarist Army in Galicia in 1915, although an officer in his unit later claimed that Hašek, when given the order to retreat, had deliberately delayed putting his boots on for such a long period that he was bound to have been caught.

When the Tsarists gave all Czech prisoners of war a chance to join the renegade Czech Legion to fight with the Russians against the Austro-Hungarian forces, many of the troops were interested. Always the pragmatist, Hašek abandoned his former allegiance and became an extremely low-key Czech freedom fighter, specialising in issuing propaganda statements.

Deciding that, despite his sedentary position, the chances of getting killed fighting for the Czechs were high, Hašek looked for softer employment. He found it by deserting from the Legion and joining the newly founded Russian Red Army after the 1917 revolution, soon making his way to Moscow. Here his bargaining skills were utilised when he was made a political commissar in the 5th Army. He also married a Russian girl, although his first wife was still alive back in Czechoslovakia.

When the war ended and Hašek returned to Prague he was treated at first with some disdain by his fellow countrymen, who considered his recent political alliances a little too scattered. He

resumed writing and produced the first of his celebrated Švejk
novels, but was so unpopular that he had to publish the first in the
series himself. However, before long the adventures of the hilari-
ously honest, naive and incompetent private soldier struck a chord
with the millions who had recently fought, with equal desperation,
in their own bloody and idiotic sections of the war.

Hašek did not live long to enjoy his unexpected good fortune.
He died from a stroke in 1923, at the age of thirty-nine.

Just as Masaryk had tried to foment a nationalistic spirit among
Czech prisoners of war, so Roger Casement attempted to draw
upon Irish dislike of England by persuading Irishmen in German
hands to join their own independence army to take part in the
planned Easter Day Uprising in Dublin in 1916.

Born in Dublin in 1864, Casement was the son of a British
soldier. He joined the consular service and achieved a reputation
for his work in exposing European colonial oppression in Africa
and South America. From an early age he became an advocate of
Irish independence from British rule. Upon the outbreak of war
in 1914, the Germans publicly declared their support for Irish
independence. Casement visited Irish prisoners in camps and then
travelled to Berlin to write a memorandum to the Kaiser stating
that every Irish prisoner would be given the opportunity of joining
an Irish Brigade similar to that which fought in Fontenay in 1745
for France against Germany.

The authorities agreed to his offer to raise a force for independence from the Irish prisoners already in German hands. It was
agreed that the unit would be transported by the Germans to
Ireland, to support the proposed national uprising.

The Roman Catholics among the Irish prisoners were segregated in separate camps. Casement made a number of visits to the
camps and did his best to persuade men captured on the Western
Front to leave the British Army and sign up for the new venture.
He was disappointed by the results. Usually he was greeted with
jeers and catcalls when he tried to address the prisoners and offer
them their freedom. Even when he wanted to give the Catholic

prisoners special privileges and rations these were turned down unless all Irish prisoners were treated in the same way.

In the end very few Irish prisoners of war joined the Irish Brigade. Those who did were moved to a separate camp. Their leaders were Sergeant Michael Keogh, Corporal Tom Quinlisk and Corporal P. J. Dowling. A former British Army warrant officer living in the USA, Robert Monteith, joined the unit as its captain.

The members of the Irish Brigade were given desultory military training, including the use of machine guns, but soon grew disillusioned with their segregation from the rest of the Irish prisoners of war. When Casement left to make his plans for the uprising, the deserters refused to carry on without him. They were dispersed by the Germans and sent to work on farms.

The disappointed Casement went ahead with his project without most of the Irish Brigade. He was sent to Ireland in a German submarine with two members of the Brigade, Monteith and Sergeant Daniel Bailey. The Germans also sent 25,000 rifles captured on the Russian front in a transport, to help the uprising. Casement stumbled ashore from a dinghy in County Kerry on 21 April 1916. He was apprehended by the British almost at once. The vessel bearing the arms was also taken.

Casement was tried and executed and the Easter Uprising was put down. In 1918, the members of the Irish Brigade were released and given passes allowing them to travel anywhere in Germany. Some of them went home; very few were punished upon their return.

14

'BE GLAD THAT YOU ARE HERE!'

We have taken the open course of severing, by our own act, all connection with the British State and army, and of giving ourselves to the service of our Country to fight for Irish Independence.
– Part of a declaration issued by the Irish Brigade

Few records survive of German deserters executed in the First World War, but it is estimated that around fifty might have been shot for cowardice in the face of the enemy. Those Germans who did desert tried to reach the safety of a neutral country like the Netherlands or Switzerland. It was not advisable to abscond while serving on the front line as soldiers on both sides were just as likely to shoot enemies running towards them, even with their hands in the air.

One deserter who did make it across no man's land only to see his luck run out more than fifteen years later was Private August Jaeger. On 13 April 1915, he sprinted across no man's land from the German trenches and surrendered to a French unit. Under interrogation he told his hosts all that he knew about his unit's dispositions and movements. He also informed the French of an impending gas attack by the Germans. This gave the French commander General Ferry time to move many of his troops and minimise the full force of the attack.

Unfortunately for Jaeger, long after the war had ended Ferry wrote a newspaper article mentioning Jaeger's assistance in defending against the gas raid. This news offended many German patriots. The long-released and demobilised Jaeger was arrested, tried, and in 1932 sentenced to ten years' imprisonment.

Perhaps the longest distance covered in a break for freedom made by a deserter in the First World War was that of an anonymous German soldier who managed to get from Germany to the USA.

In 1917, the *New Yorker Volkszeitung*, the newspaper of the German-speaking Socialists in the USA, published the first comprehensive account of a deserter's story in the First World War. The articles, published anonymously, were later translated and published in book form as *A German Deserter's War Experience*. The protagonist, a young sapper in an engineers' battalion, fought for almost a year in France. He gave a graphic description of the adversities of life in the trenches and of his growing determination to desert.

In 1915, the soldier went home on leave. Come the end of his time away, he departed in his uniform, as if he were returning to his unit. He later changed into civilian clothes, bought false identity papers and caught a train to Dusseldorf and then made his way to the borders of neutral Holland, hoping to find a way across.

He reached the frontier village of Herongen and from a villager obtained information about the frequency of German border patrols. For three days and nights the deserter hid among trees, confirming the routine of the border guards. Then he made a dash for Holland.

A patrol fired upon him but the soldier crossed the border safely. A group of Dutch soldiers gave him breakfast and helped him on his way to Rotterdam. The sergeant in charge of the Netherlands patrol said to the deserter, 'Be glad that you are here! We Hollanders wish to live in peace.'

The fugitive lived with other German deserters for some time and then, in March 1916, stowed away on a steamer leaving for the USA, taking aboard seven pounds of bread and a can of water. With most of the crew returning drunk from shore leave, he was able to make his way on board concealed among them.

For the eighteen-day duration of the voyage the deserter hid in a coal-hole. His food gave out but somehow he survived until the vessel docked in Philadelphia. He ran from the ship to a dockside warehouse and from there into the city. America was still a neutral nation and the deserter found a great deal of help from the sympathetic German community before he disappeared from public view before the USA joined in the war against Germany.

Back in Germany every available man was being conscripted into the armed forces. One of these was Béla Kiss. Kiss was thirty-six in 1913 when he arrived at the Hungarian village of Czinkota with his 25-year-old wife Maria. A purported businessman and stamp collector, Kiss had all the trappings of wealth. He bought a large house complete with servants and regularly drove to nearby Budapest in a large car. He also took particular care to make friends with the local policeman, Alfred Trauber.

Among the villagers it was common knowledge that Kiss's wife, Maria, was having an affair with a young artist called Paul Bihari and as such Kiss was regarded with much sympathy by the community. Though the villagers did not know it, Kiss was also aware of the situation. He began to arrive back from his business trips to the capital with large oil drums in the back of his car, explaining to his friend Trauber that with war imminent he was stock-piling fuel in case of future shortages.

In fact Kiss was embarking upon an orgy of destruction. He murdered Maria and her boyfriend Bihari, and put their bodies in two of the oil drums, telling concerned neighbours that his wife had run off with her lover. Then, under the name of Hofmann, Béla Kiss started advertising in the lonely-hearts column of a Budapest newspaper, claiming to be a widower. A number of misguided middle-aged women responded to the advertisements, drew most of their savings from the bank at 'Hofmann's' suggestion and went to visit him at his attractive house in Czinkota. They were not seen again.

Kiss's macabre scams were interrupted by the outbreak of war. He was conscripted and went off to fight. Life continued much as it had always done in the village, until, in 1916, news reached his friends that Béla Kiss had died of typhoid in an army hospital.

When soldiers arrived at Czinkota looking for supplies of petrol,

Alfred Trauber, the policeman, remembered the canisters of fuel that Kiss had boasted about just before the start of the war. Trauber took the soldiers to Kiss's boarded-up house and they set out to retrieve the drums. They were in for a terrible shock.

In the first instance seven oil drums were discovered. When they were opened each one contained a naked female corpse pickled in alcohol. Each one had been garrotted. Detectives arrived from Budapest and resumed the search on a larger scale, digging up the garden. In all, twenty-three corpses were discovered in the oil drums. Twenty-two of them were women, including Kiss's wife Maria. The twenty-third body was that of Paul Bihari, Maria's former lover.

Even in the heat of the war the news of the mass killings received a great deal of newspaper attention. However, as Kiss was plainly the killer and he was already dead, the case was closed. Then rumours began to spread that Béla Kiss was still alive.

When the police and military authorities made an official study of the conditions surrounding the death in action of Kiss, they found some puzzling discrepancies. A Béla Kiss had certainly died of wounds in a military hospital in Serbia, but the nurse who had attended the soldier in his last days was adamant that her patient had been a young teenager. Kiss, on the other hand, had been forty-two when he had joined up.

The investigating authorities began to suspect, although it could never be proved, that Kiss, perhaps a slightly wounded soldier in the same ward at the time, had changed identities with the dying soldier, returned to the war under the name of the dead youth and had then deserted.

For many years after the end of the First World War there were a number of unconfirmed reports of sightings of Béla Kiss. In 1919, a friend of one of his female victims claimed to have seen 'Hofmann', as she had known him, walking across Margaret Bridge in Budapest. On another occasion, in 1924, a former member of the French Foreign Legion declared that a fellow soldier called

Hofmann had boasted of his skill in garrotting people. The informant claimed that Legionnaire Hofmann had then deserted.

As late as 1936, when Kiss would have been almost seventy, a New York detective with a reputation for remembering faces declared that he had seen Béla Kiss emerging from the Times Square subway, but then had lost sight of him. Whatever the truth of these reports, Béla Kiss was never apprehended and punished for his crimes.

With so many men from so many different backgrounds involved in the armed forces, reasons for desertions multiplied. The range of reasons prompting desertion and the inevitability of such defections in both peace and war were summed up by a soldier writing over twenty years earlier. In a military magazine in 1893, Colonel Thomas M. Anderson enumerated them with a surprising degree of tolerance:

'So long as boys play hookey, so long as men drink, gamble, and make debts, so long will soldiers and sailors desert.'

15

'MY DESERT IS WAITING...'

Very plausible and bombastic. On occasion wears gold-rimmed monocle. Believed to be in possession of No. 6 revolver.
– Details on the 'Wanted' poster issued for deserter Percy Toplis, a.k.a. the 'Monocled Mutineer'

Throughout the First World War, military authorities in all armies had strict policies for dealing with deserters. They threw out nets and did their best to reel them in. Once the war had ended, however, it was a much more difficult task to recapture men who had gone missing, especially those afraid of returning home who embarked upon a life of crime. In addition to the thousands of deserters still at large there were others who deserted from other military organisations in the new period of peace.

Some lip service was paid to the rehabilitation of returning ex-servicemen but little of practical use was offered to them. Some, especially deserters, had to make their own arrangements for their futures. Their options were limited. A few embarked upon careers as soldiers of fortune, utilising the martial techniques they had acquired in action, while others expanded upon the lives of crime they had started while they were in the forces.

Some wartime deserters who had also managed to escape arrest, as well as other former soldiers, found life almost dull after the ending of hostilities in 1918 and did their best to continue to make things happen around them in the years between the two world wars. A notable example of this was Louis Phal, who became better known as Battling Siki, the light-heavyweight boxing champion of the world. Born in 1897, as a youth the wild and illiterate Phal

ran away to Paris from his home in Senegal. Unconfirmed reports
had it that he travelled as a servant to a touring French actress who
abandoned him in the French capital, forcing the West African to
earn a living as a professional boxer from the age of sixteen.

He was rescued from a life of poverty by the outbreak of the First
World War. Enlisting as a private in the army, Phal showed a natural instinct for warfare, winning both the Croix de Guerre and the
Médaille Militaire for heroism. Unfortunately Phal displayed too
much savagery even for an infantryman. After reports that Corporal
Phal had killed nine German prisoners of war by locking them in a
cellar and lobbing hand grenades down at them he was reprimanded
by his superiors. Shortly afterwards Phal overstayed his leave in Paris.
His officers leapt at the chance, court-martialled him for desertion
and in 1919 dismissed him in ignominy from the service.

Returning to the world of boxing, Phal went on to win the world
light-heavyweight championship, but his newly accrued wealth
went to his head. He lost his title and became a brawling down-
and-out on the streets of New York. In 1925 he was found murdered
after a boozy night out.

A man with a far less fiery military record than Phal's but who
caused just as much consternation to the authorities with his
wayward antics was the celebrated Percy Toplis, the 'Monocled
Mutineer'. Brought up in Mansfield, Toplis was in trouble from
an early age. He was birched at the age of eleven, worked for a
time as a pit apprentice blacksmith and then was sentenced to two
years' imprisonment for theft when he was fifteen. He enlisted in
the army at the outbreak of the First World War, and served as a
stretcher-bearer behind the lines at Loos.

He talked himself into a period of leave by claiming that a non-
existent wife had died, and turned up at his old haunts wearing
the uniform of an officer, made on credit by a gullible tailor, and
flaunting the ribbon of the DCM. Toplis then returned to his unit
in his proper rank and was posted to Gallipoli. Some reports say
that when the campaign ended his ship was turned round at Malta.
After a short stay on the island Percy Toplis returned to England.

In 1917, Toplis embarked upon his career as a serial deserter. He went absent, stole another officer's uniform and spent some weeks obtaining goods on credit and, often sporting a monocle, casually returning the salutes of other ranks. Eventually he returned to his unit but the shortage of trained manpower was so great that he was merely sent to France to work as a stretcher-bearer again.

Still only nineteen, Toplis deserted once more by the simple process of walking out of his bivouac. He made his way to the teeming base-camp of Étaples and lost himself among the thousands of soldiers in transit there, sauntering around in a variety of uniforms. It is possible that Toplis was at Étaples during the notorious mutiny there, but if he was he did not take the prominent part in the uprising later credited to him by the writers of a biography and a subsequent 1986 BBC serial.

Soon after this, however, he was caught posing as an officer in a canteen and arrested in a general roundup of deserters. He was imprisoned to await court martial but escaped with ease, hitchhiked to Boulogne in his genuine RAMC medical orderly's uniform, and smuggled himself on to a hospital ship, working his passage back to Great Britain.

Showing his usual nerve, Toplis then enlisted in the Royal Army Service Corps and was sent to Clipstone Camp in Derbyshire. The place was in a state of chaos, with thousands of soldiers waiting to be demobilised and new recruits pouring in each day. It was a haven meant for Percy Toplis. He posed as an officer in the Royal Army Ordnance Corps and lived the good life until he became overconfident and was arrested for passing bad cheques. He was sentenced to six months in prison and dishonourably discharged from the army.

Released in 1919, Toplis re-enlisted in the Royal Army Service Corps, even giving his real name. He was sent to a barracks near Bristol where he was soon operating a petrol scam, selling army fuel to local taxi firms and only bothering to return to his unit for pay parades. Finding this all too easy, the bored Toplis deserted again, in a stolen military car. The car was recognised, Toplis was arrested but escaped from the military cells at Avonmouth by grabbing a gun from a sentry and forcing his way out.

Toplis then joined the RAF but things began to get a little heavy. He was suspected of murdering and robbing a taxi-driver near Andover, and went on the run. His crime garnered great newspaper publicity and a nationwide police hunt was set in motion. The absconder kept one step ahead of his pursuers, often turning up at military canteens in stolen uniforms for meals, and even sleeping at barracks overnight as he headed across the country. A few individual soldiers recognised him in transit but kept quiet, either out of admiration or fear.

A 'Wanted' notice for him was posted in the *Police Gazette*. He was recognised and cornered in Scotland by a farmer and a gamekeeper, who sent for the local policeman. Toplis shot his way out, wounding the farmer and the policeman, before escaping on a stolen bicycle. As he left, apparently quite unconcerned, he was heard singing 'Goodbyee, don't sigh-ee, wipe the tear, baby dear, from your eye-ee'.

By now Toplis was too notorious to escape detection for much longer. After spending the night at the depot of the Border Regiment in Carlisle, he walked south towards the hamlets of Low and High Hesket. Here he overpowered a local policeman who recognised him, but soon 160 Cumberland policemen were on his trail. Toplis was ambushed by three armed officers and, after an exchange of shots, he was killed. Percy Toplis was only twenty-three years old.

To avoid the attention of the press, he was placed in a plain workhouse coffin and conveyed secretly under a pile of rags to Penrith cemetery, in a lorry usually used for carrying lemonade bottles. To the annoyance of the police present, who wanted the burial to be conducted quickly, the local clergyman insisted on carrying out a full service before the monocled mutineer's body was at last laid to rest.

Peter Kürten deserted from the German Army before the First World War began but, once it was over, achieved notoriety as a savage serial killer. Known as 'the Dusseldorf Vampire', Kürten was one of the most feared and horrific mass murderers of the twentieth century. Born in Cologne-Mülheim in 1883, the son of a vicious father who was imprisoned for attempting to rape his own daughter, Kürten was brought up in a family of thirteen who lived in a single room. He displayed homicidal tendencies from an early age. Later in life he admitted that when he was only nine he had killed two of his playmates. They had been playing on a raft on the Rhine when Kürten had deliberately knocked one of the children into the river. The second boy had dived in to save the first, but Kürten had held them both under the water until they were dead. A verdict of 'accidental death' was returned at the time.

Kürten ran away from home to scrape a living as a thief and conman, living among prostitutes. Twice he was imprisoned for fraud and he served a two-year sentence for attempting to shoot a girl with a rifle. When he emerged from the last term in 1904, Peter Kürten was at once conscripted into the army. The unwilling recruit deserted almost at once by casually walking out of a barrack room and returning to the back streets. For the next few decades, while still technically a deserter, Kürten became a mass murderer.

He was sent back to prison in 1913 for eight years at hard labour for theft. Freed again, he set out on a trail of undetected killings. He set fire to barns in the hope of killing vagrants sleeping inside, broke into an inn and cut the throat of the landlord's 13-year-old daughter, attacked one woman with a hatchet and attempted to strangle several more.

Occasionally Kürten would go back to prison for crimes unrelated to his sex attacks, but usually resumed his assaults upon his release. He married a woman who had served five years in prison for shooting her fiancée, and for several years seemed to live a relatively normal life with her.

In 1929, however, Kürten began the final deadly chapter of his stalking. He stabbed one woman twenty-four times, only to see her live, knifed a mechanic to death after a dispute, and raped and murdered an 8-year-old girl. There were other assaults which did not end in murder. He was only discovered when, in 1930, he attempted to kill a girl called Maria Budlick. Kürten had picked her up and taken her for a walk in the woods before he threw himself at her in a frenzied assault and tried to murder her. The woman had managed to fight her assailant off and flee. She gave the police an accurate description of Kürten, and he was arrested.

Kürten confessed to his crimes and talked freely. His eight-day trial began on 13 April 1931. The jury retired for ninety minutes before finding him guilty of nine charges of murder. Kürten was executed by the guillotine on 2 July 1931.

Another suspected murderer of the period was the American deserter Edward Snyder. Snyder deserted twice from the US Navy and once from the Army. In the 1920s, he achieved even greater notoriety as one of the prime suspects in a celebrated Hollywood murder scandal.

A native of Marion, Ohio, Snyder first enlisted in the navy in 1911 at the age of seventeen, having run away from home. He performed clerical duties on several ships before being court-martialled for fraud and embezzlement. He was found guilty, sentenced to a year's hard labour and dismissed from the service.

A fortnight after his release from prison in 1916 Snyder, a short, plump, glib man, re-enlisted in the navy where he served as a steward. In 1919, Snyder stole a car and crashed it. His superiors allowed him to go to New York where, he claimed, he could raise the money to pay for repairs to the car. Once he had left the base, Snyder sent his officers a message that if they wanted the money they would have to find him first.

A month after his flight Snyder joined the navy again, this time under the name of Strathmore, presenting forged papers to the recruiting office. On this occasion the authorities were a little more alert and discovered that 'Strathmore' and the deserter Snyder were one and the same. Snyder was summoned to see his commanding officer who ordered him to produce more documents if he still insisted that he was Edward Strathmore. Snyder agreed to do so at once, walked out of the office and deserted once again.

Obviously fancying a change of scene, in the same month that he had deserted from the navy he then enlisted in the army. During his sojourn in the military, Snyder was made a clerk and actually promoted to sergeant. He used his new authority to forge an army cheque, sign his own discharge papers and, in August 1919, went on the run again.

Adopting the name of Edward Sands and claiming to be an Englishman, Snyder went to Hollywood and in the following year obtained a post as cook-valet to the famous film director William Desmond Taylor, an Irishman. Luxuriating in his new post and assuring Taylor that he would be his slave for life, Snyder set out to rob his new master blind. Before the trusting director left for a holiday in England, he gave his valet a signed blank cheque to use in case of emergencies.

It must have seemed to Snyder that Christmas had come early that year. He filled in the cheque for $5,000 and cashed it, forged a number of other cheques and left Taylor's house with a large trunk, which he carried off in his master's car. Upon his return Taylor informed the police but he never saw his cook-valet again, although in a considerate gesture Snyder did post the director several pawn tickets for some diamond cuff links he had stolen.

However, the valet's chicanery was almost immediately overshadowed when, on 2 February 1922, William Desmond Taylor was found murdered at his home. The death caused one of Hollywood's greatest scandals and there was a long roll call of possible suspects, including film star Mabel Normand, one of the last people to see Taylor alive.

With his long record, one of the suspects sought by the police was Edward Snyder, alias Edward Sands, the absconding cook-valet and serial deserter. There was no evidence to link Snyder with the murder, but he might have proved a convenient scapegoat with so many Hollywood luminaries in the frame. The *Long Beach Daily Telegram* of 8 February 1922 wrote: 'Police seeking the slayer of William Desmond Taylor, movie director, were working on the theory today that his assassin was hired to kill him. It is believed that Edward F. Sands, former valet of the director, may have been the hired assassin.'

Edward Snyder was never found, and the real murderer of William Desmond Taylor was not apprehended.

Viktor Oliver von Samek, an Austrian aristocrat, may have ended his career as a top-of-the-bill musical hall comedian under the name of Vic Oliver but during the war he saw his share of action and was wounded before he deserted.

Oliver was born in Vienna 1898 and had a privileged upbringing. He showed considerable aptitude for music and also represented Austria at football against the touring Sunderland Athletic professional football team. At the age of seventeen in 1916, he volunteered for the army. His father pulled strings to get him commissioned as a cavalry officer. Because of his gifts as a pianist, Oliver was posted to the headquarters of Prince René of Bourbon-Parma, a high-ranking officer, where he led a gilded social life and soon got into debt. He married but then, as the war approached its end, he was posted to the Russian front, where he was twice wounded and decorated.

In 1918, with the Austrian Army in full retreat and revolts taking place in the streets of Vienna, Oliver, who was in the capital on convalescent leave, decided that it would soon be a case of every man for himself. This opinion was strengthened when one night he was mugged in the street by a group of revolutionaries who tore the captain's bars from his lapels. As an Austrian and technically still a serving soldier, Oliver knew that he would be shot if he was caught trying to leave the country, but he also realised that Vienna was no longer a safe place for a former member of the privileged classes.

He took his wife's silver fox furs and a gold cigarette case to a forger and exchanged the personal luxuries for a pair of Romanian passports. Bundling up their few remaining possessions and posing as Romanians, Oliver and his wife fled for Italy. He described their hasty exodus in his autobiography, *Mr Showbusiness* (1954): 'Around eight o'clock the next morning, carrying in four suitcases all our clothes and in our shoes the few pieces of jewellery that remained, we climbed in to a second-class compartment of the Trieste train.'

The next few years were desperately hard ones for Vic Oliver, as he was soon to call himself. He worked as a labourer, clerk and jazz-band drummer before emigrating with his wife to the USA. The cultured and very musical former aristocrat toured the halls as 'the piano-playing baron' and tried, with little success, to earn a living as a low comedian, delivering such limp one-liners as 'Excuse me for calling this joint a dump!'

Despairing of ever making the grade, in 1931 he decided to take his act to Great Britain. Here, to Oliver's great surprise, his laconic jokes, delivered in an attractive Austrian accent, were a great success. Before long he was topping the variety hall bills, appearing in films and on radio and even topping the bill at the London Palladium. Along the way he divorced his first wife and married Sarah Churchill, whose father Winston was to become Prime Minister of Great Britain. The relationship between Churchill and Oliver was not a good one. When the husband of the Italian dictator's daughter Count Ciano was executed for treason, Churchill was reputed to have muttered, 'Mussolini had the right idea about sons-in-law; he had his shot!'

Nothing is known about the early life of Joseph Klems, except that he was German and that he enrolled in the French Foreign Legion in 1920. The ambience of the Legion was such that a recruit's life before his enlistment was never investigated, but Klems proved such a good and experienced soldier that it is probable he had served in the German Army during the First World War.

Showing himself to be a tough, ruthless and ambitious soldier, Klems was promoted to sergeant within two years of his arrival in the Legion. He was then reduced to the ranks for some unspecified activity and became extremely bitter and resentful at what he regarded as the injustice of his treatment.

After brooding for some time, Klems deserted in 1923. He hid in the desert among wandering tribes for a time and then made his way to the Riff Mountains. Here he sought out the leading Arab insurgent of the moment, Abd el-Krim, a Moroccan leader.

El-Krim had recently gained great fame by wiping out a whole

Spanish army and capturing a vast cache of arms and ammunition. Former sergeant Klems turned up at the Moroccan's camp at just the right time. He proved himself adept at servicing the captured Spanish artillery pieces and training the tribesmen in their use. So indispensable did Klems make himself in this fashion that he was soon advanced from armourer to tactical adviser to Abd el-Krim. It did the German no harm when he also announced his conversion to Islam.

In 1925, Klems accompanied the chief on an invasion of French Morocco. The attack was so successful that other desert tribes joined in the assault. Many French forts were taken in the advance of the Moroccans and their allies before France sent reinforcements under the command of First World War hero General Pétain. In 1926, Pétain forced the Arabs back, surrounded them and accepted Abd el-Krim's surrender, although sporadic guerrilla warfare was to continue for another seven years. Ex-legionnaire Klems was captured hiding in a cave, betrayed for the price on his head by one of his more venal wives (how many wives he had is unknown). Joseph Klems was court-martialled and sentenced to death – but he was saved under bizarre circumstances.

His romantic life in the desert among the Arabs had resulted in a great deal of international newspaper exposure for the one-time sergeant. The story of Klems and his Berber chieftain Abd el-Krim in the Riff revolt in Morocco attracted the attention of a group of writers, led by Oscar Hammerstein II and the composer Sigmund Romberg. Between them they turned the story into the smash-hit musical *The Desert Song* which opened on Broadway in 1926. The plot is woven around the exploits of the mysterious Red Shadow, the leader of an outlaw band of Moroccan tribesmen. The Red Shadow is in reality a Frenchman, Pierre, the freedom-loving son of the local commanding general with a penchant for singing stirring songs and the occasional romantic ballad at the drop of a conductor's baton.

The Desert Song, with its tuneful melodies, including 'My Desert is Waiting', turned out to be an enormous success. It ran on

Broadway for over 450 performances and was equally popular all over the world. Once more the spotlight was turned on Joseph Klems, the original 'Pierre'. His death sentence was commuted to life imprisonment in the penal colony of Devil's Island.

The growing power of the Nazi regime in Germany persuaded France to release Klems and send him back home in 1934. Here the former deserter's luck finally ran out. In 1939, Joseph Klems killed himself while serving a gaol sentence in Berlin.

John Dillinger never saw military action but he became one of the best-known American gangsters of the 1930s. He was born in 1903 and spent his early years in Indianapolis. His father then moved his family to a farm, but Dillinger did not take to rural life and became mixed up in petty crimes in neighbouring towns. In 1923, on 24 July, he suddenly joined the navy. It was rumoured that he did so to avoid being charged with the theft of an automobile, but this has never been proved.

Serving as a fireman third class shovelling coal, Dillinger did not take to naval discipline. Within a few months he had been sentenced to ten days' solitary confinement on bread and water and fined $18 for being absent without leave. When his ship, the battle-ship *Utah*, put into Boston, Dillinger walked ashore and never returned. His maritime career had lasted four months. His naval record stated tersely 'left with no effects – intentions not known'.

Dillinger told any of his friends who cared that he had received an honourable discharge from the navy. Almost at once he took to a life of crime, robbing a grocer, hitting his victim with a gun and discharging it in the struggle which ensued. Dillinger was arrested and pleaded guilty, on the mistaken assumption that he would get a light sentence. Instead he was sentenced to a term of ten to twenty years in prison.

He emerged nine years later in 1933, a hardened criminal determined to get his own back on the society which had incarcerated him. He set off on a bank robbery spree, was arrested and imprisoned, and then broken out by members of his gang. During the escape a sheriff was shot and killed. Not long afterwards, Dillinger was arrested and again imprisoned. This time he bluffed his way out with a homemade facsimile gun. Later, folklore decreed that Dillinger had carved the weapon in his cell out of a bar of soap, but it is more likely that the gun was made from wood and had been smuggled into the prison to him.

Dillinger and a shifting population of associates went back to work. The gang even broke into several police stations to obtain fresh stocks of ammunition and bullet-proof vests.

The gangster was in danger of becoming a folk hero. One trait which endeared him to the populace was the fact that he obviously enjoyed his work. In a rare discursive moment he once said, 'All my life I wanted to be a bank robber, carry a gun and wear a mask. Now that it's happened I guess I'm just about the best bank robber they ever had. And I sure am happy!'

The FBI declared Dillinger Public Enemy No. 1 and began to close in on him. He was betrayed by Anna Sage, a prostitute and brothel owner, who informed the authorities that Dillinger would be with her at the Biograph Theater in Chicago on the evening of 22 July 1934. Herbert Hoover ordered that fifteen FBI armed agents should lie in wait for the reprobate. As Dillinger emerged from the show with Sage and another woman, the agents closed in on him. The bank robber fled and was gunned down in an alley.

Soldier of fortune, adventurer, film star and all-round rogue, Errol Flynn also found time in his short but hectic life to become a deserter. Born in Tasmania in 1909, the son of a professor, the handsome and charismatic youth embarked upon a life of adventure before he was eighteen and worked as a seaman, a gold prospector, plantation-manager in New Guinea and diamond smuggler. Because of his looks and physique he was even recruited to play a part in a 1933 low-budget Australian movie, *In the Wake of the Bounty*.

This aroused in Flynn a desire to become an actor and he set out to work his passage to Great Britain in order to embark upon a stage career. With a friend he got as far as Hong Kong, working as a professional gambler, only to be swindled out of his money by a prostitute. Destitute and desperate, Flynn and his companion enlisted in the Royal Hong Kong Volunteers. This was a military unit recruited to defend the crown colony against a possible attack by the Japanese, who had already invaded China.

Flynn and the other man were sent with 400 other soldiers to defend Shanghai. Instead of fighting, Flynn found himself clearing snow and digging trenches under fire from the advancing Japanese. A few days of this and the Australian's military ambitions diminished markedly. He decided to leave as soon as possible. Laboriously he forged some documents and under the pretence of visiting the camp latrines he and his friend fled for the harbour. Using what little money they had been paid for their military endeavours the pair of them bribed the captain of a small mail boat to take them on its run to Saigon.

Eventually Flynn reached Britain, begged his father to send him money and secured an acting position with the Northampton Repertory Company. He was spotted by a talent scout and given parts in several British films. So impressed, Warner Brothers brought the young actor to Hollywood. Within a year he was playing the lead in the enormously popular swashbuckler *Captain Blood*. The film made Flynn a star and launched him into a glittering career and a riotous private life, lived mainly in public, before he collapsed and died at the age of fifty. At his inquest the coroner said that the condition of Flynn's organs resembled those of an old man.

Walter Krivitsky was altogether more professional. Defecting in 1937, he became the highest-ranking Russian intelligence agent to switch to the West. Four years later his dead body was found in mysterious circumstances.

Born Samuel Ginsberg in Galicia, on the borders of Russia and the Habsburg Empire, he changed his name to avoid rampant anti-Semitism. Soon an avowed Communist, he took part in the Russian Revolution of 1917 and was then recruited by military intelligence. He worked his way up through the Soviet spy networks until, in 1933, he was serving in Vienna. He was then transferred to Holland, with the rank of general, as resident Director of Intelligence in charge of spying activities in Western Europe. A colleague and close friend was Ignace Reiss, who had fallen out with Stalin. Krivitsky was considerably shaken when Reiss was subsequently murdered in Switzerland by Stalin's operatives. He was further disillusioned with the system when he discovered that the Russians were preparing to sign the Nazi-Soviet non-aggression pact with Hitler.

In 1937, General Krivitsky defected in Paris, asking the French authorities for asylum. Fearing that Soviet SMERSH agents would find and kill him in France, he went on to the USA and was hidden in Canada for a time, while he was debriefed. He provided the Americans with a great deal of information but, perhaps because he was the first major Russian deserter, his hosts did not seem to know what to do with the intelligence he was providing.

In 1939, the Russian was brought to London, where he supplied the names of operatives working for the USSR in the British civil service. He also said that a number of Cambridge undergraduates had been recruited by Russian agents. When nothing seemed to be done about this information Krivitsky complained that no one would listen to him.

On 9 February 1941, Walter Krivitsky was found shot through the head in a Washington hotel room. An official verdict of suicide was brought in, but throughout the Intelligence community it was widely suspected that he had been murdered by his former Soviet masters.

The cause of Communism in the USA was badly shaken by the execution of Paul White, a member of an American force fighting in the Spanish Civil War. He joined the International Brigade to fight for the Popular Front government against the Nationalist Army in Spain. An American, Paul White subsequently deserted and fled for the French border. He had a change of heart and returned to his unit but was arrested, tried and executed.

White, a member of the American Communist Party, had been working on the waterfront when he joined the 3,000-strong Abraham Lincoln Battalion and sailed to take part against the

Fascists in the Spanish Civil War. White was put to work in the transport section, organising vehicles to take men to the Aragon section of the front line.

The battalion suffered heavy casualties in the early months of the campaign. In 1938, White was ordered to fetch fresh supplies of ammunition. Instead, he carried on driving, intending to escape to France and from there make his way back to the USA. While he was in transit he heard that his wife had given birth to a son. White decided that he did not want his son to hear in later years that his father had been a deserter. He turned his truck, drove back to his unit and gave himself up. He said at his subsequent trial: 'I was afraid to go into action again. I tried all this time to overcome my feeling of fear. I felt we were defeated and fighting futilely. I dropped out of the line and made up my mind to desert and try and reach France.'

Unfortunately for White, a new commissar, John Gates, whose real name was Solomon Regenstriet, had been put in charge of his battalion. Gates was determined to tighten discipline in the Lincoln Battalion and decided to make an example of Paul White. He ordered a court martial for White. The American was found guilty of desertion. In August 1938, he was executed by a six-man firing squad.

The execution caused an uproar among the Americans serving in Spain and back home in the USA. Gates faced widespread criticism for his action. He announced that he would sanction no more executions.

The execution of Paul White caused so much dissent and unease among fellow members of the International Brigade and civilians back home in the USA that political and military leaders took note of the fact, appreciating the unpopularity of such an action. In the Second World War, although thousands of US soldiers were arrested for desertion and many were sentenced to terms of imprisonment, only one US soldier was executed during the entire war.

16

'I'LL NEVER FORGIVE HITLER!'

Most of the policemen were in the Army or the Air Force or the Navy and Military Police, so you had a lot of what they called Specials. Well, they were a joke!
– 'Mad' Frankie Fraser on the joys of being a deserter in London in the Second World War

One of the strangest desertions of the Second World War concerned the hundreds of members of the Irish Army who left their units and enlisted in the British Army just to be able to take part in the war. Ireland was neutral and looked like remaining so for the duration of hostilities. The Irish volunteers served with courage and distinction throughout, but when they returned home they found that they had been officially categorised as deserters. They were often shunned by their neighbours and refused admittance to posts in the public sector. It was not until almost seventy years later that they accepted an official 'pardon' for their actions between 1939 and 1945 – by this time only about 100 of them were still alive.

During the war, many showed that they had no stomach for any sort of fight: 100,000 British servicemen were reported as having deserted, while the American total was 40,000. However, the American authorities generously counted many of their absconders only as being absent without leave – their figures would otherwise have been much higher.

The outbreak of the Second World War, with its concomitant administrative chaos in London and other major cities, was greeted with relish by criminals and the mentally disturbed, who were quick to take advantage of the blackout, German air raids and shortage of police. These men and women regarded being called up for wartime military service as a purely temporary distraction and one that could soon be put right by bribery and flight – or even a series of flights. A number of them used the war years as a time to establish gangs of like-minded criminals and to lay the foundations of personal fortunes.

Every so often the police and military police would organise sweeps, cordoning off whole areas and sometimes even whole towns, forcing every man within the enclosed area to prove his identity, but the more astute among the deserters soon bought forged papers or found reasonably secure hiding places in warehouses, bombed buildings and tenements, whose inhabitants would not take kindly to mass invasions by officers of the law. In 1943, a gang of army deserters caught looting in Kent were given prison sentences ranging from five years' penal servitude to eight years' hard labour.

'Mad' Frankie Fraser, a London dockland gangster, regarded the war years as the best time of his life. He was to spend a total of more than forty years in prison, but was in the army for such brief periods between desertions that he boasted that he had never once worn a uniform. When questioned, he could not even remember which units he was supposed to have been in.

He first made contact with the army in 1942 when he was serving a prison sentence in Chelmsford prison for breaking and entering. One day Fraser was taken to Southend in handcuffs to be medically examined for the forces so that he could be conscripted soon after his release. He passed his physical and was then taken back to complete his sentence.

Upon his release from prison, Fraser ignored his call-up papers and went straight back to a life of crime, taking advantage of the Blitz to break into shops. Sometimes he and his associates would wear the helmets of Air Raid Precaution wardens and pretend to be rescuing goods from bomb-damaged shops when in fact they were stealing them.

When Fraser received his call-up papers for the army, he automatically threw them on the fire. A few days later he was picked up by the police as he tried to pull off another robbery. When it was discovered that although he had never served in the forces he was still technically a deserter, he was escorted to the unit he should have joined in Norwich. The commanding officer informed Fraser that he was starting off with a clean sheet in the army and sent him to the stores to draw his uniform and equipment.

When Fraser arrived at the stores it was late afternoon and the building was closed. He promptly caught a train back to London. Within a month he was caught in possession of a stolen van and sentenced to three months' imprisonment. Once released, he was picked up by several soldiers and escorted back to his Norwich unit. At Norwich railway station the wily Fraser gave his guards the slip and hitched lifts back to London.

Three weeks later he was arrested for breaking into a shop. This time he was sentenced to fifteen months. He was released in 1944 and once more taken back to the army, this time to Bradford. He was ordered to get out of the van outside the barracks and at once took to his heels, losing himself in the crowd at a funfair.

As usual Fraser returned to London and as usual he was caught, this time in a routine police sweep for deserters in a pub. Ever optimistic, the army called for Fraser to be brought back to his unit, this time handcuffed to another deserter. When they reached King's Cross station the two men suddenly ran away from their police escort but were caught as they ran up a hill by their pursuers who had commandeered a taxi.

Reaching Bradford again, Fraser was put in the guardhouse with other deserters. Again he escaped, this time by diving out of a window. He was soon recaptured but by this time even the army had had enough of the reluctant soldier. Fraser was examined by a psychiatrist and discharged as mentally unfit to serve. Gleefully he went back to his life of crime, which was only temporarily interrupted by the cessation of hostilities in 1945. Frankie Fraser went on to have a long career as a criminal and an enforcer for the notorious Richardson 'Torture' Gang. He worked as a bodyguard, club owner and thief.

In his seventies he put his name to a ghosted bestselling auto-biography, appeared on television programmes and cashed in on his celebrity by conducting coach tours around London's gangland.

During the Second World War, the military authorities grew wary of the chaos likely to be caused in their units by determined and vicious thugs like Fraser, and were reluctant to take back the real hard men among professional deserters, almost turning a blind eye as they roamed the streets of the cities, reassuringly far from military bases.

The mentally unstable also used the mandatory blackout in which to prowl the compulsorily darkened streets. Reginald Sidney Buckfield, nicknamed Smiley for his perpetual grin, was a Second World War deserter who perpetrated a vicious murder for no apparent reason while on the run.

Brought up in Houghton, near Manchester, husband and father of three Buckfield was conscripted into the army. He deserted from his Royal Artillery unit because, he stated later, he thought he had made a local girl pregnant and wanted to avoid her. While on the run for a few months he earned a living as a casual labourer in the London area.

On the evening of Friday 9 October 1942, a young married woman called Ellen Symes was pushing a 4-year-old child in its pram along the Brompton Farm Road in Strood near Kent. Buckfield leapt out of the darkness and stabbed her savagely in the chest and neck before running off. Hearing screams, a neighbour ran out to find Ellen Symes already dead. There had been no attempt at a sexual assault. The 4-year-old child was later able to tell the police that the assailant had been a soldier.

The next day a police officer saw Buckley in uniform hanging around near the site of the murder. When he was questioned the gunner seemed to know a great deal about the crime he claimed not to have witnessed. He was arrested on suspicion of murder and it was soon discovered that he was a deserter.

When the police handed their prisoner over to the military police, Buckfield gave a detective a sheaf of handwritten papers entitled 'The Mystery of Brompton Road'. After further investigations, during which the knife used in the murder was traced back to him, Buckley was asked about his manuscript. 'That's all fiction,' was his reply. 'That's how I thought the murder might have been committed.'

At his Old Bailey trial in 1943, Buckley was found guilty of the murder of Ellen Symes although no motive for the killing could ever be ascertained. He was sentenced to death but later reprieved on the grounds of insanity and sent to Broadmoor.

Another deserter who committed a murder while on the run was Ernest James Kemp, a Royal Artillery deserter. Born in Gillingham he worked as a railway porter at a London railway station before joining the Queen's Royal Regiment (the West Surreys) in 1942. He served in a number of camps in Great Britain and then in 1943 transferred to the Royal Artillery.

In 1944, Kemp was sentenced to a period of detention but was allowed to visit the dentist outside the military prison area with an escort. He was allowed to go to the toilet without an escort and escaped by climbing out through a window. He made his way to London and then vanished from sight for several months. On 14 October, the dead body of Miriam Deeley, a member of the Women's Auxiliary Air Force (WAAF), was found in an allotment on the outskirts of London. She had been raped and strangled with her own scarf. Large footprints were found in the mud surrounding the body.

Police inquiries were instigated and several witnesses said that the girl, who had missed the last train back to her unit at Kidbrooke in south-east London, had been seen in the company of a young soldier who had been wearing a most impressive collection of medal ribbons. All police officers were asked to be on the lookout for such a man.

One searching constable, a former First World War soldier, noticed a young gunner with several rows of ribbons escorting a WAAF in the Regent's Park area. The policeman waited until the pair had parted and then walked over to the soldier. He realised that some of the ribbons on the man's chest had been issued for campaigns fought long before the soldier could have been born. He arrested the man, who gave his name as Gunner Kemp.

Chief Inspector Edward Greeno, who was heading the murder enquiry, questioned Kemp and soon discovered that he was a deserter. The soldier had no alibi for the night of the murder and some of Miriam Deeley's possessions were found in his rucksack. When Gunner Kemp's boots were found to fit the footprints left in the mud in the allotment, he was arrested for the murder.

Ernest Kemp's trial at the Old Bailey began on 18 April 1944. He was found guilty, with a recommendation for mercy. He was hanged at Wandsworth Prison on 6 June 1944.

One murderer of the time was actually saved, at least for a time, by a sudden German victory. Walter Burridge, a private in the 1st Battalion of the Welsh Regiment in the British Army in Crete in 1941, went absent without leave, was recaptured and then killed a provost sergeant major, but by a strange quirk of fate was not tried and punished for almost four years.

Burridge, an irascible, moody man with a record of insubordination, was put on fatigues at Paragoria camp and ordered to dig latrines. He absconded and went into the town. When he did not report on a defaulters' parade, military policemen, led by a Corporal McCullough, were sent to find him. Burridge was arrested drinking in a wine shop and brought back to his unit.

When Private Burridge was brought before Provost Sergeant Major Samuel Victor Sims, responsible for discipline in the camp, he picked up a rifle which had been left lying against a tent pole. On his way to the provost tent the deserter took two rounds of ammunition from another soldier. Quickly he loaded the rifle and shot and killed Sergeant Major Sims. When he was overpowered by other troops Burridge asked, 'Who did I shoot?' When he was told that he had killed the sergeant major, he muttered, 'I'm sorry it was him.'

Burridge was placed under close arrest to await a court martial on a charge of murder. Before the court could be convened the

Germans attacked and took Crete. Burridge was sent as a prisoner of war to Silesia, where he was made to work in the mines until 1945. He twice made escape attempts and then with other prisoners was forced to take part in a 1,000-mile march to Bavaria. He was released on demobilisation leave in England when the papers concerning the charge of murder levelled against him turned up.

Burridge could no longer be court-martialled, as more than three years had passed since the original offence. Instead he was tried at the Old Bailey in 1946 under civilian law. Burridge pleaded that he had been so drunk at the time of his arrest for absence without leave that he could remember nothing about the matter.

Not all of the witnesses to the murder could be found and Burridge's defence barrister made the most of the fact that so much time had passed since the murder far away in Crete, that Burridge should be given the benefit of any doubt going.

The jury obviously agreed with this sentiment. Its members found the accused guilty of manslaughter, not murder. Sentencing Burridge to five years' imprisonment, the judge, from his affronted remarks, made it clear that he considered that the prisoner should have been convicted of murder. Nothing was heard of him after his release.

The American authorities had their own problems with men of military age who preferred not to serve. When the USA entered the war after the attack on Pearl Harbor in 1941, the Joint Chiefs of Staff estimated that it would need an army of nine million men successfully to fight both the Japanese and the Germans. The draft was put into action and by 1942 huge military training camps were in operation all over the country. This new urgency proved too much for some career soldiers and conscripts alike.

In 1942, two GI deserters went on a shooting rampage, dominating newspaper headlines across the country despite the ongoing war. Twenty-one-year-old Charles Joseph Lovett and James Edward Testerman, 22, were both members of the Machine Gun Troop of the Third Cavalry, stationed at Fort Oglethorpe in Georgia. Neither man was regarded as a good soldier by his superiors. Lovett, who

often ran away from home as a youth, had a record of petty thefts
before enlisting in the army in 1939. In the relatively short time
he had been in the forces he had been court-martialled twice, for
absence without leave and drunken behaviour. Testerman had also
been court-martialled for desertion.

In the early hours of the morning of 12 March 1942, the two
GIs knocked the sergeant in charge of their billet unconscious by
striking him over the head with an iron bell from the mess hall.
They stole four revolvers from the barracks and escaped by stopping a passing taxi, robbing the driver and driving to Sweetwater
in Tennessee. They continued their journey by bus to Abingdon in
Virginia, where Testerman hoped to secure the assistance of
a girlfriend.

Details of the deserters had already been circulated. Two FBI
agents who happened to be driving into Abingdon saw a couple
of soldiers entering a restaurant resembling the descriptions of the
wanted men. The agents, Hubert J. Treacy and Charles Tignor,
followed the soldiers inside and asked them for identification.

Lovett suddenly produced a revolver and shot both FBI men.
Tignor was struck in the arm while Treacy received a bullet in
the face. The two deserters fled for the door. As they left the café,
Lovett fired two more shots at Tignor and one at Treacy. Out in
the street, the deserters commandeered a car but were cut off by
a police vehicle responding to alarm calls. Lovett and Testerman
abandoned the vehicle, firing a number of shots as they ran, and
hid in the basement of a house.

In a short time the building was surrounded by an armed force
of policemen and FBI agents. The latter were reinforced by other
agents who had been attending a course nearby. A few shots were
fired and tear gas was pumped into the basement. The *Utica Daily
Press* of 14 March 1942 described the ending of the siege: 'Abingdon
VA: Two young Army deserters, waving an improvised white flag,
after a gun battle which resulted in the death of one FBI agent and
the wounding of another, stumbled from a tear gas filled house
here yesterday and surrendered.'

Agent Treacy died from his wounds. Charles Tignor was severely wounded by shots to the head, chest and arm, but recovered. Because it was difficult to call some service witnesses back from duty in Europe, Charles Lovett and James Testerman were found guilty and sentenced to life imprisonment.

There were also a number of examples of serious crimes committed in Great Britain by American deserters. Karl Gustav Hulten was a Swedish-born wartime deserter from the US Army who was hanged for what became known as the Cleft-Chin Murder.

The 22-year-old Hulten deserted from his paratrooper unit in August 1944 and made his way to London, where he lived by his wits for six weeks. On Tuesday 3 October, in a café in Hammersmith Broadway, he met a Welsh girl called Elizabeth Jones, separated from her soldier husband, who had been working at a variety of jobs, including barmaid, waitress and striptease dancer. She had been out of work since the beginning of the year and was greatly attracted to Hulten, who claimed to be 'Ricky', an officer in the US Army.

When he took her out on a date that evening Hulten arrived in a military truck. As they drove, he regaled her with fanciful tales of his pre-war life in Chicago. He also claimed, with no foundation, to be 'Chicago Joe', the leader of a London gang. Elizabeth Jones told him that she had always longed to be something exciting, like a gangster's moll. At this Hulten came clean and told the girl that he was on the run and that the truck was stolen. To demonstrate his prowess he stopped the vehicle, jumped out, stopped a girl cycling past and stole her purse before driving off again.

Hulten and Jones started living together, and on 5 October they decided to rob a taxi they had followed to Cricklewood. They stopped the vehicle and Hulten threatened the driver with a pistol before noticing that there was a passenger in the back of the cab. Hastily he abandoned the raid and he and Jones drove off. On the Edgware Road they gave a lift to a girl who wanted to get to Paddington railway station. Hulten hit the girl with an iron bar, half-strangled her and robbed her of five shillings before leaving her lying in the road.

The next night they decided to try to rob a taxi again. They hailed a private cab driven by 34-year-old George Edward Heath, who took them to Chiswick roundabout. Here Hulten and Jones got out. Hulten produced his pistol and shot the driver in the spine, paralysing him. He died twenty-five minutes later.

Hulten ordered Elizabeth Jones to go through their victim's pockets. All that she could find was 19/- (95p), a watch, a silver pencil and a cigarette case. After dumping Heath's body in a ditch in Staines the two abandoned the car and went back to Jones's place.

Because of the taxi driver's cleft chin the case became known in the newspapers as the 'Cleft-Chin Murder'. Hulten and Jones were not at liberty for long. An alert policeman noticed the stolen Ford V8 parked on Fulham Palace Road. He telephoned his station and was joined by an inspector and a sergeant in a police car. As they kept observation an American Army officer left a nearby house and entered the parked car. It was Hulten. He was arrested and taken to the police station.

The arrested man, who was found in possession of a pistol and ammunition, insisted that he was Richard John Allen before finally admitting to being Private Gustav Hulten. At first he was charged with being absent without leave and being in possession of a stolen pistol. Hulten denied being responsible for the murder of the taxi driver and said that Elizabeth Jones would provide him with an alibi for the time of the murder.

Unfortunately for the American, Jones was beginning to suffer pangs of conscience. She told a friend, 'If you had seen what I had seen, you would not be able to sleep.' Her confidante informed the police and Elizabeth Jones was arrested. After questioning she admitted that Hulten had murdered George Heath while she looked on.

Although the American Army Criminal Investigation Department had questioned Hulten in the initial stages of the investigation the US military authorities waived their right to court-martial the private. The trial of Hulten and Elizabeth Jones began at the Old Bailey on 16 January 1945. After six days they were both found guilty and sentenced to death. Hulten was hanged at Pentonville Prison on 8 March 1945. Jones was reprieved two days before she was due to be executed. She was released in 1954.

A fatal disturbance involving US deserters, but on a larger scale, occurred in Devonshire in 1944. Ten black American soldiers of the 3247 Quartermaster Service Company left their posts without permission outside the village of Kingsclere in Devonshire and shot and killed a black, American military policeman and the landlady of one of the village pubs.

The ten soldiers had left their camp without permission earlier on the afternoon of 5 October 1944. Having no leave passes, they were turned back by four US military policemen. The piqued troops returned to their unit and discussed the matter at some length. They decided to return to the village with their loaded carbines, disarm the military policemen who had humiliated them and then beat them up. They paraded through the public houses, searching for their targets. They found some of them in the Crown Inn. One of the military policemen left the pub and there was a volley of shots. When the drinkers went out to investigate, they found the dead bodies of one black US soldier and one black military policeman. Another military policeman was fatally wounded. A little later the landlord's wife, Rose Napper, was found dying in one of the rooms of the public house, shot through the jaw, presumably by a stray round of ammunition.

The soldiers were arrested and brought to trial just over a month later. They were accused of being absent without leave, riotous assembly and murder. Nine of the men were found guilty on all charges and sentenced to life imprisonment. The tenth man was found guilty of being absent without leave from his unit.

Efforts were made to hush up the incident, but a number of newspapers got hold of the story. General Eisenhower, the US commander in chief, asked his second in command to apologise to the inhabitants of Kingsclere for the dreadful events of the night of 5 October.

Throughout the Second World War, and indeed long before

that, as in the case of Paul White during the Spanish Civil War, the matter of desertions were recognised as being a hot political potato and a contentious issue to be avoided whenever possible. Members of the public did not like to think that soldiers were not fully committed to fighting for their country or, as in the case of the Kingsclere murder, that any of the troops surrounding them at home were capable of going on the rampage and causing harm. This was true of every nation concerned in the war and government departments and military censors did their utmost to prevent any mention of unauthorised military absences in the media.

17

'THEY'RE NOT SHOOTING ME FOR DESERTING!'

There were 20,000 Australian troops in Singapore, so where did the others go?
– General Henry Gordon Bennett claiming that most of the troops under his command refused to fight the Japanese

During the Second World War, 21,049 American military personnel were convicted of desertion and forty-nine were sentenced to death. Only one was executed. The ultimate misfit and the one who paid the highest price for his inability to cope with war was Private Eddie Slovik. Not only was he the only US soldier to be executed for desertion, he was also the first US serviceman to face a firing squad for the offence since the end of the American Civil War.

Born in 1920 to immigrant parents, Slovik spent much of his youth in the Michigan Reformatory School for stealing sweets and cigarettes from the drugstore where he worked. He was released on parole in 1942 and went to work for a plumbing supplies firm. On 7 November 1942 he married Antoinette Wisniewski and soon began employment in a factory.

Slovik believed that his criminal conviction would safeguard him from the draft, but the war in Europe was approaching its climax and on 24 January 1944 he was called up for basic infantry training at Camp Wolters in Texas. Slovik was bitterly unhappy in the army and proved to be a misfit combat soldier; so afraid was he of weapons that during his training he had to be equipped with dummy grenades.

Nevertheless, he was shipped to the front line in France, soon after the Germans had made their celebrated last push at Bastogne in 1944 where they launched fourteen infantry divisions and five Panzer tank divisions along a thinly defended fifty-mile front in the Ardennes, hoping to drive through to the port of Antwerp. Many Americans fought and died bravely, but some did not. There were mass desertions in the face of the enemy and 7,500 troops surrendered, the largest mass capitulation in American history.

Unable to cope with the constant German shelling, Slovik deserted his rifle company in the 28th Division on the night of 24 August 1944. For weeks he wandered aimlessly behind the lines, living as best he could. In October he was discovered, arrested and returned to his company. He was warned by his commanding officer that if he went AWOL again he would be charged with desertion. Several days later, still unable to cope with the constant bombardment, Slovik departed once more. This time he reached Belgium where, starving and wretched, he turned himself in to the authorities and signed a confession.

Slovik was tried by a court martial for desertion under fire and sentenced to death by firing squad. It was generally expected that the Supreme Allied Commander Dwight D. Eisenhower would commute this sentence to one of imprisonment but at the time Eisenhower was desperately worried by the number of desertions that had taken place during the Ardennes offensive. He decided that an example must be made of Private Slovik and ordered that the verdict of the court should stand. At his execution at Sainte-Marie-Aux-Mines, on 31 January 1945, a member of the twelve-man firing squad begged Slovik to make it as easy as he could for himself and his executioners. 'Don't worry about me,' muttered the accused man. 'I'm OK. They're not shooting me for deserting the United States Army – thousands of guys have done that. They're shooting me for the bread I stole when I was twelve years old.'

Mass desertions occurred in the Far East, especially after Japan launched attacks on British-held territories there. By February 1942, the invading Japanese were advancing on Singapore down the Malay Peninsula. The Allied forces were in full retreat. Many of the 90,000 Allied troops present had discarded their weapons, left their units and were trying desperately to get out of Singapore before they were killed or taken prisoner by the Japanese.

The few remaining ships in the harbour were ordered to take onboard as many fleeing civilians and forces personnel as they could carry. One of these vessels was the SS *Empire Star*, under the command of Selwyn Capon, which was moored alongside the Keppel Harbour wharf waiting to leave after delivering a consignment of tanks to the garrison. The crew worked frantically to cram hundreds of desperate civilians, nurses, soldiers and airmen onboard, while the Japanese shelled the harbour, destroying a number of buildings and setting fire to others.

Towards the end of the day groups of drunken Australian deserters began to close in on the moored vessel. British military policemen had been stationed on the wharf, in case of attempts by unauthorised soldiers to embark, but were overwhelmed by about 100 deserters, who swarmed up the gangplank of the *Empire Star* and even climbed hand over hand up the mooring ropes to reach the crowded decks.

Captain Capon looked on helplessly as the ferocious yet terrified Australians determined to escape mingled with the women and children, pushing their way to safety. When there were more than 2,000 people crammed standing shoulder to shoulder on his vessel, he gave orders for the gangplank to be raised. Early on the morning of 12 February, the *Empire Star*, with its heaving human cargo, left Singapore, three days before the Japanese captured the island. Conditions aboard were atrocious, with only sixteen cabin spaces available to accommodate several thousand people.

The vessel was able to sail with other ships in the last major convoy to leave the stricken crown colony but at 9 a.m. the small flotilla was attacked by Japanese aircraft.

The *Empire Star* was one of the vessels bombed and sustained a number of dead and wounded. A handful of RAF members turned a machine gun on the attackers, bringing down one of the low-flying Japanese aircraft. Some sixty Australian nurses among the passengers distinguished themselves by their devotion to duty and the care they took of the stricken on deck while under fire themselves.

It was not until the aerial attacks had ceased and the *Empire Star* was approaching Batavia (now Jakarta) that Captain Capon was able to turn his attention to the problem of the Australian deserters lurking on board his ship. He radioed ahead and asked for a contingent of British soldiers to be waiting when his vessel docked. Then he ordered a large, armed group of seamen and marines onboard to round up the Australians.

His move took the deserters by surprise and they surrendered without a fight, giving up their arms. When the ship docked the now subdued and sober men were herded down the gangplank and handed over to the waiting escort.

Little is known about what happened to the deserters after that. Batavia itself was invaded and taken by the Japanese a short while later and in the confusion that followed little notice was taken of the hundred or so unwelcome Australians. A number were imprisoned to await courts martial. Few records of the period survived the Japanese attack and for years afterwards the Australian authorities did their best to hush the incident up to avoid despoiling the good name of their forces

It is certain that some of the deserters were discovered in prison and hustled off to prisoner-of-war camps with other captured Allied troops by the Japanese. Although the Australian forces did not impose the death penalty for mutiny, for years rumours persisted that a number of the *Empire Star* deserters had been shot summarily by British troops soon after they had been disembarked from the vessel which they had hoped had been carrying them to safety. After the war ended there were demands for a public enquiry into the whole *Empire Star* incident, but these were rejected by the British government.

As the imminent fall of Singapore looked increasingly likely, Winston Churchill issued an urgent order from London: 'There must at this stage be no thought of saving the troops or sparing the

population ... Commanders and senior officers should die with
their troops.'

General Henry Gordon Bennett, a senior Australian soldier, did
not see eye to eye with the British Prime Minister on this point
and his conduct came under considerable scrutiny at Singapore and
afterwards.

Bennett was a career soldier who fought bravely in the First
World War at Gallipoli and France, becoming, at twenty-nine, the
youngest general in the Australian Army. He left the army briefly
after the war but rejoined and was made a major general. Despite
his achievements, the ambitious, acerbic and envious Bennett had
made enemies and was at first passed over for active command
when the Second World War broke out.

In 1941, he was placed in command of the Australian forces in
Malaya to stem the Japanese advance but did not get on with his
overall superior, the British lieutenant general, Percival. When in
February 1942 the triumphant Japanese entered Singapore, Percival
announced his intention to surrender. During the defence of
Singapore, 2,000 Allied troops had been killed and 5,000 wounded.
An astonishing 70,000 had surrendered; the largest capitulation of
troops in British military history. Following his Prime Minister's
order, Percival stated that he expected his officers to remain with
their men. Gordon Bennett repeated this order to his own officers,
handed over the Australian command to a subordinate, and with
a small group took over a sampan by force and travelled by sea to
the east coast of Sumatra. Here Gordon Bennett, two other officers
and some expatriate planters were taken on board a small launch
which conveyed them round to the west coast of Sumatra. When he
landed, Bennett started demanding preferential treatment, claiming that he had information of vital importance to the Allied cause.
The group took a plane to Java, where Bennett left his companions
and flew on ahead of them to Australia. He arrived in Melbourne
on 2 March 1942.

Bennett's sudden reappearance, safe and well when so many
Australian troops had been killed or were in Japanese prison camps,

was not greeted kindly by the majority of his fellow countrymen. Questions were asked in Parliament about his actions, but Prime Minister John Curtin defended the general, saying that Bennett had escaped, not deserted. For a time Gordon Bennett was placed in charge of the defence of Western Australia, but it became apparent that his army career was over. In 1944 he virtually retired.

After the war, General Percival, released from his prison camp after surrendering in Singapore, accused Gordon Bennett of giving up his command without permission. In answer to the clamour a court of inquiry was convened in Australia. It reached the decision that Bennett had not been justified in leaving Singapore in the manner in which he did. This was followed by a 1945 Royal Commission, ordered by Prime Minister J. B. Chifley, which decided that Gordon Bennett had been under orders to surrender at the time he left Singapore. There the matter was left.

Gordon Bennet, his reputation ruined, wrote articles on military topics. He was not complimentary about the actions of many of his troops in Singapore. On one television programme he claimed that when the Japanese attacked the fortress he had only 2,000 Australians with which to defend the perimeter.

Over a million Canadian men and women served in the armed forces during the Second World War. They fought with distinction in Italy and Sicily, at Dieppe and on D-Day. Some 44,093 were killed in action, most of whom were volunteers. When conscription was introduced, in some quarters there was less enthusiasm to serve and over 7,000 went absent without leave in Canada before they could be sent overseas. In January 1945, the first conscripts embarked for the war in Europe. Many dropped their rifles over the sides of the troopships. Of the 13,000 Canadians who reached Europe in the last year of the war fewer than 3,000 reached their units.

Private Harold Pringle was the only Canadian soldier to be executed for desertion in the Second World War. In 1939, he enlisted in the Hastings and Prince Edward Regiment. His father, who had fought with the regiment in the First World War, joined up with him, but was sent back from England for medical reasons.

Harold Pringle did not take to army life and while he was training in England he went absent without leave on a number of occasions. When finally he completed his training, he was posted to Italy and saw action. His unit suffered heavy casualties.

In March 1945, Pringle walked away from the front line and followed the well-travelled deserters' route to Rome. There were already over 1,000 Canadian deserters in custody in Italy and many more on the loose in the capital, together with thousands of other absconders from most other Allied armies and a number of German and Italian former soldiers.

Pringle managed to link up with one of the many gangs of deserters which were terrorising the Italian capital. These groups of desperate men robbed houses, hijacked vehicles and were heavily involved in prostitution, counterfeiting, drug dealing and the black market. One of these organisations, known as the Lane Gang, was particularly notorious for the ruthless manner in which it killed and robbed, almost with impunity. The Allied authorities were anxious for success in dealing with the flourishing mobs of deserters.

Harold Pringle's group, made up of British, Canadian and American deserters, was known as the Sailor Gang. It was much less successful and efficient, and therefore much easier for the military police to cope with. Receiving information that its members were meeting in a house in a part of the city, the police launched a raid on it.

Pringle was present with the others when the raid took place. He and his fellow deserters tried to shoot their way out. In the ensuing gun battle one of the deserters, a friend of Pringle's, was shot and killed. Pringle was apprehended almost immediately and charged with the death of the gang member, although witnesses stated that he was drunk at the time of the shooting.

After a long period in a military compound, Harold Pringle faced a court martial on a charge of murder. It was alleged that he had shot his accomplice, already wounded and disabled by the military police, in order to stop him talking after he was arrested.

Pringle denied the charge. His lawyer had only six days in which to prepare his case.

Private Harold Pringle was found guilty and sentenced to death. Appeals for clemency were turned down. Pringle was executed by a firing squad on 5 July 1945.

He met his end bravely, telling members of his firing squad: 'Come on, do what you have to do. Let's get it over with!' His body was buried in Caserta War Cemetery in Rome.

There was no general public response in Canada to the news of Private Pringle's execution because for years the government denied that it had ever happened. Not wishing to blunt the joy of the news of the end of the war in Europe, and with a national election about to be held, the government denied that any of its soldiers had been shot for desertion. It was years before an enterprising author unearthed and published the true story of the executed Canadian deserter.

Not all deserters were cowards, opportunists or self-serving villains. A number deserted for much more noble and surprising reasons, such as wanting to be able to fight. In 1940, Jean Offenberg, a Belgian fighter pilot, left occupied France without official permission to serve bravely with the RAF.

Born in Brussels in 1916, Offenberg became a pilot in the Belgian Air Force. Upon the outbreak of the Second World War, flying a Fiat biplane he took part in a number of aerial combats against the invading Germans. When France surrendered, Offenberg stated his intention of escaping to North Africa. His commanding officer forbade any such move, saying that without official sanction this would make the pilot a deserter.

Offenberg was still determined to continue his fight against the Nazis. He and a friend each took an aeroplane and, without any maps, flew first to Corsica and then on to North Africa, although he was not sure what he would do when he got to French-occupied territory. There he joined up with a group of pilots from a flying school.

Again the French authorities warned the young flyers against any displays of initiative. The pilots ignored their superiors and,

Offenberg among them, caught a train to Casablanca. Because they were still technically deserters, the French consul in the town could not help them.

However, Offenberg and twelve others linked up with a bunch of like-minded Poles, who smuggled the French and Belgian flyers on to their ship and transported them to England. The Belgian was made a pilot officer in the RAF and fought in the closing stages of the Battle of Britain with a Belgian squadron. Offenberg was awarded the Distinguished Flying Cross (DFC) and promoted to flight lieutenant, but was killed in a flying accident on 22 January 1942.

A deserter who displayed equal initiative was Prince Emanuel Galitzine, a member of an exiled aristocratic White Russian family which had retained its titles. Galitzine was born in the Caucasus, the son of a White Russian general, in 1918. When the Reds took over Russia in 1919, Galitzine's father took his family to England. He was able to pay Emanuel Galitzine's school fees by selling paintings he had smuggled out of his country.

After he left school the well-off Galitzine formed his own film production company and embarked upon a life as a playboy. His extravagant lifestyle soon came to an end, however, when in 1939, after signing a pact with Germany, the Soviet Union invaded its neighbour, Finland, without declaring war.

Almost half a million Russians, supported by 900 aircraft, poured over the border. To the amazement of the world, the Finns defeated the Russians in a series of battles with only 160,000 troops. Against the relentless Russian Army, however, it soon became apparent that they would not be able to hold out much longer on their own. Propelled by his anti-Communist beliefs, Prince Emanuel Galitzine volunteered to fight for the Finns against the Russians and enlisted in the Finnish Air Force.

Galitzine had only just arrived in Finland when he encountered a family friend, the great Finnish leader Carl Mannerheim. One of his country's most revered generals and statesmen, Mannerheim had the unfortunate task of informing Galitzine that the prince's mother had recently been killed in the London Blitz.

Mannerheim also told Galitzine that Finland would shortly be allying itself with Germany in an effort to repel the Russians. Should this happen, Prince Galitzine would probably find himself fighting with the Germans against Great Britain. Mannerheim offered to help the Russian return to England, if that was what he wanted.

Emanuel Galitzine agreed to the proposition with alacrity. Through Mannerheim's contacts he was able to obtain a Finnish passport, under an assumed name, and sail for the USA. The British consul in Boston could not help Galitzine return to Great Britain to join the RAF, so the prince travelled on to Canada. The *Ottawa Citizen* of 31 March 1941 announced his arrival: 'Prince Emanuel Galitzine, 22-year-old son of Prince Vladimir, head of one of the oldest families of the Russian nobility, is in Ottawa, awaiting acceptance by the British Air Mission here of his application to enlist in the Royal Air Force.'

The authorities in Canada were no more helpful, so Galitzine signed on a ship as a deckhand and worked his passage back to Scotland.

When he landed, his story was considered so unlikely that he was arrested as a spy. Fortunately for the Russian, by this time his father had been co-opted by the British Intelligence Service, and he was able to secure his son's release.

Prince Emanuel Galitzine joined the RAF, trained as a pilot, and from 1941 flew a Spitfire. He served in Great Britain and Italy, attaining the rank of squadron leader. After the war he worked as an airline pilot and then for a time sold aircraft for the Avro Company. Eventually he founded his own aircraft company.

Less exalted in background but still perhaps two of the great unsung Allied hero-deserters of the Second World War were Peter King and Leslie Cuthbertson. Both Dental Corps soldiers, the two tired of inactivity in wartime England, went absent without leave and invaded France on an unauthorised commando raid in a small boat.

In 1942, fed up with doing nothing to assist the war effort at their

Aldershot barracks, Sergeant King, a fiery New Zealand-born drill instructor who was always vague about his real age, and 19-year-old dental technician and devout former Church Lads' Brigade member Private Cuthbertson decided to leave their unit and launch their own private attack on the coast of German-occupied France. They prepared for the expedition by withdrawing a total of £30 from their bank accounts and began to accumulate equipment, purchased or stolen, such as pistols, bayonets, hand grenades and knives.

They then went into training for their raid, going for long runs and route marches together after lights-out in their barracks. King stole a number of blank railway warrants from the orderly room and on 11 April 1942, the two men were ready to leave their unit.

Before they left the two men decided to safeguard their position by writing to Prime Minister Winston Churchill, sending him their pay books and explaining that they fully intended to return to their units, if they survived. They also informed the Prime Minister that their intentions in France would be to kill Germans, destroy military buildings, generally disrupt the enemy and then return with as much information as they could gather.

The two deserters made their way to a Cornish village. They spent over a fortnight posing as soldiers on leave, spending most of their time climbing secluded local cliffs in case they should land in a rocky area of France. To keep alive they stole vegetables from fields, a diet supplemented by buying sweets at an exorbitant rate from a local schoolboy who attached himself to them for a time.

They managed to hire a 30-foot-long boat, the *Sea Bird*, with a sail and a small engine, by claiming that they were going out fishing in the bay and left England for France on 29 April. Before long they were lost in a thick fog, but eventually managed to reach the Cherbourg peninsula. Beaching their craft, they scaled a cliff and set off inland on foot in quest of the enemy.

It took them almost a full day before King and Cuthbertson saw their first German: a passing soldier. They had no firm plans, so were forced to improvise. On the spur of the moment, they decided that the best thing that they could do in the first instance was to cut some telephone wires, blow up a railway line and attack a signal box with grenades. Altogether they spent four days on French soil. At one stage they encountered a German patrol and exchanged fire with the enemy, before running off into the night back to their boat.

On their way back across the English Channel their craft was damaged by a mine, putting the engine out of action. They drifted back in the general direction of the Channel Islands and were fortunate enough to be picked up, tired, wet and hungry, by a Norwegian destroyer.

King and Cuthbertson were returned to their unit to await punishment. Though the absconders were court-martialled, they were saved by the intervention of Winston Churchill, who had been tickled by the enterprise of the two unlikely heroes. King was reduced in rank to corporal, while Cuthbertson served twenty-eight days' detention.

In case they hatched up any more bizarre plots, the two men were separated. Private Leslie Cuthbertson was transferred to a fighting unit, the Durham Light Infantry, and ended the war as a warrant officer physical training instructor. In post-war civilian life he became a successful businessman and Deputy Lord Mayor of Newcastle. He died in 1996. Peter King was commissioned in the Commandos and went on to win the Military Cross. After the war he joined the New Zealand Army and served in Korea, where he was awarded the Distinguished Service Order (DSO) for gallantry and was wounded several times in hand-to-hand combat while serving in a forward artillery unit. He was killed in a car crash in 1992.

Another genuine hero was Marine Bill Sparks, who was decorated for his part in the celebrated two-man canoe raid on enemy shipping later celebrated in the film *The Cockleshell Heroes* (1955). Yet on several occasions during his service career, Sparks went absent, each time in unusual circumstances.

Sparks was born in 1922 and brought up in the East End of London. He left school when he was fourteen and became a cobbler. Upon the outbreak of war he enlisted in the Royal Marines and served at sea for several years. His brother, serving in the Royal Navy, was drowned at sea. Sparks was so overcome with grief that he overstayed his period of compassionate leave and was charged with being absent and sentenced to a spell in the cells.

Upon his release he applied for hazardous duties and was selected for the small group of volunteers to be trained to paddle canoes into German waters and destroy shipping. On 11 December 1942, ten Royal Marines, under the command of Major 'Blondie' Hassler, embarked on the submarine *Tuna* with their kayaks, known as cockleshells. For five days they went south, to the Bay of Biscay, ten miles from the mouth of the river Gironde. After a 24-hour delay due to bad weather, the five cockleshells were launched, with instructions to paddle up the Gironde and destroy German-armed merchantmen stationed at Bordeaux.

The tiny force was soon reduced in numbers. The occupants of two canoes were caught and shot and two other Marines were drowned. The two remaining canoes, one of which was the *Cachalot* containing Hassler and Sparks, continued on their journey, eighty-five miles up-river, paddling by night and hiding during the day. Reaching Bordeaux, they concealed themselves among the tall reeds on the fringe of the harbour. Then the four surviving Marines paddled out to the ships and placed limpet mines with nine-hour fuses on the hulls.

The resultant explosions severely damaged four vessels and sank another. Hassler, Sparks and the other two Marines, Corporal Laver and Marine Mills, paddled back to the shore, sank their canoes and set out for freedom on foot.

Laver and Mills were captured by the Germans and shot, but Sparks and Hassler, aided by the French Resistance, made an arduous three-month trek across France and Spain to reach Gibraltar. When they arrived Major Hassler was flown back to England. There was no one left to confirm the marine's story and his appearance was treated with suspicion by the local authorities. Sparks was placed under close arrest, in case he was either a deserter or a spy, and taken back to England in a troopship.

With some justification Marine Sparks was now extremely disgruntled by his treatment. He was placed on a train and taken to London with an escort of military policemen. At Euston, Sparks gave the redcaps the slip and returned home for a few days of self-imposed rest and recuperation. Feeling a little better he then reported to the Admiralty. His successful escape-bid from the railway station had annoyed his superiors, however, and Sparks was threatened with imprisonment for going absent without leave.

Fortunately, at this point Marine Sparks encountered a sympathetic and resourceful naval intelligence officer. This officer advised Sparks to absent himself again by way of a back door to the building and report to Combined Operations Headquarters and hope for a better reception there.

At last it was realised who the doughty marine really was and what he had done. Sparks was awarded the DSO medal and went on to serve in Burma, Africa and Italy for the remainder of the war. Upon demobilisation he became a bus driver and then served as a police lieutenant in Malaya during the Emergency period there.

After time in the forces, Sparks became a garage inspector at a bus depot. When his invalidity pension was reduced he was forced to sell his medals for £31,000. He returned on a number of occasions to France to meet his wartime benefactors who had helped him on his long journey to Gibraltar. When the film *The Cockleshell Heroes* was made about the raid, Sparks was played by the actor-singer Anthony Newley as a cheerful Cockney Jack-the-lad. At the age of sixty-one, for charity, he re-enacted his canoe trip from the mouth of the Gironde river to Bordeaux.

18

THE LOST DIVISIONS

I swear by God this holy oath, that I will obey the leader of the German State and people, Adolf Hitler, as commander of the German Armed Forces, in the fight for the freedom of India.
– Part of the oath taken by members of the Indian National Army, 1942

A typical army division contains between 10,000 and 15,000 men. During the Second World War so many troops deserted for different reasons that they became known unofficially as the lost divisions.

Occasional efforts were made in German prisoner-of-war camps to persuade Allied prisoners to defect and fight for Germany. In order to accomplish this, prisoners were offered preferential treatment, holidays in special camps and a promise that they would never be called upon to fight against troops from their specific native countries. Others were bullied into defections if they had committed crimes, especially ones carrying the death penalty, like consorting with German women

While the Czech Legion recruited thousands of former deserters eager for patriotic reasons to fight for their new country, other nationalist organisations found it much more difficult to attract incarcerated prisoners to fight for them. Between 1943 and 1945, the British Free Corps comprised a small group of renegade British and Commonwealth prisoners of war persuaded by the Germans to fight against the Russians. Initially, the organisation was the brain child of John Amery, son of Leopold Amery, the Conservative Secretary of State for India and a member of the War Cabinet. John Amery, who had strong fascist sympathies, left

England for Germany at the outbreak of the war. An ineffectual man with more interest in social activities than politics, he tried to curry favour with high-ranking Germans with his proposal for the formation of a pro-German legion of men recruited from prisoner-of-war camps.

It took two or three years for the concept of the Legion of St George to take root, but in 1943 officers in the Waffen-SS took an interest in the idea and began to send recruiters to the camps. They promised that any prisoners of war who would forsake their allegiance to the Allied cause would be given money, a certain amount of freedom and access to prostitutes in specially constructed establishments.

The British Free Corps, as it was renamed, never really took off, but a few malcontents, opportunists and pre-war anti-Communists took advantage of the offer and moved over, at least temporarily, to the Axis cause.

It is believed that as many as 300 prisoners of war may have volunteered initially, but by the time the German recruiters had weeded out the drunks, the incompetents, the untrustworthy and the mad, only about thirty volunteers were left. Of these at least two had one German parent; several had been blackmailed into joining because they had impregnated German women, the punishment for which was death.

Two relaxed camps with English-speaking guards were set up and the volunteers were issued with German Army uniforms with special insignia consisting of a Union flag shield worn on the left arm and a collar patch bearing lions resembling those on the British Royal Banner. Later a British Free Corps cuff title was added to the ensemble.

At first the authorities did not seem to know what to do with the rather pathetic group of Britons, Canadians, South Africans, Australians and a solitary New Zealander they had been saddled with. There were not enough of the misfits to form an individual fighting force, and Hitler was known to distrust the idea of incorporating the volunteers into a German military unit.

Some of the volunteers were sent on tours of prisoner-of-war camps to persuade others to join them. They received such a rough reception that the project was soon abandoned. One unfortunate volunteer for the British Free Corps with boxing experience, the former circus strongman Eric Pleasants, was unfortunate enough to find a niche fighting exhibition contests with the German ex-paratrooper and former world heavyweight boxing champion, Max Schmeling.

German hopes were raised for the moment when a British officer, Lieutenant William Shearer, joined the ranks of the Free Corps. However, he turned out to be mentally unstable and seldom left his quarters. He was eventually invalided home. Some of the original deserters began to drift away, either asking to be returned to their camps or trying to escape. By the end of 1944, there were only about fourteen volunteers left, and by the spring of the following year this number had been reduced to eight.

These eight, fearing the consequences from loyal prisoners of war if they were to go back to their first camps, actually offered to fight. They were sent to the Russian front but were soon taken out of the front line and used as drivers and in other non-combatant duties. There seem to have been only six of the volunteers remaining by May 1945, when the ill-fated unit was officially dissolved.

After the war, John Amery was tried for treason and hanged. Some of the former British Free Corps members were also arrested and tried. Their sentences varied. Francis McLardy was sentenced to penal servitude for life, Edwin Martin received twenty-five years and Roy Courlander was given fifteen years. At the other end of the scale, Kenneth Berry, who had been little more than a child when his ship was sunk and he was taken prisoner, was given only nine months in prison by a merciful judge.

A number of individual prisoners of war were also known or suspected to have aided the enemy while in captivity. Walter Purdy was born in Essex in 1918, the son of a dockworker. A pre-war member of the British Union of Fascists, he served in the merchant service before transferring to the Royal Navy upon the outbreak of war. He had been serving as an engineer officer on board the cruiser HMS *Van Dyck* when the vessel was sunk near Narvik, off the north coast of Norway. Purdy was one of the survivors.

While imprisoned in the Marlag camp, Purdy was spotted by a German guard reading a book written by the traitor and broadcaster for the Nazis, William Joyce (nicknamed Lord Haw-Haw). Purdy was soon introduced to Joyce and he agreed to broadcast for the Germans himself. He was given a certain amount of freedom by his captors and was even allowed out of his camp occasionally but he earned their displeasure by going absent without leave in Berlin. As a punishment he was sent to the famous Colditz prison camp, on the understanding that he could work his way back into favour by informing on his fellow prisoners. Purdy did so, but conducted his relationships with the German guards too blatantly.

The other prisoners soon suspected that Purdy was a traitor and he was moved constantly for his own protection. His suspect reputation preceded him to such an extent that when Purdy had been imprisoned in Colditz, the Senior British Officer in the castle informed the German Commandant that he could not be responsible for Purdy's safety there. Purdy was moved again. In the chaos of defeat he simply walked away and surrendered to a British unit.

Walter Purdy was tried for high treason at the Central Criminal Court in London and found guilty. He was sentenced to death but this was later commuted to life imprisonment. He served only nine years and was released in 1954. He changed his name, married several times and died of cancer in Southend in 1982.

A much more complicated character than Purdy was John Henry 'Buster' Brown. He was one of the great enigmas among the chronicles of Second World War desertions. Though recognised by his government as a successful spy and awarded the Distinguished Conduct Medal (DCM) for his activities, there were many prisoners of war who always regarded him as a German collaborator.

A university graduate, a dedicated Christian yet a paid-up member of the pre-war British Union of Fascists, Brown, a battery quartermaster sergeant in the Royal Artillery, was captured in May 1940 as he tried to reach the evacuation beaches of Dunkirk.

He was imprisoned at Stalag VIII-B at Lamsdorf in Germany, where he volunteered to become foreman of a group of British prisoners labouring at an artificial oil and rubber plant. A glib, self-confident man, Brown soon established good relationships with his German masters while simultaneously building a flourishing black market business. Brown was later to claim that he did this in order to pass on better food to his fellow prisoners, but many of the men who worked under him later disputed this fact and pointed out that Brown himself lived the good life, surrounded by a protective coterie of former BUF members.

Brown was sent to a prison camp at Steglitz, where the Germans housed Britons of special interest. It was here that he encountered a Scottish prisoner, former Glasgow dentist Captain Julius Green. Green was proving a real handful for his captors and was shortly to be transferred to Colditz, the camp for escape-prone British officers. Before he left, however, he gave Brown details of MI9-devised secret codes to be incorporated in letters home. MI9 was the section of the Secret Service devoted to setting up an espionage network among British prisoners of war.

No one is certain why Green entrusted Brown with such vital material. The quartermaster sergeant later claimed that it was because the captain saw in him a potential British agent, although it is just as likely that Brown was the one prisoner encountered by Green of sufficient intelligence to master the workings of the code.

Brown's next move led to subsequent accusations from fellow prisoners of desertion. In 1943 he agreed to act as the leader of one of the holiday camps set up by the Germans on the outskirts of Berlin to provide better treatment for volunteers of the British Free Corps and other collaborators with the enemy. Visitors to the camp were sent there in batches from among the original and rapidly dwindling 300 members of the organisation. Brown took care never to join the Free Corps, and claimed that he only took on the position to get close to such major traitors as the aforementioned

John Amery and William Joyce, and then pass on information to British Intelligence.

With the war going badly for the Germans, Brown next joined a long forced march of prisoners westwards with his German guards, away from the advancing Russian Army. Wherever he encountered Britons who knew him he was threatened with beatings and even death as a traitor and friend of the Germans. In April 1945, finally he was able to surrender to an American unit, which handed him over to the British.

Back in Great Britain, Brown was interrogated fiercely. A number of returning prisoners of war had given his name as a traitor. For his part, Brown reiterated his story of keeping in contact by letter with MI9 and acting as their agent. Brown's powers of persuasion prevailed. Not only was he exonerated and decorated but he was also called upon to give evidence against a number of former members of the British Free Corps at their trials, before he returned to his pre-war occupation of office manager.

Later Brown wrote a self-justifying book, *In Durance Vile*, about his time in Germany but it is still a matter for debate as to whether he was a German collaborator, a brave and resourceful British agent or just an opportunist with a gift for playing both ends against the middle.

There were no such doubts about Douglas Webster Berneville-Claye's loyalties while a prisoner of war in Germany. A handsome, glib and charismatic rogue, Berneville-Claye was commissioned in the West Yorkshire Regiment and then transferred to the Special Air Service. He proved too eccentric even for that idiosyncratic unit and was regarded as a bit of a loose cannon. Because of his constant references to the peerage he claimed he would one day inherit – he was the son of an earl – his men would refer to him mockingly as Lord Chuff. After his capture in 1942 while serving in the SAS in Libya, he was interned in Italian and German prisoner-of-war camps, but on more than one occasion he had to be moved on hastily for his own safety, as he was regarded by fellow prisoners as being a stool-pigeon for the guards.

Berneville-Claye soon joined the traitors of the British Free Corps, but appears to have done little in that organisation. He was captured in Germany in the closing days of the war, proudly wearing an SAS panzer uniform, one of the survivors of the original 300 members.

Douglas Webster St Aubyn Berneville-Claye was court-martialled and sentenced to a term of imprisonment. In the 1950s, he resurfaced as a photocopier salesman, based in Leeds. He became a leading light of a local amateur dramatic society, married a German *au pair* and emigrated to Australia, where he died in 1975.

Subhas Chandra Bose ('Give me blood and I will give you freedom!') was a much more important instrument in the cause of persuading prisoners of war to defect to the German side during the Second World War. Bose was one of Mahatma Gandhi's more bellicose challengers in the fight for Indian independence. He was instrumental in persuading Indian prisoners of war to change their allegiance and join the Indian National Army in an effort to secure independence for India after the war.

Originally known as the Indian Free Legion, the army was formed in 1942, after an intensive recruiting campaign by Chandra Bose in German prisoner-of-war camps. About 300 Indian prisoners volunteered to serve the Germans.

By May 1943, the Indian troops were serving in Holland on coastal defences before being moved to occupation duties in France. There were suggestions that they should be sent to fight under Rommel in the North African desert but the German commander rejected the idea. A suggestion by Chandra Bose that he lead an invasion of India was also turned down.

After the Allied invasion of Europe, the Indian National Army troops retreated to Germany, never having fought as a unit. They finally surrendered to the advancing Americans near Lake Constance.

Chandra Bose was reported to have been killed in an aircraft crash in Taiwan in 1945. There were allegations that the crash had been staged, either for him to be taken prisoner by the Allies or so that he could continue his fight for Indian independence. Several commissions investigated the allegations but came to no definitive conclusions. After the war, as had been the case with Roger Casement's Irish volunteers in the First World War, very few returning members of the Indian National Army were court-martialled.

In Europe, Andrey Andreyevich Vlasov, a highly regarded Russian general in the Second World War, also went over to the Germans and led an army of Russian deserters against his own countrymen.

The son of a Russian peasant, Vlasov had been conscripted in 1919 and fought against the White Russians in the closing days of the Soviet Civil War. He remained a soldier and rose steadily during the interwar years. At the outbreak of the Second World War, as commander of the 37th and 20th Soviet Armies, Vlasov distinguished himself by fighting in the defence of Moscow. Fighting at Sebastopol, his unit was trapped after five days' continuous attack by the Germans. A special aircraft was sent to rescue Vlasov but he was so disillusioned with the incompetence of his superiors that he refused to escape and was taken prisoner.

However, Vlasov became leader of a deserter army almost by accident. German military intelligence agents discovered that their prisoner was no admirer of Stalin and set out to ingratiate themselves with the charming Russian. They transferred Vlasov to a camp for special prisoners and saw to it that he had preferential treatment and privileges.

While he was being held, Vlasov had time to formulate his opinions about Joseph Stalin, regarding him as the architect of the USSR's misfortunes. He wrote down his thoughts in a pamphlet, demanding that the Russian leader be overthrown.

Hardly able to believe their good fortune, German Intelligence leaders dropped thousands of these leaflets over the Russian lines. Many Russian deserters requested to join General Vlasov's army.

At this time there was no such unit but intelligence officers saw both the propaganda and military advantages of recruiting thousands of Russians to fight on their side. Neither Hitler nor his senior advisers were in favour of such a unit, but individual intelligence officers continued to woo Vlasov and encourage him to regard himself as the chosen leader of free Russians against Stalin. One of the leaflets, 'Order No. 13 of the German High Command, 1943', promised Russian deserters that they would be well fed and looked after and immediately separated from the other prisoners of war: 'Every man in the Red Army service (officer, political officer, soldier, etc.) who deserted alone or in a group must be considered not a prisoner of war but a person who voluntarily moved to the side of the German Army.'

Unofficially, many Russian deserters were already being used in, mainly, non-fighting capacities behind the German lines. Known as *Osttruppen*, they wore German uniforms, performed guard duties and were even used occasionally to combat partisan raids.

The German Intelligence Service had much grander plans. They envisaged a large army, nominally led by Vlasov, which would be hurled against the Russian lines. Ignoring the disapproval of Hitler and Field Marshal Keitel of the German High Command, in 1943 Vlasov was allowed his freedom to visit large cities and expound his views.

Finally, with the situation on the Eastern Front growing steadily worse, Vlasov was given his command. Between 200,000 and 400,000 Russian deserters and prisoners of war were recruited for the Russian Liberation Army. They were armed and sent into battle.

By this time the Russians were beginning to break through. Despite its large numbers, the Liberation Army could do little to stem the advance out of Moscow and Stalingrad. It began to retreat, along with the regular German forces. Hitler, always an opponent of the scheme, was furious, blaming his new Russian allies for breaches in the line. Many of the newly recruited Russians were taken out of uniform and sent to France to work in the coalmines.

Vlasov retreated across Russia with the remnants of his force. Eventually, in the closing stages of the war, the Russian Liberation Army found itself stationed in German-occupied Czechoslovakia. The advancing Americans were only a few miles away. In a frantic

last effort to save something from his parlous situation, General
Vlasov changed sides again. With his now depleted unit he led an
attack on the German SS unit defending Prague, hoping to take it
and curry favour with the Americans by handing the garrison over
to them. The attack failed. Soon the Americans arrived and took
the city for themselves. Vlasov surrendered to the new arrivals.

Vlasov hoped to find some sort of security as a prisoner of the
Americans, but he did not know that it had been secretly agreed
by Stalin, Churchill and Roosevelt at the 1945 Yalta Conference,
that all prisoners of war would be handed back to their home
nations. General Patton sent Andrey Vlasov and other members of
the Russian Liberation Army back to Russia. In 1946, Vlasov was
hanged as a traitor.

As well as Chandra Bose and Andrey Vlasov, other leaders and
would-be leaders tried to utilise the war to advance the causes of
nationalism in their countries. Aung San was a Burmese nationalist
hero who devoted his life to securing independence for his country.
As an undergraduate at Rangoon University, Aung San was one
of the leaders of a 1936 student revolt and as a result was excluded
from the university; he was later reinstated so that he could resume
his studies. He then went to work for a nationalist organisation.

In 1940, after the outbreak of war, Aung San took the opportunity
to form alliances to help secure the independence of his country,
which then was a crown colony. He was convinced that only an
armed uprising would secure Burma's freedom. Regarding him as a
thorn in their sides the British authorities tried to arrest Aung San,
but he escaped to China, hoping to enlist its aid in his struggle.

Instead he was contacted by the Japanese and taken to Japan for
military training. Upon his return to Burma, he enlisted the aid of
thirty other young Burmese men, creating the Thirty Comrades.
They were the kernel of the Burma Independence Army and
supported the Japanese invasion in 1942 which drove the British
back after a series of bitter battles. The British abandoned Rangoon,
first releasing the inmates of the prison, leper colony and zoo, and
began the long, thousand-mile retreat to the Chindwin River.

Some Burmese troops picked off stragglers from the retreating British column, but mostly policed areas taken and occupied by the Japanese. Aung San soon began to resent the scorn with which the Burmese troops were regarded by the Japanese and to distrust the assurances of the latest invaders of his country that after the war Burma would be granted full independence.

Between 1943 and 1945, Aung San, who had received the Order of the Rising Sun, served as Minister of Defence in the puppet government established by the Japanese. He was also a general in the local army, now known as the Burma Defence Force, whose numbers had grown from several hundred to 40,000. Aung San had fresh cause for worry when the Japanese, believing that the Burma Defence Force was growing too powerful, reduced its strength and changed its title to that of the Burma Defence Army.

Slowly, by 1943 the tide of the war turned and the Allies began to advance. Aung San realised that the Japanese were now unlikely to win the war, and that they would be of no further use to him or his country.

Aung San had started to make contact with the small groups of British troops hiding in the hills of his country when the Japanese first started to pull back. Having approached Lord Louis Mountbatten, the Allied commander in south-east Asia, Aung San offered to bring his troops over to the Allied side. In March 1945, Mountbatten accepted the Burmese offer.

On 26 March, the Japanese ordered Aung San to leave Rangoon and take his army to the assistance of the beleaguered Japanese. Aung San appeared to obey the command, leading his force out of the capital, but at the same time he issued orders to his people that they should do all that they could to hamper the Japanese.

No pitched battles ensued, but groups of Burmese conducted jungle warfare operations against the now retreating invaders. The war virtually came to an end in Burma when an RAF pilot flying over Rangoon noticed that there were no signs of Japanese activities on the ground. He landed his aircraft and walked into the city to discover that the Japanese had fled. The pilot released Allied troops held prisoner in the city and informed his superiors that he had taken Rangoon.

On 15 June 1945, Burmese forces took part with Allied troops in a victory parade through the streets of Rangoon. In August of that year the Japanese surrendered.

The British attempted to incorporate the Burma National Army into the regular army, but Aung San was too shrewd to allow that. Deliberately he held many of its members back in a unit known as the People's Volunteer Organisation, in theory to help with the post-war rehabilitation of the country but really as his own private political force.

Aung San's pragmatic policy worked. He had supported the Japanese when they had been in the ascendancy in his country, and then the Allies when they had started to advance. He made no bones about his policy. When he offered to help the Allies, a senior commander accused him of doing so because the Japanese were losing the war. The Burmese leader replied, 'There wouldn't be any point in leaving them if they were winning, would there?'

Aung San became Prime Minister of the independent nation in 1947. But his success was short-lived. In the same year, along with six others, including his brother, he was murdered in the Rangoon Council Chamber.

19

STARS OF STAGE, SCREEN AND GLASSHOUSE

I don't want to be a soldier,
I don't want to go to war.
I'd rather hang around Picadilly Underground,
Living off the earnings of a high-born lady.
– First World War trench song

Most deserters needed a certain amount of resolution and determination in order to accomplish their aims of achieving freedom, but one category came more under the heading of creative artists, the square pegs in round holes who travelled through their service careers in a fog of misunderstandings and incomprehension. They were the showmen.

A surprising number of future show business and sporting stars proved unable to cope with service life. Others were just unfortunate. Those itinerant folks touring the halls of Britain could quite easily not receive their call-up papers and were punished as a result.

The comedian and a founder member of *The Goon Show* radio programme, Michael Bentine, often claimed to have been the only Peruvian Old-Etonian born in Watford. Because of his Peruvian father's nationality he was rejected when he tried to join the RAF upon the outbreak of war. While appearing in a Shakespearean play in London's Hyde Park, it came as something of a surprise to him, therefore, when two RAF military policemen strode across the grass and arrested him because he had not responded to his mobilisation orders which had been following him around the country. The worst was not yet over. A little later, when lining up for a service typhoid vaccination, Bentine was given an accidental overdose. He collapsed and lay in a coma for six weeks. After he recovered, his overdose was regarded as having done Bentine so much harm that he was unfit for flying duties. He served out the war as an intelligence officer in the RAF.

Leading British television comic Benny Hill began his career as an assistant stage manager, playing small parts in girlie revue 'Send Him Victorious' in the opening years of the Second World War. He enjoyed the life so much that he tried in vain to avoid being conscripted. In 1942, the 18-year-old Hill received his call-up papers. By this time the tour was well into its stride, playing weekly engagements up and down the country. He decided to ignore his summons to the colours, hoping that his peripatetic life would make it impossible for the military authorities to catch up with him.

The young comic was soon to be disabused of this notion. One night while stood innocently in the wings of the New Theatre, Cardiff, he was arrested by two military policemen. For several nights he was lodged in the cells of Cardiff police station before being transported under close arrest across Britain to an army barracks in Lincoln. He began his military career sentenced to a short term of confinement to barracks for not reporting on time, while concurrently undergoing his basic military training. 'They treated me like a criminal,' he said aggrievedly in one of his rare interviews later in his life.

Hill spent most of his three-year army career as a driver in the Royal Electrical and Mechanical Engineers, although towards the end of his service he managed to transfer to the Central Pool of Artists and spend some time entertaining troops in touring shows.

After his demobilisation, Hill toured the variety theatres as a stooge to Reg Varney, another comic, and took part in summer shows before he was enlisted by the developing British television industry. In the early 1950s he became one of television's first major stars, writing most of his own material – although he did gain a reputation for 'borrowing' material, unaccredited, from other performers. His comedy series attracted audiences of many millions of viewers, and were sold to over ninety different countries, although throughout his life Hill continued to live a frugal and solitary existence. Towards the end of his career his ITV contract was not renewed, his bawdy shows considered too sexist and anti-feminist for their times. When he died, unmarried, he left a fortune of £7 million.

Dick Emery made a much more determined effort than Hill to distance himself from military life and actually went on the run. Five-times married, the diminutive Emery became one of Britain's favourite post-war television comics, his leering 'Ooh, you are awful!' entering the lexicon of show-business catch-phrases. His career received an initial boost during his wartime service in the RAF, when he became a member of the well-known services entertainment group, the Ralph Reader Gang Show. Prior to this, however, he found service life something of a trial.

Born in 1915, the son of music hall stars, Emery chose to follow his parents' example and entered the world of show business. Having progressed to understudying the celebrated tenor Richard Tauber in the musical *Land of Smiles* in the West End, Emery was standing in the wings watching the star singing when the stage door keeper handed him a special delivery letter containing his call-up papers.

From the start, Emery hated RAF life. Married and with a young son, on his periods of leave Emery would find his wife tearful and depressed, and finding it difficult to make ends meet. The comedian-cum-singer decided that if only he could get out of the RAF he could secure a well-paid stage job which would put matters right at home.

In 1942, Corporal Emery left his station at St Eval in Cornwall one evening, calmly carrying a kit bag, and took a train to London. Knowing that the RAF police would first look for him at his home, he met his wife at Paddington station and told her to open a post office box in her maiden name, so that he could send her money when he found work.

Emery then made his way by train to Glasgow, moving from

one cheap lodging house to another, working in pubs and cafés in the evenings. He was but one of thousands of deserters inhabiting large cities at the time. The comedian soon decided that this itinerant life would never help him fulfil his ambition of being able to provide for his wife and child and mother. He took a chance and went back to London, where he auditioned for a role in the chorus of a revival of the operetta *The Merry Widow* at His Majesty's Theatre.

For several months Emery danced and sang in the background, his features obscured by a large fake moustache. He was able to support his family again and even began to wonder optimistically if he could see out the rest of the war in this fashion. Unfortunately, two sergeants from the chorus boy's station came to see the show while on leave. They informed the military police, who waited in the wings to grab the deserter as soon as he came off stage. The redcaps did not even give their prisoner time to change, but took him into custody attired in his exotic stage costume and false moustache.

Dick Emery spent nine months in Stanmore military prison. Upon his release he auditioned successfully for the Gang Show and spent the rest of the war entertaining troops in Europe and North Africa – hard work but far more congenial than being in the glasshouse. 'I was better in drag than I was in uniform,' he admitted ruefully.

After his demobilisation he struggled to get a toehold in show business, but managed to get an engagement as a comedian at London's famous non-stop nude revue shows at the Windmill Theatre. He then broke into radio and television, attracting attention as Private Chubby Catchpole in the forces TV comedy *The Army Game*. In 1963, the BBC offered him his own series. He became a huge success though in his later years he suffered from ill health and depression.

Actor Stewart Granger played dashing military officers in a number of films, including *Bhowani Junction* (1956), but his real wartime career was less glamorous. Born James Stewart in 1913, the tall, dark and handsome London-born actor broke into British films in the 1930s, but before he could really establish himself on screen he was conscripted into the army.

Lance Corporal Granger was posted to Cruden Bay, north of Aberdeen in Scotland. With a family to support, Granger was fortunate to book a room for his pregnant wife Elspeth at a neighbouring hotel. They were eating in a restaurant one evening when Elspeth went into labour. The panic-stricken Granger hurried back to his barracks but could find no one there to grant him compassionate leave. He hired a car and driver from a garage to make the three-hour journey to a hospital in Aberdeen, where their baby boy was born but unfortunately died within hours. After several days Granger left the hospital. He was picked up by military policemen and taken back to Cruden Bay. He spent a few anxious days in the guard house but was released with a reprimand.

Granger was later commissioned in the Black Watch Regiment but was invalided out with a stomach ulcer before he could see action. After the war he went to Hollywood and achieved success as a dashing leading man in such action movies as *King Solomon's Mines* (1950) and *The Prisoner of Zenda* (1952). He divorced Elspeth and married actress Jean Simmons, divorcing her in 1960 and later marrying for a third time. He died at the age of eighty.

Austrian-born actor Oskar Werner never achieved the same success as Stewart Granger, but he was a distinguished stage actor in his home country and for a while it looked as if he might also become an international film star.

Werner was a convinced pacifist who regarded the Second World War as an unnecessary encroachment upon his theatrical career. Nursing a devotion to the theatre as soon as he first took part in school productions, Werner had roles in radio plays and joined the Vienna Repertory Company during the early stages of the war when he was only eighteen. He was to appear in over fifty productions and become a leading man with the company. Obsessed with his career, he had no interest in the war and, like many Austrians, was fiercely anti-Nazi. In 1941, he was conscripted into the German

Army, but for a time managed to combine his tenuous military duties with his stage appearances.

This happy state of affairs was not to last long. Werner was selected for officer training, which would entail a full-time military career. He thought deeply about his convictions and realised that at heart he was a conscientious objector, although he knew that to express such opinions would not get him far in the prevailing conditions in Austria. He managed to prove, however, that he was not officer material by failing his training.

The actor was given further time for reflection in hospital, when he was injured in an American bombing raid. Deciding that he would rather die than continue to serve in the army, Werner deserted by swimming across a river and spent the rest of the war hiding in a forest, living hand-to-mouth until the war ended.

Oskar Werner resumed his acting career and began to earn a considerable reputation on stage. In the 1950s he started to make films and was even summoned to Hollywood, where he received a best-actor Oscar nomination for his role in *Ship of Fools* (1965). He was not to win but his performance led to offers of leading roles in *Fahrenheit 451* (1966) and *The Shoes of the Fisherman* (1968). He also claimed to have rejected several hundred offers of film parts as Nazi officers.

Werner's main love was always the stage, and he accepted film roles only for the money. He became a heavy drinker and a recluse, and slowly his acting career petered out. He died of a heart attack at the age of sixty-two, just as he was about to deliver a lecture at a German dramatic society.

It might have been thought that boxers, by definition, would be the bravest of the brave, but several leading fighters have been found among the ranks of deserters in the Second World War. One of the best known was Rocky Graziano, the ring name of Thomas Rocco Barbella. He was a savage street fighter and hoodlum who went on to win the world middleweight boxing championship. In the service, however, Graziano's fighting was confined almost exclusively to striking officers and NCOs, before his hasty departure.

A New York tearaway and petty thief, he served several terms in reformatories and approved schools, where he partook in a little amateur boxing. He turned professional but his embryonic career was cut short when he returned to prison for another stretch for stealing. He was released in 1942 and was at once inducted into the US Army.

Like many of his street and ring fights, Graziano's military career was short and brutal. On his first morning in the service, at Fort Dix in New Jersey, he overslept and then floored a corporal who gave him an order to pick up rubbish. Brought before a captain he knocked the officer out for good measure and went on the run, hitchhiking back to Brooklyn. In his autobiography, *Somebody Up There Likes Me*, he described his escape: 'I walked across the fields and through some woods and then I come to a highway. A truck picks me up which is going to Hoboken, and I'm on my way home.'

With no other way of earning money except by stealing, Graziano returned to boxing while he was hiding in New York. It was here that he adopted the name of Graziano, so that his real name of Barbella would not feature on the fight bills. He had seven fights, one of them in front of 2,000 soldiers, before the military police caught up with him.

Graziano was court-martialled, dishonourably discharged and sentenced to a year's imprisonment in a military prison, where he became a star of the boxing team. In 1943, he was released and resumed his boxing career. With his all-action style he became a great success, his career peaking with his win against Tony Zale for the world middleweight championship, before losing it to the same boxer in the third of three thrilling fights between the pair. He retired with a record of eighty-three contests and sixty-seven wins, fifty-two of them by knock-outs.

After his retirement Graziano gave his name to a bestselling ghosted autobiography and enjoyed a successful career in show business, mainly on television and as an after-dinner speaker.

A ring contemporary of Graziano's was the British fighter Freddie Mills, one of Great Britain's best-ever boxers among the heavier weights. Mills was born in Bournemouth in 1919 and worked as an apprentice milkman when he left school at fourteen, by which time he had already fought a number of bouts. He turned professional, achieving early success, and had toured the country with a boxing booth, taking on all-comers, before he was called up into the RAF in 1939. He became a sergeant physical training instructor, fought exhibition bouts at troop shows and continued with his professional boxing career.

In 1942, he challenged Len Harvey, an RAF officer, for the latter's British light-heavyweight title and won in two rounds, knocking Harvey out of the ring. It should have been a good time for Mills, but the boxer suddenly went into a fit of acute depression. Training, fighting and performing his RAF duties proved too much of a strain. In June 1942, just a few days after his fight with Harvey, the 22-year-old Mills deserted. He hitchhiked from his camp at South Witham in Lincolnshire to London. He wandered about the capital, half in a dream, visiting St Paul's, the Tower of London and other tourist attractions. He stayed away for a week and then, overcome with remorse, travelled back to his camp.

Mills's commanding officer told the errant boxer that he was liable to face a court martial for desertion. However, at a higher level it was decided that such an event involving a famous sporting personality would result in bad publicity for the RAF. Mills was posted to another unit and later sent on a tour of troop camps in India, fighting exhibition bouts.

After the war Mills resumed a full-time boxing career, winning the world light-heavyweight title from the American Gus Lesnevich. He was less successful in a number of lucrative heavyweight contests, taking several bad beatings against much bigger men. He lost his title in 1950 and retired from the ring after ninety-seven bouts, of which he lost seventeen.

He dabbled in boxing promotion, took small parts in films and on television and opened a restaurant-cum-nightclub in the West End. Mills had a number of financial problems and in the early hours of 25 June 1965, he shot himself in his car outside his club, although rumours persisted that he had been murdered by under-world connections.

Julian MacLaren-Ross was one of the famed Soho drinking set of the 1940s and 1950s, which also included poet Dylan Thomas and artist Francis Bacon. MacLaren-Ross was a gifted writer with a chaotic private life. Unable to cope with the discipline of wartime military life, he deserted and was sentenced to twenty-eight days in a military prison before being discharged on psychiatric grounds.

Born in South Norwood in London in 1912, the son of a wealthy businessman, the bombastic would-be writer added a hyphenated MacLaren to his surname of Ross and in the 1930s embarked upon a career as a freelance writer. He was gifted enough to attract the attention of Cyril Connolly, editor of the literary magazine *Horizon*, and publisher Rupert Hart-Davis, then working for the Jonathan Cape publishing house.

Even so, cast adrift from his parents, MacLaren-Ross found it difficult to earn a living from his pen and embarked upon what became a lifetime habit of borrowing from his friends while undertaking a number of poorly paid jobs including one as a door-to-door salesman of vacuum cleaners.

In 1940 he was conscripted into the army. Despite his poor eyesight, puny physique and total lack of coordination, to his surprise he was posted to the Suffolk Regiment. He turned up for his basic induction course with two cases containing unfinished literary manuscripts.

MacLaren-Ross soon proved completely incapable of coping with the demands of infantry training. Within weeks he had injured an already damaged knee and was sent to a military hospital. To overcome his boredom he spent his weeks in the ward learning the military manual by heart and further antagonising his superiors by quoting military orders verbatim whenever he was in trouble. Returning to his unit he was made an orderly room clerk where he further disturbed the military establishment by writing a series of humorous and subversive articles on his army activities, which were published in such magazines as *Lilliput* and *Horizon*.

Managing to talk himself into a selection course for would-be officers, MacLaren-Ross was thrown off the course after an exercise in which his squad was supposed to traverse a log bridge across an imaginary ravine. Unable to negotiate the logs because of his bad knee, MacLaren-Ross made a loud noise simulating an explosion and informed the supervising officers that he had sacrificed his life by blowing up the bridge. Within days he was an orderly room clerk again, this time in Southend.

By this point, the writer was thoroughly disillusioned with the army. He went on leave to London, determined to find himself a job in one of the government ministries or a film unit. He spent his days writing letters to everyone he thought might find him employment and his evenings drinking heavily with like-minded cronies in Soho.

When his leave period came to an end, MacLaren-Ross did not return to his unit but continued his search for more congenial employment. After he had been absent without leave for several weeks, one of his acquaintances gave him away to the authorities. He was arrested by two military policemen while in bed with a girlfriend, and returned to his unit in Southend. He was sentenced to twenty-eight days' detention, but first was sent to a military hospital outside Birmingham for psychiatric evaluation.

In his memoir of the poet Alun Lewis, killed in action during the war, MacLaren-Ross described the aftermath of his arrest. 'In March 1943, I was travelling to hospital under escort, for I was at the time awaiting court martial: as the RSM predicted, I had gone a little bit too far at last.'

MacLaren-Ross was then sent to Colchester Military Prison to serve his time, before being discharged from the army. With considerable relief he resumed his career as a part-time author and full-time Soho drinker. He continued to write articles for *Punch* and other magazines but frittered away his talent on drink and drugs. He lived in a succession of seedy rooms and hotels, constantly dunning editors for advances on unwritten manuscripts and moving to avoid his creditors. Most of his time was spent in

The Wheatsheaf and other London hostelries, laying down the law and antagonising many who tried to help him. He died at the age of fifty-two of a heart attack after an altercation over a fare with a taxi driver. After his death, his unfinished account of his life and literary and artistic acquaintances in Soho, *Memoirs of the Sixties*, was published, confirming his unfulfilled talent.

A much braver soldier than MacLaren-Ross but one who ultimately found army life just as intolerable was Vernon Scannell. A prize-winning poet and novelist, as a young soldier Scannell deserted twice.

Scannell was born John Bain in 1922. A former schoolboy boxing champion, he joined the London Scottish Regiment and then transferred to the Gordon Highlanders. He saw action at Dunkirk and then in the North African campaign at El Alamein.

Scannell first deserted in 1942 when, after a battle, he saw fellow soldiers from his unit looting watches and rings from the dead bodies of German and British troops as they lay on the sand. Sickened, he turned and walked back from the front line. In his book *Argument of Kings*, Scannell describes in the third person the first steps of his desertion.

> Then he turned away and started to walk back down the slope towards the foot of the hill where they had dug in on the previous night. No one attempted to stop him. No voice called out, peremptory and outraged. He walked unhurriedly, but quite steadily, not looking back, his rifle slung on his right shoulder.

Scannell hitched a lift in a truck to divisional headquarters and then continued to walk away. On one occasion he was given food and drink by a group of Gurkha soldiers; later he begged a lift as far as Tripoli in an RAF truck, claiming to be an escaped prisoner of war sent back to be re-located. On the outskirts of the city he was picked up by a military police patrol.

At his court martial, Scannell was sentenced to a term of fifteen years' imprisonment, to be served at a military prison in Alexandria.

This was later reduced to a three-year term. He was released early, on a suspended sentence, when, as an experienced and battle-hardened soldier, he agreed to volunteer to take part in the Normandy landings in 1944. He was wounded in both legs near Caen, and spent some time in a military hospital in England.

He was still recuperating in the hospital when the Germans surrendered in May 1945. As far as Scannell was concerned, his war was over. He packed a haversack and walked out of the hospital gates, going absent without leave once again.

This time he was on the run for two years before he was arrested and court-martialled for a second time. Instead of being sentenced to imprisonment Scannell was co-opted as an unwilling guinea pig at a hospital where experimental treatment for shell-shock and battle fatigue was being tried.

Vernon Scannell went on to become one of Britain's leading poets and the author of several novels. Among the literary prizes he won were the Heinemann Award and the Cholmondeley Award for poetry.

Most deserters who later became celebrities tried to keep quiet about their inglorious military careers. Film star Burt Lancaster was a former serviceman who claimed to have gone on the run, although his boast seems to have been little more than a film studio publicity stunt.

A former circus acrobat, Lancaster was called up in 1942 at the age of twenty-nine. He was drafted into a Forces Entertainment Unit and spent much of his war performing to troops with a touring revue in North Africa and Italy. In 1944, Lancaster met a dancer from another touring Forces Entertainment show. Her name was Norma Anderson and Lancaster was smitten with her; by all accords they were set to marry but Norma's show was sent on to Caserta. According to a Universal Studios publicity handout issued in 1947, when Lancaster was embarking upon his glittering screen career, the soldier then went AWOL in order to be with his girl. The military police were informed and Lancaster was apprehended and brought back to his unit. The blurb went on to say that Norma in turn went AWOL in order to be with Lancaster, who had been taken to Montecatini.

It made a good story and painted Lancaster favourably as an ardent suitor willing to risk imprisonment for love. Unfortunately there is probably no truth in it. There is no mention in Burt Lancaster's military record of his ever being charged with desertion.

After the war, Lancaster secured a small role as a sergeant in a Broadway play, was spotted by a film producer and taken to Hollywood where he starred in his first movie *The Killers* (1946). He went on to become a major star in such films as *From Here to Eternity* (1953), *Gunfight at the OK Corral* (1957) and many others. In 1960, he won an Oscar for his performance as a fast-talking, dishonest evangelist in *Elmer Gantry* (1960).

A similar apocryphal story was told by Robert Mitchum, another film star. He claimed that when he was caught in the draft in 1945, he struggled so hard to stay at home that when he reached his unit the splinters from the fence he had been clinging to were still embedded under his fingernails.

On the other hand, Royal Marine Harry H. Corbett had a much tougher war than Mitchum, who never left the USA. Corbett took part in hand-to-hand jungle combat in Malaya but when he reached Australia at the end of the war, the 21-year-old took a well-deserved rest and went absent without leave for twenty days. He knew that one more day's absence would officially class him as a deserter so he surrendered at a police station just in time. He served eight weeks' detention for being absent without leave, and returned to Britain to embark upon a career as an actor, becoming a television star in the hit comedy series *Steptoe and Son*.

Hollywood tough guy Steve McQueen deserted on more than one occasion before he attained fame as a Hollywood star of the 1960s and 1970s. He would later appear in such mega-hit movies as *The Magnificent Seven* (1960), *Bullitt* (1968) and *Papillon* (1973) and also portrayed courageous if undisciplined military types in *The War Lover* (1962) and *The Great Escape* (1963). His own forces career, with one exception, was relatively undistinguished and included at least one spell in the brig for being absent without leave.

McQueen, who was born in Indianapolis in 1930, had a troubled childhood, spending time in a reform school, running away from home and generally drifting before enlisting on a whim in the Marines in 1947. McQueen already had one desertion to his credit, or discredit, before his enlistment in the Marine Corps. In a drunken moment he had signed on as a deckhand on the merchant vessel *Alpha*, sailing from New York for Trinidad. He stood it for a week and then jumped ship in San Domingo. Making his way back to the USA he wandered into a bar in Myrtle, South Carolina, saw a recruiting poster and decided the Marines was for him.

McQueen was posted to the Second Recruit Battalion at Camp Lejeune in North Carolina. He soon decided, however, that service life was as bad as his civilian career had been – only with added discipline.

He met a girl while on a two-day pass and stayed away with her for two weeks before he was rounded up by a shore patrol and sentenced to thirty-one days in the brig, the first twenty-one on a diet of bread and water.

Private First Class McQueen spent the remainder of his three-year hitch in a state of subdued mutiny, although he distinguished himself on one occasion, organising a rescue attempt when a number of marines were thrown into the water after a transport vessel capsized.

He left the Marines having secured no promotion at all. He wandered into acting, as he had drifted into so many episodes of his life, and found that not only did he enjoy it but he also had an aptitude for it. He broke into television and in 1958 secured the lead in Western series *Wanted Dead or Alive* as a laconic, tough bounty hunter.

He became enormously popular with the public, although few of his co-workers liked him, regarding the former marine as a bitter, selfish loner. This perception wasn't all true, however: with memories of his own upbringing, McQueen was always generous in donations of his time and money to charitable causes involving troubled children.

Sensitive artists, temperamentally unsuited to life in the forces have often had a hard time of it when brought in to contact with the coarse texture of military life.

The services have long recognised the problems of those unlikely to adapt to military conditions but have been plagued by the fact that it is almost impossible to detect such traits during the initial recruitment process. These are only revealed with the passing of time – and often not too much time. It became generally acknowledged that there were four main factors that led to mental breakdown or desertion: separation from family and familiar conditions, inability to respond to military discipline and hierarchy, lack of self discipline and a phobia about living at close quarters with others, all of which are part and parcel of daily life in the armed forces.

20

'FOR YOU THE WAR IS OVER!'

So long as you command one soldier you are to continue to lead him!
– Order given to Lieutenant Hiroo Onoda, who did not surrender until 1974, twenty-nine years after the official end of the Second World War

When it became apparent that the war was drawing to an end in 1945, a number of deserters hastily started to make their own arrangements for the future. For some, further flight was the only solution. A number of agents and double agents had particular cause to consider their positions.

One of the most resourceful and courageous of German agents was Theodore Schurch, a German operative who on several occasions joined the British Army to gain information and then deserted again.

Schurch was born in London in 1918 to a Swiss father and an English mother. When he left school he worked for several firms as a junior accountant, developing fascist sympathies and encountering a number of German sympathisers living in London. It was suggested to him that if he joined the regular army he might one day be of considerable use to the German cause.

Accordingly, in 1936 he enlisted as a driver in the Royal Army Service Corps and was posted to Palestine. He was contacted in Jerusalem by German agents, who had been given his name by his former London contacts. Schurch was able to provide them with details of troop movements.

When the Second World War broke out, Schurch was posted to North Africa and was taken prisoner at Tobruk. At a prisoner-of-war camp he made himself known to the authorities and gave an account of his pre-war fascist contacts. With the blessing of Italian military intelligence he was used by the guards as an agent in the camp, was given an officer's uniform and began introducing himself to Allied prisoners of war as Captain Richards. He ingratiated himself with a number of Allied officers and succeeded in worming a certain amount of information out of them.

Schurch was no stranger to departing unceremoniously from duty; while serving in Egypt in 1941 he went AWOL to make contact with an Italian agent called Homsi for a briefing. Upon his return he had been given a term of field punishment.

After his activities in the prisoner-of-war camp, Schurch's intelligence activities were intensified. He was sent across to the British lines, with his real identity documents, posing as a British prisoner of war who had escaped from the Italians. He was posted to a transit camp where he ferreted out more information from bored soldiers and then slipped back across to the Italians.

Next, with the British advancing, Schurch was asked to stay on in Benghazi, again in his role as a British prisoner of war, to find out what he could about the plans of the occupying forces. Once more Schurch was accepted by the military at his face value, and once more he deserted and rejoined the Italians. This was a pattern he was to repeat on at least one more occasion, travelling both ways across the front line.

Schurch was soon transported to Italy and resumed his role as Captain Richards in a prisoner-of-war camp in Rome. By this time Italy was on the brink of surrendering to the Allies. When the armistice was signed, Schurch was working for the Italians in the town of Perugia and was captured by the Germans, under the assumption that he was an escaped British prisoner of war. He was sent to Germany in a train carrying other British troops who had been rounded up but before the train could leave, he leapt from the carriage, damaging his ankle in the process. Making his way back to Rome, Schurch reported to the German Intelligence Service. They checked his credentials and were more than happy to employ such a courageous and resourceful agent in their service. Before Schurch could prove his worth to the Axis cause once more, however, he was captured by the Americans and handed over to the British.

Schurch freely admitted to his activities and gave a detailed account of them. On 12 September 1945, his court martial began in London. He was found guilty of nine counts of treachery and one of desertion and was sentenced to death. On 4 January 1946, at the age of twenty-seven, Theodore Schurch was hanged at Pentonville Prison.

A much less successful and more venal agent than Schurch, but one who lived considerably longer, was George John Dasch. He was a member of an eight-man team of German saboteurs who landed in the USA in 1942. Having all lived in the USA and able to speak English, the men were trained by the *Abwehr*, the German Secret Service, and split into two groups. The project was named Operation Pastorius, after a pioneer seventeenth-century German settler in America.

Dasch was put in charge of one of the groups. He was thirty-nine years old and had served in the army in the First World War. After the war ended he had reached the USA as a stowaway and worked as a waiter. He had also been arrested on several occasions for violating the Prohibition laws and running a brothel. In 1941 he returned to Germany and offered to enlist in the army; considering his background, however, he was instead recruited as a potential saboteur.

The main missions of Dasch and his group were to blow up the hydroelectric plants at Niagara Falls and to destroy nominated factories in Illinois, Tennessee, Philadelphia and New York. The other four-man group was tasked with blowing up the Pennsylvania railway station and strategic sections of railway lines across the country, as well as wrecking the water-supply system in New York City.

The teams were transported across the Atlantic in two U-boats. The submarines submerged during the day and raced across the surface at night. Each group of saboteurs was supplied by the Germans with almost $60,000 in cash and crates of explosives.

Dasch and his three companions were landed on Long Island, near East Hampton, at 11 p.m. on the night of 12 June, after a fifteen-day voyage. During the landing they were dressed as German Marines to avoid being shot as spies if they were caught coming ashore. Once they had reached the coast they buried their uniforms and donned civilian clothes.

As they were digging in the sand, intending to leave their munitions boxes and retrieve them later, John Cullen, a young, unarmed coastguard seaman, stumbled across the four Germans. Dasch accosted him and pretended that he and his companions were fishermen forced ashore by bad weather. When the young American looked dubious, Dasch changed tack and gave him $300 to keep quiet about what he had seen.

The coastguard took the money and disappeared into the night. He ran to his station only half a mile away and told his superiors of his strange encounter. A group of coastguards ran to the spot, but Dasch and the others had disappeared. However, the Americans were in time to see the U-boat disappearing into an offshore fog. They found freshly dug holes and discovered the ammunition crates and discarded German uniforms. The coastguards alerted the authorities and news of the buried crates soon reached the FBI.

In the meantime, Dasch and the others had caught an early Saturday morning train from Long Island to New York. There they split up. Two of the saboteurs, Richard Quirin and Heinrich Heinck, registered at one hotel, while Dasch and Ernest Burger booked in at the Governor Hilton.

On this their second night in the USA, Dasch and Burger began to talk uneasily and realised that each of them harboured grave reservations about the task ahead of them. They were bothered by their encounter with the coastguard on the beach at Long Island, and decided that their arrival was now probably known to the American authorities.

Dasch was later to state that he was a fervent anti-Nazi and had intended to desert to the Americans all along, but this is doubtful. He told Burger that he would go to Washington and engage the assistance of Edgar Hoover, the head of the FBI at the organisation's headquarters, while Burger remained in New York and tried to allay any suspicions of betrayal that Quirin and Heinck might have.

Accordingly, Dasch took a train to Washington, booked into a hotel and telephoned the FBI. His call was regarded as a fake, but because of the news of the Long Island landing an agent was dispatched to collect the German. Dasch spent many hours telling the FBI everything he knew about the plans of both teams of saboteurs, although he was only granted the briefest of meetings with Hoover himself. The FBI realised that they had a genuine deserter on their hands and went into action.

Agents were sent to the Governor Hilton hotel in New York to follow Berger. Almost at once he led them to Quirin and Heinck. The three Germans were arrested at a clothing store. Burger at once claimed that he had been a co-conspirator with Dasch to betray the others. The four other saboteurs were picked up in Cincinnati, thanks to the information provided by Dasch. All eight Germans were accused of being spies, horrifying Dasch who had thought that he would be treated as a hero by the FBI. He was to discover that he was to receive no preferential treatment.

The men were brought before a military tribunal in July 1942. All eight of them pleaded that they had never had any intention of actually blowing anything up. Six of them were not believed, were sentenced to death and consequently executed. Because they had betrayed their companions, Dasch was sentenced to thirty years' imprisonment, while Burger received a life sentence. They both spent a little over five years incarcerated. The two men were then deported to Germany, where Burger accused his colleague of being responsible for the deaths of the six other saboteurs.

Dasch was shunned by many Germans for his betrayal. In 1959, he published a self-justifying book, entitled *Eight Spies Against America*, about his mission. He worked intermittently as a travel agent and tour guide. He applied for a presidential pardon, hoping to return to the USA, but it was never granted.

A number of spies sent to undertake work for Germany in the war were captured by or surrendered to the Allies, and were coerced or volunteered to become double agents. One of the best known was the safe-cracker Eddie Chapman.

Born near Tyneside in 1908, Chapman took to a life of crime early in life, becoming a member of a gang of safe breakers, specialising in the use of the explosive gelignite to break open locks.

Chapman was arrested in Scotland but given bail. He and other members of the gang fled to Jersey in the Channel Islands, but were re-arrested and imprisoned there. While Chapman was in a prison cell, the Germans landed and occupied the islands.

The ingenious and opportunistic Chapman asked for an interview with the German commanding officer on Jersey. He offered to abandon his country and spy for the Germans in England, if he was well paid for his work. Chapman was promptly transferred to a French prison and from there to Germany, where he received training in espionage and sabotage techniques.

In 1942, he was dropped by parachute in Cambridgeshire, under orders to blow up a de Havilland factory in north London. No sooner had he landed did Chapman surrender to a policeman in Littleport and demand an interview with British Intelligence. When this was granted, the German agent offered to swap sides again and work for the British. His offer was accepted with alacrity. Chapman was promised that his criminal record would be expunged and that he would be given enough money to set himself up in business after the war.

In an immediate effort to give Chapman's sabotage efforts credibility, MI5 used the talents of Jasper Maskelyne, a pre-war professional magician, to simulate an explosion and the resultant destruction at the de Havilland factory. Aerial photographs of the 'damage' taken by the Luftwaffe duly reached the German Intelligence authorities, who began to regard Chapman as one of their top agents.

For a time Chapman remained in London, maintaining radio contact with his German masters and feeding them misinformation supplied to him by MI5. Using forged papers, he then made his way to Lisbon in neutral Portugal, and from there travelled back to Germany. The Germans were delighted with the former criminal's success in England and used him on a number of secret missions to such neutral countries as Turkey and Switzerland. In 1944, his Nazi spymasters sent Chapman back to Great Britain, with instructions to discover the precise landing points of the anticipated Allied invasion of Europe.

Once more Chapman reported to MI5. British Intelligence officials then embarked upon a game of double bluff. They knew that the Germans had already discounted Normandy as a potential target. Accordingly, they provided Chapman with locations close to the actual forthcoming attacks to be transmitted by the double agent to Berlin.

The Germans thought that Chapman had failed them and called him back. However, after D-Day, when the beaches of Normandy had been stormed as Chapman had predicted, he was reinstated in their estimation as a master-spy. By then, the German forces were retreating into Germany. Chapman went with them, until he saw a chance to slip away, surrender to the advancing Allies and be returned to Great Britain. He returned to civilian life with a clean record, the sum of £25,000 from British Intelligence and whatever survived of the £100,000 originally negotiated with the Germans.

A less opportunistic double agent was Jack Berg. Of mixed Norwegian and British parentage Berg became a pre-war fascist in Norway and was recruited by the Germans to serve as an agent in Great Britain. He was captured, and agreed to work for the British.

In 1941, Berg and another Norwegian agent, Olav Klausen, were put ashore off the coast of Scotland by a German submarine. Both men had orders to blow up any military installations they could get near. Unfortunately for them by the time both men had set out on their mission experts at the celebrated Bletchley Park code and cipher school had broken the German codes by cracking the German Enigma coding machine. Armed troops were waiting ashore for Berg and Klausen. Both men were arrested and conducted under conditions of great secrecy to a former mental home.

Berg and Klausen both admitted that they were spies and gave up as much information as they could about their intentions. The two men also agreed to work as double agents, although Berg did so with more alacrity than his gruff accomplice.

Under strict supervision the turncoats were installed with their radio equipment in a safe house. For most of the remainder of the war, Berg and Klausen provided the Germans with a stream of misinformation about their non-existent sabotage operations. They were backed up by British Intelligence operatives who organised a series of faked explosions at the appropriate locations.

The double agents were also instructed to transmit demands for money and ever more expensive equipment. Accordingly these were dropped over the stipulated areas from low-flying German aircraft.

Berg, a pragmatic *bon viveur*, grew to like his easy life of deception, but Olav Klausen's conscience was more troubled. In the end he refused to cooperate further. He was arrested and sent to prison. Berg, by this time happily domiciled in Scotland, continued to do as he was told.

At the end of the war Berg was sent back to Norway. Perhaps wisely, in view of his wartime exploits, he adopted an extremely low profile and was soon lost from sight.

Harold Cole also served on both sides during the war, but he did not survive as long as Chapman or Berg. Conman and housebreaker, Cole joined the Royal Engineers immediately after his release from prison in 1939. With his usual opportunism he soon became a sergeant and was posted to northern France with the British Expeditionary Force. Caught stealing mess funds he was put in the guardroom to await trial.

While his guards were eating their dinners, Cole picked the lock of his cell and walked out of the camp. He was soon found in a local café, brought back to his camp and put in a room above a stable. But Cole couldn't be contained: he discovered a hole in the floor and used a blanket as a makeshift rope to climb down to the ground. Pausing only to steal the uniform of a company sergeant major, he fled into the night.

He was caught again, this time wearing the uniform of an officer he had acquired along the route, having discarded his purloined sergeant major's uniform. He was thrown into a seventeenth-century fortress under 24-hour guard. However, the Germans broke through the Allied lines and the British, Cole among them, fled. But the Germans were close behind them. Apprehended by the Nazis again, he was escorted back to Brussels railway station. In the chaos he escaped once more but was recaptured before he had got too far. The German advance had temporarily been stemmed, so Cole was conducted back to the fortress.

The German halt was only made in order to regroup and soon they started thrusting forwards towards Lille again. Cole's guards unlocked his cell door, told their prisoner that it was a case of every man for himself, and vanished.

Cole needed no second bidding. He lost himself among the thousands of retreating troops and civilians choking the roads before the German advance. Some brave French men and women were trying to establish groups to help with the escape routes already springing up. With his usual quickness of mind Cole linked up with one of them. Gradually he took over the network and began to organise and escort groups of downed airmen and escaped prisoners of war.

For a while, Cole did good work, at times putting his life at risk, something recognised by British Intelligence, which backed his efforts pragmatically, neglecting to inform the French Resistance of Cole's criminal background. Eventually, however, his true nature took over. He began to steal money from escape funds and even took cash from pilots in his escape parties, claiming that they would not need it. He also solicited funds from wealthy Frenchmen wishing to help the escape plans. His colleagues in the underground movement caught him with unauthorised sums of money and subjected Cole to an unofficial court martial. He was found guilty and it was decided the sergeant would be sent back to England to face punishment. Before this could be done, however, Cole escaped through a bathroom window and went on the run again, on this occasion making his way to Paris.

By this time the Germans were aware of the activities of the mysterious British non-commissioned officer and were eager to find him. Finally, he was picked up by the *Abwehr* in 1941. At once Cole offered to become a double agent. His offer was accepted, albeit with some suspicion on the part of the Germans. Cole began to betray all the French agents he knew and even helped to round up British pilots on the escape routes he had established.

After the invasion of France in 1944, Cole went on the run again, hunted by both the Germans and the Allies. For a time he masqueraded under a false name as a British secret service agent, and even managed to attach himself as such to an American unit. He was given a uniform, vehicle and driver, and distinguished himself by the severity of his interrogations of captured Germans.

By now Cole was pushing his luck too far. British Intelligence was piecing together an accurate record of his traitorous activities. He was arrested at the American camp and put into a detention barracks in Paris, while the British, Americans and French disputed as to which nation should have the pleasure of trying the sergeant.

Even now Sergeant Harold Cole had not finished. In the barracks he claimed he wished to write his autobiography but that his cell was too cold to do so. His credulous captors provided their prisoner with a typewriter and permission to write in the guardroom. One night, after he had finished his typing stint, Cole picked up his typewriter and made his way towards his cell. On the way he picked up a sergeant's overcoat from a peg on the wall and strode casually past the guards out of the building and on to the nearest metro station.

'Wanted' notices displaying his photograph were put up all over Paris, but by now there were reputed to be 30,000 Allied deserters in Paris. Cole adopted the identity of a British soldier waiting to be posted home and took up with a female owner of a bar in the city, who let him rest in a room above the premises.

By this time, descriptions of the British stranger hanging around the bar had been passed on to the police by some of its regular drinkers, who suspected that Cole might be an escaped German prisoner of war. Two armed inspectors of the French police were sent to investigate. Cole answered the door to their knock and fired at the police officers when they announced who they were. Airey Neave, who worked in the department organising clandestine operations in occupied Europe, wrote of what occurred next in his book *Saturday at MI9*: 'Cole fired three times, wounding one of them, but they returned the fire and shot him dead. There is an unconfirmed report that he hesitated in a last gesture of chivalry because the proprietress was in the line of fire.'

Towards the end of the reign of the Third Reich, a number of its senior members made last-minute efforts to desert, with varying degrees of success. Hermann Fegelein was a career SS officer who cemented his ties with Adolf Hitler by marrying Gretl Braun, the sister of Eva, the Führer's mistress and later, for a very short time, his wife.

Born in Ansbach in 1906, Fegelein served in the cavalry and then the Bavarian police force. He hitched his wagon to the Nazi cause and was rewarded by being made director of the SS riding academy in Munich. Upon the outbreak of the Second World War, Fegelein commanded the SS cavalry brigade in occupied Poland. He became notorious for his treatment of Red Army prisoners of war; during his period in command some 20,000 Jews were murdered in Poland.

In 1942 he was promoted to the rank of SS-Oberführer but a year later he was wounded in action. At the beginning of 1944 he was appointed Himmler's SS liaison officer at Hitler's headquarters, where he met Gretl Braun, his future wife. As a new member of Hitler's inner-circle further promotion came his way and he reached the rank of SS-Gruppenführer.

In April 1945, realising that all was lost, Fegelein slipped quietly out of the bunker, returned to his house in the city and changed into civilian clothes before attempting to escape to either Sweden or Switzerland, both neutral countries. His absence was noticed and troops were sent to bring him back to the bunker. Fegelein tried in vain to persuade the commander of his arresting party to

desert with him. His offer was spurned and he was brought back in
ignominy to face the wrath of Hitler. In vain Fegelein begged his
sister-in-law to intercede on his behalf. He was accused of desertion
and of conspiring with Heinrich Himmler, who was endeavour-
ing to negotiate with the Allies, to commit treason. He was found
guilty and shot.

Another high-ranking German to make a bolt for it as the Allied
forces closed in was the aforementioned Heinrich Himmler, head
of the Gestapo and for a long time one of Adolf Hitler's most
trusted associates.

When he first left school, Himmler worked as a salesman for a
firm of fertiliser manufacturers and then as a poultry farmer, before
joining the Nazi party in 1925. Four years later he was appointed
head of the SS, an elite guard surrounding Hitler. By 1936, he was
commander of the unified police forces in Germany. His fortunes
rose with those of his master and in 1943 he was placed in charge of
the Ministry of the Interior.

A ruthless man and an advocate of racial purity, he was responsible for the Nazi concentration and death camps in which
thousands of Jews were tortured and exterminated in the gas cham-
bers. Towards the end of the war, Hitler turned over command of
the remaining German armies to his loyal associate, but Himmler
proved no tactician. In despair he tried to negotiate a separate
peace with the Allies. When Hitler heard this he was furious
and ordered that Himmler should be arrested. He decreed that
his former close colleague be stripped of his offices, but did not
condemn him to death.

In those final days of the war, Himmler tried to make his escape
from his headquarters at Flensburg. He shaved off his moustache
and adopted the identity of one Heinrich Hitzinger, one of his
murder victims. Himmler also wore a patch over one eye and put
on the uniform of a sergeant major in the Secret Military Police,
a sub-division of the Gestapo. It was later thought that he had
been heading for Switzerland, where he was suspected of hiding a
fortune in gold.

Unknown to Himmler, the Allies had issued orders that members of all branches of the Gestapo should be arrested. On 22 May he was detained crossing a bridge with hundreds of other refugees near Hamburg by a British patrol. In contrast to the other fugitives, who were more concerned with shuffling on, Himmler meticulously offered his papers for examination. He was detained and was soon identified.

His request to be taken to Field Marshal Montgomery was denied. Himmler was stripped and placed in a cell. While he was being examined by a doctor he committed suicide by biting down on a vial of cyanide concealed in a dental cavity. His last recorded words were 'I am Heinrich Himmler!' His naked body was wrapped in camouflage and buried anonymously in a forest near Luneburg.

A much more successful and well-organised high-ranking German deserter was Major General Reinhard Gehlen. Towards the end of the Second World War, knowing that Germany's final defeat was only a few months away, Gehlen, a German spymaster, surrendered to the Allies with all his files and became a leading operative in Western Intelligence.

Gehlen, a former artillery officer and German Army Intelligence chief, specialising in the study of Russian military political leaders, had laid plans to desert to the Allies as early as 1944. Disliked by Hitler for what the German leader regarded as his unnecessarily pessimistic reports, Gehlen felt no loyalty to his superiors. He began to lead his staff to the west, away from the advancing Russian forces, at the beginning of 1945. First, in March, as a possible future bargaining counter with the Allies, he gave orders that all his laboriously obtained files should be transferred to microfilm, placed in fifty-two steel drums and buried in three different caches near Lake Spitzing in Upper Bavaria.

Ignoring Hitler's directive that all military officers should assemble in northern Germany on 22 May 1945, Gehlen and his senior officers surrendered to a team of US counter-intelligence officers. His opening remarks should have attracted the attention of his captors and got his desertion off to a flying start: 'I am Head of the

Section Foreign Armies East in German Army Headquarters. I have information to give of the highest importance to your government.'

In fact, at first the Americans did not appreciate the value of what their German captive had on offer, but when Gehlen wrote a 129-page report on what he knew and also turned over the contents of the steel cases, he was welcomed into the Allied fold. He was flown to the USA where he offered to establish a national intelligence agency pending the establishment of a government in western Germany.

The Americans did not have the resources or the knowledge to launch their own intelligence operations in Germany against the USSR on a large scale, but in Reinhard Gehlen they had a ready-made operative. The former major general was placed in charge of the local espionage network, first under military auspices and then in the control of the CIA.

Before long, Gehlen was in charge of an organisation of over 3,000 people and was given permission to recruit former army and SS officers from internment camps. In 1956, Gehlen's organisation was transferred to the newborn West German republic, where he remained until his retirement in 1968.

One German soldier who joined in the flood of deserters clogging the roads of Germany in 1945 was Joseph Ratzinger, an 18-year-old youth. His story is no more compelling than thousands of others, but he is one of the most famous of deserters for what he later became.

Born in 1927, the son of a policeman, Ratzinger enrolled in the Hitler Youth movement but was released to study for the priesthood. In 1943, his studies were interrupted when he was called up to serve with an anti-aircraft battery outside Munich. Two years later Ratzinger deserted with others from his unit.

In his book *The Salt of the Earth*, he recalled of this period, 'In three days of marching, we hiked down the empty highway in a column that gradually became endless.' Ratzinger and his companions were very nervous. Even this late in the war the SS was still carrying out summary executions of deserters by shooting them on the spot or hanging them from the nearest lamppost.

His fears were realised when he was stopped by an SS unit. 'Thank God they were men who had had enough of the war and did not want to become murderers,' Ratzinger wrote in later years. He was allowed to continue on his way. After the war he resumed his studies and entered the priesthood. In March 1977, he was made Archbishop of Munich and Freising. He became a cardinal in Rome and in 2005 he was elected to be Pope Benedict XVI.

On the other side of the world, in the Pacific theatre of operations, a few unfortunate, highly dedicated Japanese soldiers went on the run simply because they did not know that the war had ended. For many years after the end of the Second World War occasional reports were issued of the discovery of yet another Japanese soldier who had refused to believe that hostilities had ceased and had doggedly established himself in some remote jungle, grimly prepared to fight on to the end. Literally they did not know when they were beaten.

Private Yuichi Akatsu was an exception to this rule: he deserted from a band of post-war Japanese survivors and gave himself up. In 1945, Akatsu and three others were stationed on the small island of Lubang in the Philippines, unaware that the Japanese in the Philippines had surrendered. They retreated into the deepest part of the jungle and fortified a position. There they existed on rice, coconuts and bananas and the occasional cow captured and slaughtered during raids on Philippine villages. They lived on in this fashion until 1949. The American authorities, aware that Akatsu's party was raiding villages, dropped leaflets over the jungle, declaring that the war was over and urging any surviving Japanese troops to surrender. The officer in charge, Lieutenant Onoda, refused to believe the leaflets and ordered his men to remain together.

One day, Private Akatsu, fed up with the isolation, meagre rations and constant illnesses, simply walked away from the others. He lived on his own in the jungle for another six months, unable to pluck up the courage to surrender in case he should be shot. Eventually he walked into a village and gave himself up. Its inhabitants handed Akatsu over to the American authorities, who treated the Japanese survivor with great kindness, informing him that the war had been over for four years.

Akatsu stayed on the island for some time. Hoping to find his former colleagues, he led a fruitless search party and wrote a note in Japanese which was copied and dropped all over the island of Lubang, confirming that the war was over.

Private Akatsu was then flown home to resume his former civilian life. Of his three former colleagues, one was shot and killed by villagers in 1954, while another was later shot by a Philippine patrol. Lieutenant Onoda survived on his own until 1974, thirty years after he had first led his party into the jungle. He was found by a persistent journalist but even then he would not surrender until his former commanding officer was brought back to the islands to assure the officer that the war was over.

21

'MAKE MINE A DOUBLE!'

Never obey an order, and if things get really bad, pretend to be barmy.
– Advice from Second World War deserter Charlie Kray to his two
sons Ronnie and Reg, shortly before they deserted from the National
Service army

When the war ended in 1945 it was estimated that over 20,000 deserters of all nations were on the run in Britain. By this time most of them had attained fake identity cards and papers, and were holing up inconspicuously all over the country. It was recognised that deserters were contributing significantly to the national crime rate and spasmodic and largely unsuccessful attempts were made to round them up. In January 1946, hundreds of police were involved in manning a series of check-points on major roads leading in and out of London and various crossings on the river Thames. The success rate of the operation was minimal.

Meanwhile, deserters-cum-criminals continued to flourish, until the numbers of available able-bodied police officers were swelled by returning servicemen. Nevertheless, absconders from the forces continued to contribute significantly to crime statistics in Britain. Most were petty thieves but one or two of their number began to appear in the headlines. One of these was Neville George Heath, a vicious murderer who, earlier in his career, had been cashiered from three different branches of the services, twice for desertion and once for bad behaviour.

He was born in Ilford in Essex in 1917. The glib and personable Heath soon embarked upon a life of crime in the 1930s. He was imprisoned at various times for such white-collar crimes as theft, fraud and obtaining money by false pretences. A gifted mimic, one of his favourite aliases was that of Lord Dudley, apparently a moneyed aristocrat.

With things getting a bit hot for him in civilian life, Heath joined the RAF. He was soon promoted to flying officer and posted to 9 Fighter Squadron at Duxford. In 1937, he was court-martialled and dismissed from the service for stealing money from a mess fund, being absent without leave, escaping while under arrest and stealing a car.

The last charge related to the fact that, while under arrest, Heath had given his word as a gentleman that he would make no attempt to escape. While his escort relaxed the prisoner stole a car belonging to a sergeant and fled.

Released from prison upon the outbreak of war, Heath tried to re-enlist in the RAF but was rejected because of his previous conviction. Instead he joined the army and was commissioned in the Royal Army Service Corps. Posted to Egypt and reaching the rank of captain he was soon in trouble again. Somehow he got hold of two pay books, drew a double salary, passed bad cheques and finally made the mistake of trying to pull a scam on a vengeful brigadier. Not for the first time Heath went on the run. He was caught and sent home in disgrace on a troop ship.

Reaching Cape Town on the troop ship, Heath deserted yet again, married a wealthy heiress and enlisted in the South African Air Force, using the name Armstrong. The persuasive and handsome recruit became an officer for the third time and was trained as a bomber pilot. He served well in action. Forced to bail out on a raid over Europe, he made his way back to Allied lines but even when his previous record was revealed inadvertently he was allowed to retain his position.

As usual, Heath betrayed his trust and before long was arrested and found guilty of undisciplined conduct and wearing unauthorised decorations. He was dismissed from the service and his wife's family paid him over £2,000 to divorce her.

Heath returned to London and resumed his criminal activities, haunting the drinking dens of the capital and claiming at different times to be a peer of the realm and a high-ranking officer in mufti. He also revealed a sadistic side to his character when on several occasions he was found engaged in bondage sessions with prostitutes in cheap hotels.

In 1946, Heath picked up a woman in the Panama Club in South Kensington and took her back to a Notting Hill hotel. The next morning the woman's body was found, bound, badly beaten and slashed and suffocated. Heath was missing.

Next he moved the scene of his activities to Bournemouth, now calling himself Group Captain Brooke, where he took up with another unfortunate young woman. One night he took her out to dinner. The girl was never seen again alive.

The police interviewed 'Group Captain Brooke' about his assignation with the girl and he was most helpful and solicitous. However, at the police station it was noticed that the man being interviewed resembled the circulated description of someone wanted for questioning for the Notting Hill Gate murder.

When Heath made the mistake of complaining of feeling cold an inspector went back to his hotel, ostensibly to fetch the officer's coat. While he was there the police officer instigated a search of Heath's room and found a left-luggage ticket for a suitcase deposited at Bournemouth West railway station. The case was found to contain clothes with Heath's labels on them, a bloodstained neckerchief, a scarf with female human hairs stuck to it and a blood-spattered riding crop.

Heath was arrested for the Notting Hill Gate murder. Soon the mutilated naked body of his second victim was found in a copse near Heath's hotel. The girl's throat had been cut.

Neville George Heath pleaded guilty but insane to both murders. His pleas for mitigation were ignored by the jury, which, after deliberating for an hour, found him guilty of murder. On 26 October 1946, Heath was hanged at Pentonville Prison. Insouciant to the end, it was reported that on his last night, when offered a whisky by the governor, he accepted with the words, 'You might make that a double!'

Two other murders which occupied much space in newspapers in the post-war period, although a decade apart, were those committed by deserters Donald George Thomas and Michael Dowdall. Thomas was called up into the army in the last year of the war and went on the run almost immediately. Eventually he gave himself up, served 160 days' detention and then deserted again. The deserter was stopped by a police officer while in the process of undertaking a series of burglaries. Thomas shot and killed the officer, PC Nathaniel Edgar, and ran away. However, before he had been shot, Edgar had written the name and address of Thomas in his notebook while questioning him. A massive police search followed and Thomas was arrested in a Clapham boarding house, still in possession of the Luger he had purchased on the black market and with which he had killed PC Edgar. Thomas was found guilty of murder at his trial in April 1948 and sentenced to death. Because of a four-year political experiment with a no-hanging policy he was given instead a term of imprisonment. He was released fourteen years later, in 1962.

A decade after Thomas had started his sentence, another deserter, Guardsman Michael Dowdall, murdered a prostitute while on the run from the Pirbright Camp of the Grenadier Guards. He returned to his unit, served his punishment and then, while serving by day, committed a series of assaults on young women at night. He was soon caught after attacking a woman in her Fulham flat. The woman, a Mrs Hill, was able to give the police a description of her assailant. The 19-year-old Dowdall was arrested and brought to trial in 1962. He pleaded guilty to manslaughter on the grounds of diminished responsibility and was sentenced to a term of life imprisonment. In 1975, he was released after serving fifteen years but died a year later.

Ensio Tiira was a Finn who, maintaining the long tradition of the French Foreign Legion, deserted successfully from a troopship on a raft. He drifted for thirty-two days across the Indian Ocean under horrifying conditions before being rescued.

He was brought up in Rauma in Finland. In 1944, at the age of sixteen, he fought with the Finnish Army against the Russians. He married but then left his wife and became a fireman on a number of ocean-going vessels. On one trip he fell out with the engineer and deserted at Rouen. Soon he met a group of other unemployed Finns and, unable to get work and acting on impulse, five of them joined the French Foreign Legion.

After a tough period of basic training Tiira was separated from the other Finns and sent to French Indochina to fight against the Vietminh. On the voyage out on the transport *Skaubryn* the 24-year-old Finn became friendly with a Swedish legionnaire, Fred Ericsson. The pair of them decided to desert.

Enlisting the aid of several members of the crew, Tiira and Ericsson collected a little food, some wine in a rubber water bottle, a torch and several knives. At 3 a.m. on 23 February 1953, they threw overboard one of the four feet square life rafts belonging to the transport vessel and jumped into the sea after it. They hoped to paddle to the tip of the island of Sumatra, which they believed to be only a few miles away.

Almost at once they were swept away by a strong current, which took them far from Sumatra across the Indian Ocean. It was the start of a dreadful voyage. Sharks pursued the tiny raft constantly, sometimes attacking the frail structure and threatening to capsize it.

The two men soon ran out of food and their supply of wine dwindled alarmingly. The rays of the sun blistered their skin and the raft was too small and too low in the water for them to lie comfortably in it.

At night they were sometimes seized by storms and carried helplessly even further out into the ocean. They were able to collect drinking water from the occasional downpours, but soon they became too weak to hold open their water bottle.

Ericsson was the first to despair and became increasingly apathetic and refused to help with the paddling. Soon the two deserters lost all sense of direction and had no idea where they were. Now and again they were passed in the distance by ships but were unable to attract their attention.

Sometimes they had strokes of good fortune. From a tree trunk, which floated past their raft, they were able to take and eat some crabs clinging to the roots. Once they even managed to capture and kill a turtle. Having lost their knives overboard, they were able to cut up the flesh with glass from a broken mirror but soon found that they could not swallow the meat and instead were forced to drink the turtle's blood.

On the seventeenth day of their voyage Fred Ericsson died. Tiira tried to retain the corpse on board the raft, but it soon turned black and began to stink. Sadly he pushed the body of his friend over the side and watched the circling sharks dispose of it.

The legionnaire had almost given up hope. In his account of his desertion he wrote: 'If I have ever been certain of anything in my life it was that on March 25, 1953, my thirty-first day at sea, I was about to die.'

On 26 March, the thirty-second day of the dreadful voyage, he was picked up by a British freighter the *Alendi Hill*. The crew managed to transfer the exhausted Tiira on board from his raft, but even then the leaping sharks made one last effort to catch him as he was helped up the side of the vessel. His weight had shrunk from 132 pounds to 55 pounds but Tiira responded to the nursing of his rescuers. He was transferred to a hospital in Singapore and looked after by members of the Finnish community there. In spite of his poor physical state Tiira's main worry was that he would be handed back to the French Foreign Legion.

His compatriots assured him that they would not allow this to happen. They were as good as their word. They managed to secure a berth for the ex-legionnaire on a Finnish vessel returning home. The captain promised the agitated Tiira that he would not be putting in at any French port en route.

It was estimated that the two deserters drifted for some 700 miles after failing to land at Sumatra. Ensio Tiira recovered his health and wrote *Raft of Despair*, a bestselling book about his dreadful experiences. It was translated into a number of different languages.

After the end of the Second World War, the British government continued to retain conscription for another fifteen years, until 1960. In the Act of 1947, it was officially called National Service. After experimenting with shorter periods it was decided that all fit 18-year-old youths would serve in one of the armed forces for two years. For years afterwards the wall of at least one NAAFI canteen at a barracks in the south of England displayed a large jagged hole caused in the riot which ensued after the assembled conscripts had been informed that their period of service arbitrarily had been increased from eighteen months to two years.

Over a million young men served between 1948 and 1960. Some of them served and died in such battle zones as Korea, Malaya and Burma; most suffered agonies of boredom in such Siberias as Aldershot and Catterick. A few took matters into their own hands and deserted.

Kit Wilkes-Chase was one of the last conscripts to be enrolled before the official rebranding of conscription as National Service. He served longer than he anticipated, but not in the British Army. He was born in Boston, Lincolnshire in 1929 and joined the Royal Artillery in 1947 where he was soon posted to Palestine. As an impressionable 19-year-old guard at an internment camp for illegal immigrants he was so appalled at the state of Jewish victims of the Holocaust imprisoned behind the wire that he decided to fight for the cause of a free Jewish state.

Wilkes-Chase left his unit and hid among the luggage on top of a bus going to Tel-Aviv. His offer to serve with the Jews was accepted. He was kitted out with a rough uniform, rifle and grenades and sent to join the elite commando unit *Hayot Ha'Negev*, or the Beasts of the Negev.

Soon Wilkes-Chase was taking part in a series of battles against the Egyptians and Jordanians in the Negev desert. He was twice wounded in action and commissioned in the Israeli Defence Force. In 1952, he was appointed bodyguard to David Ben-Gurion, the Prime Minister of Israel, attaining the rank of captain.

In 1958, after more than ten years in Israel, Kit Wilkes-Chase returned to Great Britain and surrendered to the military authorities.

He was sentenced to a year in a military detention centre and then honourably discharged.

He embarked upon a business career and became managing director of a fruit-packing firm. In 1985, he was awarded a special Israeli citation: 'Your fighting spirit and readiness to help us in our fight for existence was a personal example of moral courage to your fellow soldiers and officers in the Israeli Defence Force.'

At the other end of the scale, peacetime conscription housed, sometimes briefly, a number of young men who were later to become famous, or notorious, outside the confines of military life. One of these was Jeffrey Bernard, a witty, volatile, self-destructive alcoholic who spent most of his time in Soho pubs and earned his living by writing magazine columns depicting his Bohemian existence.

He was born in Hampstead in 1932, the son of a stage designer who died while Bernard was only seven. He attended a number of schools, rejected his mother's attempts to make him a naval officer and, when he was sixteen, drifted with delight into the artistic life of Soho pubs frequented by writers and artists. In 1950, he was conscripted into the 14th/20th King's Hussars as a trooper and trained as a tank driver.

Disliking the discipline of life in the Hussars, Trooper Bernard deserted in February 1951, three months after he had been conscripted. He left his camp at Catterick in Yorkshire on leave and simply did not return. For four months Bernard hid in London, staying with a variety of old drinking cronies. Finally, bored and depressed, he gave himself up. He telephoned the military police from the Gargoyle nightclub and waited to be picked up and escorted back to his unit.

He spent most of his time awaiting trial by shovelling dirty snow away from the purlieus of his cell and replacing it with the more pristine variety. All the time he feared the worst, expecting a long prison sentence for desertion. He was saved by the actions of his brothers Oliver and Bruce who wrote to Bernard's commanding officer claiming that their sibling had deserted because he was distraught at the death of his mother some time before.

Their appeal worked. Instead of being court-martialled for desertion Trooper Bernard was only charged with overstaying his leave and given a week in the guardhouse. Nevertheless he was determined to get out of the Hussars. He attempted suicide by taking an overdose of sleeping pills and was sent to a military mental hospital. He was soon discharged from the army; the inscription in his papers read: 'Mental stability nil.'

After his premature release from the army, Bernard embarked upon a career as a full-time Soho 'character', spending most of his days drinking with cronies. When he had to he would undertake such casual work as labouring and dishwashing. He became an illegal bookmaker and for a brief period he even toured with a fair as a booth boxer, taking on all-comers.

Fortunately he discovered, or others discovered in him, a talent for writing short magazine pieces. Seldom leaving his convivial corner of the bar, he became an erratic racing tipster, a television critic who seldom watched programmes and then a columnist, first for the *New Statesman* and then *The Spectator*. In this latter activity he really found his niche, recording the disasters of his daily life and describing graphically the strange denizens of his favourite Greek Street public house, The Coach & Horses.

Bernard was often too intoxicated to deliver his articles to the editor of *The Spectator*, who would then explain the absence of the column by stating 'Jeffrey Bernard is unwell'. This phrase was used by Keith Waterhouse as the title for his hit play about the alcoholic's life, starring Peter O'Toole. At one point Bernard tried to write his autobiography but was reduced to asking anyone who remembered what he had been doing between 1960 and 1974 to contact him. Jeffrey Bernard married four times. He died at the age of sixty-five.

Many temporary soldiers who later became infamous criminals first displayed their intrinsic anti-establishment feelings when called upon to serve their country in the post-1945 period. Ronnie Biggs was a member of the gang of sixteen, which pulled off the Great Train Robbery of 1963, taking £2,631,784 from the

Glasgow-to-London mail train. He was arrested for the crime, but then, infamously, escaped from prison and remained at liberty for thirty-five years. Earlier in life he had achieved some rudimentary practice in avoiding the law when he absconded from the RAF.

Biggs was born in Lambeth in south London, in 1929, the youngest of five children. During the war he was evacuated to the West Country, returning to London in 1942. When he was fifteen he was arrested for stealing pencils from the chain store Littlewoods. It was the first of three court appearances he was to make for pilfering in the same year. In May 1947, he joined the RAF on an eight-year engagement. He failed an electricians' course and was re-mustered as a cook.

Biggs first went AWOL soon after being posted to a cookery course near Aylesbury. He was picked up by the RAF police in Brixton but while a sergeant and a corporal were taking him back to his camp Biggs ran away from them at Baker Street underground station. He thrived by stealing from shops but soon tired of this and returned to his camp at RAF Halton. He was sentenced to a few weeks' confinement to barracks but still managed to get out of his camp occasionally to rob tobacconists' shops, selling the cigarettes to his camp mates on credit at inflated prices.

It was not long before Biggs went on the run again. Once more he went back to stealing. With several accomplices he robbed a chemist's shop, but the mother of one of the thieves gave the gang away to the police. In February 1949, the 19-year-old Ronald Biggs was sentenced to six months' imprisonment and was dishonourably discharged from the RAF.

Upon his release from prison in 1949, Biggs entered a career of petty crime. Over the next fourteen years he was often caught and sentenced to terms of imprisonment. During one of his gaol sentences he met and befriended Bruce Reynolds, who was to mastermind the Great Train Robbery. During this period he also married and had three children.

Biggs was recruited by Reynolds for the mail-train robbery and received about £150,000 as his cut, but was arrested within a month when his fingerprints were found on some stolen notes. He was tried and sentenced to thirty years. After a little more than a year Biggs escaped.

He fled to Paris where he underwent plastic surgery and purchased forged documents, which admitted him to Australia. He worked for a few years there as a builder and then went on the run again, this time to South America. He left his wife behind in Melbourne, settling in Rio de Janeiro in Brazil with a local girlfriend.

Biggs was discovered there in 1974 and efforts were made to deport him back to Great Britain. By this time his girlfriend was pregnant. Under Brazilian law Biggs could not be extradited. He scraped a living from his notoriety, entertaining tourists for a fee, cooking them meals using the expertise he had garnered on his RAF course, and regaling them with tales of his experiences. He even made a record as a guest singer with the Sex Pistols. On one occasion an effort was made by bounty hunters to kidnap him. Biggs was trussed up and transported as far as Barbados in a sack marked 'Live Snake', but the Barbadian authorities released him and allowed him to return to Rio de Janeiro.

In 1998, Biggs suffered a stroke and after that remained in poor health. In 2001, he tired of life on the run and gave himself up, returning to Great Britain on a stretcher to serve the remainder of his long-delayed prison sentence.

Biggs's cohort, Bruce Reynolds, was a conman and thief who got twenty-five years for masterminding the 1963 railway theft. Although he often claimed to have been the youngest major in the British Army, Reynolds's actual length of military service was of only a few days' duration before he deserted.

Born in 1931 and brought up in London, the scholarly look-ing Reynolds, son of a trade union organiser, had a number of token jobs when he left school, including working in the accounts department of the *Daily Mail*, but soon drifted into crime. He had already escaped from a borstal institution for young offenders and served a sentence in Reading Prison before he was called up to do his National Service in the army.

Because of his several digressions en route, Reynolds was twenty-one, three years older than the average conscript, when he turned up at the Royal Army Medical Corps centre at Ash Vale Barracks in Aldershot. He was late arriving and within a few hours had deserted, after a sergeant referred to his borstal background in front of the other recruits in his squad.

Reynolds followed the first set of railway tracks he encountered, on the principle that they were bound to reach somewhere, and caught an early train home from Weybridge. He left his army uniform with a relative to sell and met up with his former associates at a Lyon's Corner House café. Unfortunately this was an established staging post for absconders of all sorts and within a few hours Reynolds had been rounded up in a routine police sweep and returned to his unit.

Back in the army he slashed his arm repeatedly with a knife, hoping that the action would get him discharged as being mentally deranged. However, when he reached a military hospital he found the beds fully occupied and a long queue of recruits ahead of him with similar intentions.

Returned to his unit once more Reynolds went on the run almost immediately. He met up with some of his old criminal friends and started stealing fur coats by the simple method of smashing the windows of shops containing them. One day he was detained in the street by two plain-clothed police officers who recognised him. He managed to escape, but a detailed search for Reynolds had been launched. He was arrested while leaving a café in Tooting, charged with breaking and entering, and sentenced to three years in Wandsworth Prison. His brief military career was over.

After his release from Wandsworth, Reynolds soon graduated from shoplifting to housebreaking and gradually, between prison sentences, attained a reputation among fellow villains as a shrewd planner of criminal operations. While he was not serving time he lived in luxury and in 1963 he became involved in his biggest operation yet, helping to plan and taking part in the Great Train Robbery.

Such a massive crime merited an equally huge response and most of the train robbers were soon rounded up in an all-embracing police operation, although a number were able later to finance at least temporary escapes from prison. Reynolds went to ground for a while and then travelled to the south of France when the British police began to close in on him. From there he and his family flew to Mexico City.

When his share of the proceeds from the Great Train Robbery began to dwindle, and unable to operate as a conman in a country in which he could not speak the language, Bruce Reynolds moved to Canada. He heard rumours that the police suspected his presence in Vancouver and, panic-stricken, moved back to France and then to England, to try to get hold of some of the supply of stolen money he had left there.

Back in London he found that, as one of the country's most notorious wanted criminals, most of the people he met were either likely to turn him in or blackmail him. In an effort to get away from his low-life associates he moved with his wife and children to Torquay. Too many rumours about Reynolds's reappearance in Great Britain were floating about and in 1968 he was arrested and brought to trial.

Reynolds pleaded guilty and was able to hand over £5,500, all, he claimed, that remained of his share of the train robbery proceeds. He was sentenced to twenty-five years' imprisonment and was released in 1978, after serving ten years. Later he published an autobiography, *The Autobiography of a Thief*, and earned a living on the crime media and lecture hall circuit.

Even more notorious than Reynolds and Biggs were the Kray twins, Reggie and Ronnie, who ran a successful but brutal criminal empire in London. They deserted together when they were called up to do their National Service.

They were born in the London district of Hoxton in 1933 and left school when they were fifteen. For six months they worked in Billingsgate fish market; Reggie trained as a salesman while Ronnie collected empty fish boxes. In their spare time they fought with some success as amateur boxers and then turned professional for a few bouts. Early in 1952, the brothers were conscripted to do their National Service in the Royal Fusiliers at Waterloo Barracks in the Tower of London.

After a few hours in the army, the Krays decided that they did not like the discipline being imposed and walked out of the barracks. When a corporal naively asked where they were going, they said that they were on their way home to see their mother. Unwisely the corporal tried to detain Ronnie by clutching his arm. Ronnie knocked him out and he and his brother continued on their way.

The following morning they were picked up at their mother's house and returned to the barracks. There they were sentenced to seven days in the guardroom. While they were in the cells they met a kindred spirit, a former borstal boy called Dickie Morgan who came from Mile End. When their period of detention was over, the Krays walked out with their new friend and stayed with him in the London docks area, where they made some useful criminal contacts. On a day trip to Southend the twins sent to the commanding officer of the Royal Fusiliers a postcard, saying 'Wish you were here!'

The Krays were arrested once more, this time after a struggle. They were sentenced to a month in Wormwood Scrubs for assaulting a policeman who had recognised them and tried to arrest them, and a further nine months at Shepton Mallet military prison for striking a non-commissioned officer and being absent without leave. Here they met other criminals, including Charlie Richardson, before being discharged in 1954.

Back in civilian life, the Krays began to build their criminal empire. They started by renting a snooker hall called the Regal in Mile End, which rapidly became a centre for all sorts of nefarious activity. They gained respect by beating off an armed attack from a Maltese gang which had demanded protection money. The twins then started their own protection rackets. Known as 'The Firm', their organisation spread until it controlled a large area of London.

The brothers finally overreached themselves when they committed two spectacular murders. Ronnie shot and killed a fellow criminal, George Cornell, in the Blind Beggar public house, apparently because the other man had alluded to his homosexual activities. Reggie stabbed and killed another crook, Jack 'the Hat' McVitie.

They were sentenced to a minimum of thirty years. Ronnie died of a heart attack in prison in 1995; his brother died five years later, having been released because he was suffering from an incurable illness.

Military prison mate Charlie Richardson, a London gangster who, like a number of his kind, found army life a little too much for him also went on the run. Always wheeling and dealing, Richardson managed to avoid conscription until he was brought before a magistrate's bench on a minor criminal charge. An astute Justice of the Peace noticed that the 19-year-old youth standing before him had not reported for National Service and ordered the matter to be investigated. Almost before he knew what had hit him, Richardson was in uniform and disliking the experience considerably.

Richardson decided to 'work his ticket' and be dismissed from the armed forces as soon as possible. He began by refusing to sign the Official Secrets Act, declaring that in the unlikely event of his ever being told any military secrets he would at once pass them on to the Russians. A kindly but misguided senior officer told Richardson to go to the canteen and have a cup of tea and think matters over before returning and signing the papers. Richardson went, had the tea and promptly left. He walked past the guard on the gate and caught a bus home.

The two policemen who were sent to bring Richardson back to his unit refused the youth's offer of £5 apiece to go away, and made sure that the deserter was returned to his camp.

Once deposited in the cells, Richardson launched a campaign to convince the authorities that he was insane. He ripped up his uniform, indulged in screaming fits and finally set fire to his cell. He was overcome by the fumes and lapsed into unconsciousness but celebrated being revived by striking the hapless medical officer who brought him round.

Released from military prison in 1954 at the age of twenty, Richardson resumed his life of crime. He built up an enormous underworld empire, including scrapyard businesses and West End drinking clubs, and became notorious for the way in which he would kidnap and torture rival criminals. Eventually Richardson was arrested on various racketeering and assault charges. He was sentenced to twenty-five years' imprisonment.

Over in Europe, another conscript, one who became even more famous than the Krays, was Arnold Schwarzenegger, but he too would go on the run although for an altogether more amusing reason.

Austrian-born Schwarzenegger achieved fame first as a body-building champion and won his first major physique title by going absent without leave from his army unit. The son of a police official, Schwarzenegger was brought up strictly. When he left school to become an apprentice carpenter he was already training in a gymnasium seven days a week to develop his already impressive muscles.

In 1965, 18-year-old Arnold Schwarzenegger was called up to begin his mandatory twelve months' service in the Austrian Army. His father pulled strings to get him posted to a tank unit, but the youth was interested in little other than bodybuilding.

While he was still in the early weeks of his basic training, Schwarzenegger received an invitation to participate in the Junior Mr Europe physique competition, due to be held in Stuttgart. He knew that he would be refused permission by the army to take part, so he went absent without leave on Friday night by climbing over the wall of his camp and catching a train to Stuttgart.

He won the competition with a perfect score and, a few days later, tried to get back into his barracks without being observed. He was seen and arrested by the base police and placed in a cell for seven days.

Schwarzenegger was convinced that he would receive a court martial and a heavy sentence. He was saved by newspaper reports making much of a major national bodybuilding title being won by a serving Austrian soldier. The private was released from his cell and encouraged by his officers to continue with his training and enter more contests.

He went on to win every major physique contest, including the Mr Olympia title six times from 1970 to 1975. His growing fame secured him movie roles, at first in low-budget productions like *Hercules Goes to New York* (1970). To the amazement of many who have seen this, Schwarzenegger went on to become a major film star. His acting skills were below par and his thick Austrian accent made him sometimes difficult to understand, but after a few walk-ons as bodyguards and football players he began to be cast in action movies, where he could flaunt his incredible muscles and directors could lessen his dialogue. He later married a niece of the former President John F. Kennedy and served as Governor of California, before slotting almost seamlessly back in to the movie business.

Most deserters, like Schwarzenegger, have blundered almost blindly through their attempts to defect, but some, accustomed to living by their wits outside the law, like the Krays, Charlie Richardson and Frankie Fraser have found that their anti-social skills have suited them quite admirably to deserting and living comfortably while on the loose.

The deserters who particularly annoyed the military authorities were those who had been taught certain skills in the forces, which they then used to defect and stay at liberty. One of these was US Air Force specialist James Pou. He had been a member of a search and rescue unit in which he had been taught skills of evasion and how to live off the land. Tired of service life he absconded, faked his own death and undertook a bigamous marriage, but after a tempestuous liaison was turned in to the Air Force by his second wife.

Pou was sentenced to eighteen months' detention for desertion and bigamy. Completely unfazed he told his guards, 'When I want to, I'll just walk out!' He was as good as his word. In June 1993, he escaped from his detention quarters at March Air Force Base, San Diego. No one ever worked out how he had made his departure.

22

'UNTRUSTWORTHY AND INCAPABLE'

He's very important, and at this stage it's still possible that someone might want to eliminate him.
– US official commenting on the defection of Brigadier Rafael del Pino from Cuba to USA, 30 May 1987

With the unconditional surrender of Japan in 1945, Korea was divided into two occupation zones, divided by a line drawn across the 38th Parallel. This was intended to be a temporary measure until Korea could be resettled as a nation.

It was agreed that North Korea would be administered by the USSR and South Korea by the USA. Hence the once united nation was now being influenced in the north by a Communist regime, while the south was introduced to the joys of capitalism. Hopes of uniting Korea as a whole came to nothing.

This was a certain recipe for antagonism. In June 1950, South Korea was invaded by its neighbour, supported by Chinese troops. The USA went to the aid of its allies and the conflict was soon called a police action under the supervision of the United Nations, with the USA, South Korea and Great Britain supplying most of the troops, with smaller forces from fourteen other nations. By the end of the conflict over a million US troops were serving in the country. A ceasefire was declared in July 1953, although officially the war has never ended.

The desertion rate of individual soldiers from the countries making up the United Nations force in Korea was remarkably low, perhaps because in such an isolated and barren country there was nowhere to go. However, a considerable number of troops deserted in their home countries rather than be sent to fight in Korea, and there were many absences among UN troops sent on rest and recuperation leave in Japan, who had to be rounded up by military police and sent back to their units. By the end of the three-year campaign it was estimated that over 30,000 US troops had deserted rather than be shipped to Korea. At first the conflict did not go well for the Americans and one unit in particular, the 24th Infantry Regiment, a regiment of segregated black US soldiers led by white officers, received such a bad reputation for its wholesale desertions in the face of the North Korean Army that in 1951 it was officially disbanded.

In 1950, the UN forces in Korea were pushed back as far as the coastal pocket around the coast of Pusan. In July, the 24th Infantry Regiment went into action and acquitted itself well, fighting to regain the town of Yech'on. This was to prove one of the few battle honours to fall to the lot of the ill-fated 24th. The regiment did not have a sparkling history of combat experience and had been used mainly to police rear areas in the Pacific and accept the surrender of small pockets of Japanese survivors during the Second World War. After the war, it performed garrison duty guarding the docks of Kobe in Japan, before being dispatched hastily to Korea in 1950.

In September of that year, the 2nd Battalion of the regiment cracked before a determined enemy attack. Hundreds of troops fled and replacement units had to be used to plug the gaps left in the line. In Pusan many of the deserters were rounded up by the military police.

This was the first of a number of similar incidents. Soon the regiment became a byword for deserting in the face of enemy attacks. An official account accused the unit as being 'frightened and demoralised'. A divisional commander followed this up by stating that the 24th was unreliable and a drag on other units fighting with it.

There were a number of reasons for the state of the regiment. Many replacements were barely trained and had to be shown how to load and fire their rifles. There was great mistrust between the white officers and black soldiers, and accusations of racial intolerance and poor leadership. Those brave soldiers who remained at post often suffered a needlessly high casualty rate because their comrades were not there to support them.

In September 1950, Major General William B. Kean requested that the regiment be broken up, as it was 'untrustworthy and incapable of carrying out missions expected of an infantry regiment'. On 1 October 1951, the 24th Infantry Regiment was disbanded.

Otherwise there were relatively few desertions during the Korean conflict, mainly because there was nowhere in such an inhospitable and tightly controlled country for deserters to hide. The desertions that did take place were almost entirely by United Nations troops who had been taken prisoner and brainwashed in captivity, so come the ceasefire they declared that they did not wish to return home.

The only Englishman in this category was Marine Andrew Condron. When he chose not to return from captivity in 1953 he was cited by the Admiralty as a deserter.

Born in Bathgate, twenty miles from Edinburgh, in 1928, Condron grew up during the war. His older brother Samuel fought in the RAF and was taken prisoner by the Japanese. Condron took a wireless course at Edinburgh College and in 1946 enlisted in the Royal Marines. Almost as soon as he had completed his basic training he volunteered for service in Korea with 41st Independent Commando unit.

Immediately the Marines were rushed into action. In November 1950 a force of twenty-five Marines, including Condron, found themselves surrounded by the Chinese. Condron surrendered and was the only survivor. He spent most of his subsequent time in a prisoner-of-war camp near the Yalu River, where he attended indoctrination classes held by his Chinese and North Korean captors.

Gradually, Condron came under the influence of his lecturers. Later he was to claim that he could see no future for himself back in the United Kingdom and refused repatriation.

Along with twenty-one US prisoners of war who also refused to go home, Condron was moved to a compound at Panmunjom on the 38th parallel. He dismissed entreaties from British military representatives to return home, saying that Britain was now no more than an American colony.

By 1956, Condron had been sent by the Chinese authorities, operating through the Chinese Red Cross, to Beijing University to study Chinese and International Relations and made a few friends among the British community in the city. He helped edit an anthology of poems and essays by some of the ex-prisoners of war. Gradually he grew disillusioned with his life in North Korea and after many years in China he returned home.

Richard Corden became the leader of the twenty-one US prisoners of war who, like Andrew Condron, refused to return home. The son of a railway worker in Providence, Rhode Island, Corden was orphaned at the age of six and went to live with a grandmother. He had an intelligence quotient of 134 but got into some minor scrapes at school and left at the age of fifteen to work as a welder in a shipyard. When the shipyard closed down at the end of the war, Corden enlisted in the army. He was rejected for officer training because of his juvenile petty crime record. He served for four years and then reenlisted in 1950, just in time to be sent to Korea with the US 2nd Division. He was taken prisoner by the Chinese in November of that year.

Corden seems to have collaborated with his captors almost from the beginning and was given special treatment. He was allowed to live with the Chinese at several prison camps and received extra rations. In return, other US prisoners later claimed, he informed on American personnel and wrote pro-Communist articles for various publications.

At the end of the war, Corden was one of twenty-three US servicemen who elected initially not to return home, though two of these defectors changed their minds in time and were allowed back into the USA. The remainder, together with the British renegade Marine Condron, spent three months in a compound in neutral territory close to Panmunjom.

It was here that Sergeant Corden emerged as the natural leader of the defectors. He refused to allow United Nations negotiators to talk to the other Americans and gave defiant press conferences, stating that he and the others wanted to live in North Korea. In January 1954, Corden and the other deserters were taken to China.

Little was heard of Corden after his desertion, although there were rumours that many years later he returned quietly to the USA.

Lowell D. Skinner was another of the twenty-one Americans. One of five children of an itinerant plasterer, Skinner attended a number of schools but made few friends in the process. He finally dropped out of school after his sixteenth birthday. He worked at a number of poorly paid jobs before enlisting in the US Army in 1949, the year before the outbreak of the Korean War.

Posted to the 8th Regiment of the 1st Cavalry Division, Skinner spent eighty-seven days in combat in 1950, attacking the North Korean capital Pyongyang, before being captured in a Chinese counter-attack in Unsan on 2 November.

Skinner's letters home from his prison camp indicated that the loner was increasingly becoming influenced by Chinese propaganda. When the war ended in 1953, Private Skinner took part in a press conference in Panmunjom. He accused Americans of being warmongers and stated that he intended to settle in China.

For ten years, Lowell Skinner worked in a paper mill in the city of Tsinan. During this period he married a Chinese schoolteacher. In 1963, Skinner asked if he could return to the USA to see his elderly parents. When permission was forthcoming he left China, abandoning his wife who had contracted both polio and tuberculosis.

As he had been granted a dishonourable discharge by the army during his absence, the 32-year-old Skinner did not have to face a court martial for desertion on his return. He underwent a hostile reception from those who had known him, however, and became a heavy drinker; despite his puny physique, he took part in a number of well-reported bar room brawls. He was featured in the media again when he fired shots at two teenagers who were harassing him. He changed his name, married and died in San Bernardino, California in 1995.

A decade after the end of the Korean War, American servicemen were still patrolling the 38th parallel region and a few of them were still deserting. Charles Robert Jenkins was one of four US servicemen to defect to the North Koreans during this period.

In 1965, Sergeant Jenkins was with a three-man patrol reconnoitring an area close to the demilitarised zone between North and South Korea. Ordering his men to remain where they were, the young sergeant went forward on his own. He was not seen again. It later transpired that before going on patrol he had gained his courage by drinking ten cans of beer.

Back at his unit a note was found from Jenkins to his mother, in which he apologised for the trouble that he knew he was going to cause. It was surmised that Jenkins had deserted because he feared that he was going to be posted to Vietnam.

In North Korea, Jenkins shared a house with three other US deserters, where their conversations were bugged. Jenkins said later, 'We found microphones everywhere!' He and the others believed that they had been planted by the North Korean 'political leader' charged with looking after them. The deserters did little but attend lectures and study. Eventually all four were granted North Korea citizenship. Jenkins was put to work teaching English and married and remained in the country.

Another US soldier who deserted from Korea during this period was James Joseph Dresnok, who reached the North Korean lines in 1962 by walking across a minefield. He described the confused state of mind which led to his defection: 'I was fed up with my childhood, my marriage, my military life, everything. I was finished. There's only one place to go.'

As the Ancient Greeks and Egyptians had done thousands of years before, both sides fighting the Korean War devoted units to the task of persuading troops on the other side to surrender. On the UN side the effort was led by the less than ferociously named First Loudspeaker and Leaflet Company of the US Army, which came into operation in 1953 and consisted of eight officers and ninety-nine men. Its task was to issue leaflets printed in Chinese and Korean intended to persuade ordinary soldiers that they had been duped by their leaders in China and the Soviet Union. Loudspeaker messages were also broadcast to Korean and Chinese troops, telling them that their compatriots were being slaughtered in large numbers in other areas of the front line and urging them to desert and make their way back home. The North Koreans responded with similar broadcasts and leaflets suggesting that United Nations troops stop fighting for the capitalist cause in such a distant area and go back to their homes. Both sides continued their paper warfare fusillades until 1953. The Korean War never ended officially. To this day, both sides are still staring at one another across the line drawn along the 38th Parallel.

The Cold War was the name given to the protracted mainly non-violent antagonism between the Soviet Union and its satellite nations and the West, led by the USA. It is generally regarded as having lasted from 1947 to the collapse of the USSR in 1991. Among the political and economic manoeuvring and subsidised military coups of this period, a number of deserters, wittingly and unwittingly, became pawns in the struggle between East and West.

An unusual deserter whose motives are still debated was Nikolai Artamonov, a destroyer lieutenant commander in the Russian Navy who fell in love with a Polish girl. When he heard that he was going to be posted far away from her, Artamonov decided to flee to the West.

In June 1959, Artamonov obtained a small launch in Gdynia, pulled rank on a Russian seaman and forced the man to help him pilot the boat to Öland Island, off the coast of Sweden, where he surrendered to the authorities.

As soon as they heard about the young deserter, the Americans offered Artamonov asylum in the USA. He was debriefed and regarded as a considerable catch, especially after he had passed a number of credibility tests. One of these consisted of controlling an American destroyer, under careful supervision. For a time Artamonov's star was in the ascendancy in the espionage community of his new country. Slowly, however, doubts arose as to whether he was a genuine defector or not. These were heightened when another defector accused the ex-destroyer commander of being a Russian agent.

Efforts were made to 'turn' Artamonov, in case he was a Soviet plant. In 1975, he was encouraged to meet some Russian representatives in Vienna, with a view to his becoming a double agent. Almost at once the commander disappeared. It was never ascertained whether he had been murdered by the Russians, in which case he was a genuine defector, or had been a plant and had returned home because the Americans no longer trusted him.

Other Russian defectors of the period proved to be of equally dubious provenance. One of these was Vitaly Yurchenko, a senior Russian Intelligence agent. He defected to the Americans in 1985 but returned to the Russians in the same year, leaving the Americans to wonder if he had been a plant, a double agent or had experienced a change of heart.

Yurchenko had been in charge of the Russian Internal Counterintelligence Depot of the First Directorate, responsible for spying activities against the USA. Visiting Italy on 'diplomatic' business, he told his companions that he was off to visit local museums. Instead, he walked into the American Embassy in Rome and announced that he would supply information in return for sanctuary.

His stay in the West did not get off to a good start when by chance he was debriefed by Aldrich Ames, a US official spying for the Russians. The defecting colonel was placed in a safe house while he was interrogated. During this period he betrayed several Americans working as Russian agents. Three months after his initial desertion, Yurchenko and his CIA agent were eating at a restaurant in Georgetown. While the agent left him to pay the bill, the Russian slipped out of the restaurant and vanished. Yurchenko later turned up at the Soviet residential compound in Washington and asked to be taken back. At a subsequent press conference he claimed that he had been drugged and kidnapped by American agents and then held in isolation at a CIA safe-house near Fredericksburg in Virginia. Yurchenko returned to the USSR and was not heard of again.

Amid the two-way traffic between East and West, the most senior Communist to abandon his homeland was Rafael del Pino, a leading Cuban air ace and a general in his country's air force. The fiery del Pino commandeered an aircraft and defected with his family to the USA.

Coming from a well-to-do family, which owned several cinemas, del Pino became a student activist against the dictator Batista, incurring the displeasure of the secret police. After one public demonstration, del Pino was arrested and only saved from a prison sentence when his father sent him to study in the USA.

His absence did nothing to cool del Pino's political ardour. Upon his return home in 1956, he joined Fidel Castro's revolutionary movement. Again he made no secret of his political affiliations and once more he was arrested. With the use of his parents' influence and money, he escaped for a second time, on this occasion to Venezuela.

Del Pino was nothing if not whole-hearted in whatever he undertook. Once he was in Venezuela he joined a revolutionary group plotting the overthrow of that country's dictator, Pérez Jiménez. As irascible as ever he was discovered, arrested and thrown into gaol. His life was saved when the dictator was overthrown and political prisoners released – del Pino among them.

He returned secretly to Cuba and joined in Castro's uprising. Having learned to pilot an aircraft, he was assigned to his country's air force, with the rank of lieutenant. He later served with distinction at the Bay of Pigs invasion, shooting down several US aircraft.

After this his progress was rapid. He was appointed aviation adviser to Fidel Castro during the Cuban Missile Crisis and then sent to the Soviet Union for advanced training on Russian MiG fighter jets, returning to Cuba in 1965. In that year, he was sent to Florida to bring back a Cuban MiG 17, in which a pilot had defected to the USA.

Del Pino's next assignment was as a colonel in the Angolan war, supporting the Communist government against the rebels. It was here that his hot-headedness let him down. Although he was told not to fire on other aircraft without specific instructions from Havana, he went to the aid of a Cuban reconnaissance patrol surrounded by enemy aircraft. For this disobedience of instructions del Pinto was relieved of his command.

Slowly he began to climb back up the ladder, but he was growing disillusioned. He was particularly upset when increasingly poor health meant that he had to give up flying.

On 28 May 1987, del Pino, accompanied by his third wife, young daughter and son, coolly appropriated a small Cessna-402 aircraft belonging to the airline Aerocaribbean. He told the airport authorities that he and his family were merely going for a joy-ride around the island. Instead, the general headed straight for Key West, ninety miles from Cuba.

As soon as he entered US air space, del Pino was intercepted by two American F-16 fighters, who escorted the Cessna to Homestead Naval Airbase, near Miami. When the aircraft had landed, del Pino turned himself over to the authorities and asked for shelter. He was the highest-ranking officer to have defected from Cuba.

The Americans were delighted to be in possession of a man who knew so much about Cuban defences. For their part the Cubans tried to play down del Pino's importance as a defector, claiming that he had only been a disgruntled flight instructor, recently grounded for psychological reasons.

After a thorough debriefing del Pino was allowed to settle in the USA. He wrote several books and founded the Cuban American Military Counsel, intended to help exiled Cuban military personnel.

Throughout the Cold War, Berlin, occupied by both Russian and Western troops and divided by the Russian-constructed Berlin Wall, was a centre for desertions. Most of the Americans who went over to the Russians were of low rank. Sidney Ray Sparks was one enlisted man in the US Army stationed in West Germany who deserted to East Germany only to be imprisoned by the Russians.

Born in 1932 and brought up in Wrightsville, Georgia, Sparks joined the army in March 1950, having left school after the ninth grade. He was stationed in West Germany where he had a German girlfriend and young baby. Short of money, he assaulted and robbed a German taxi driver, was caught and imprisoned in the guardhouse to await a court martial.

In December 1951, Sparks managed to break out of the slackly supervised guardhouse and cross over into East Germany. He begged the Russians for political asylum. They held him in custody for three months while they investigated his case before giving him an unskilled job in an East German town.

In July 1952, Sparks was allowed to make a clandestine return to West Berlin for five days to visit his girlfriend and child. While he was there, the deserter encountered a corporal from his old unit. The corporal suggested that Sparks expunge his crime by working for US Intelligence. The former enlisted man promised to think about it and went back to East Germany.

The Russians were already suspicious of Sparks's motives for desertion so they arrested him and began investigating him once again. This time Sparks spent six months in the cells while a case was mounted against him.

On 14 April 1953, Sparks was convicted of trying to persuade other deserters to spy for the USA. He was sentenced to fifteen years' imprisonment. He served three years and was then returned to the US Army.

The Americans were not overjoyed to receive their errant enlisted man. They charged Sparks with desertion and his original crime of assaulting and robbing the taxi-driver. The soldier was sentenced to a ten-year term of imprisonment.

Another American defector was Robert Lee Johnson, an army sergeant who went over to the Russians while he was stationed in Berlin, supplying them with information. Upon his return to the USA he deserted but was caught and tried.

In 1952, Johnson, a heavy drinker and dissatisfied with his lot, contacted the KGB through his Austrian wife and offered to spy for them. The Russians trained him in elementary espionage techniques. He was not very successful and even left the army, but the Russians caught up with him and ordered him to re-enlist. This time Johnson became much more useful to his spymasters. He was posted to the armed forces courier station at Orly airport near Paris, the nerve-centre of most secret communications between Washington and the US Army in Europe,

Acting under orders from his KGB superiors, Johnson made a wax impression of the locks of the high-security vault. These were used to fashion keys and Johnson was given an X-ray device that would help him penetrate the inner sections of the vault containing cipher systems devised in Washington for US NATO bases in Europe.

By volunteering to work at weekends, the sergeant was unimpeded in his activities. He stole documents and gave them to a KGB contact, who took them to the Russian embassy, photographed them and returned them to the Orly military unit before Johnson was due to go off duty.

The sergeant broke into the secret installations on at least seven occasions before he was posted back to the USA. But the pressure became too much for Johnson and his wife. He was drinking more than ever and his wife was in the throes of a nervous breakdown.

In October 1964, the drunken Johnson deserted and caught a bus to Las Vegas. The FBI interrogated his wife and she gave him away, telling them all about his Paris spying activities. Johnson surrendered at a police station. He was tried with a military accomplice, Sergeant Mintkenbaugh and was sentenced to twenty-five years' imprisonment.

After he had served seven years Johnson was visited in prison by his son who had just returned from serving in Vietnam. The son had not seen his father for years and, in an appalling act of violence, son stabbed Robert Lee Johnson to death, 'for personal reasons'. The guards had not seen the knife that Johnson's son had brought into the visiting room until it clattered to the floor after he had stabbed his father with it.

Jeffrey M. Carney was yet another American serviceman to go over to the Russians. Born in Cincinnati in 1963, Carney, a homosexual, joined the US Air Force in 1980. He was trained as an intelligence linguist and between 1982 and 1984 he served at a West Berlin listening post as a signals specialist.

One night, after a solitary drinking session because a love affair with another NCO was going badly, the 19-year-old Sergeant Carney made contact with an East German border post at Checkpoint Charlie and asked to speak to a senior officer. He was soon smuggled into East Berlin, where he was interrogated. Carney informed the East Germans that he hated his life in the US Air Force and could not bear to lead the double life of a closet homosexual. He offered to spy for the East Germans.

The East Germans investigated Carney's background, decided that he was genuine and enlisted him as a spy. For two years the sergeant supplied the East Germans with secret information, leaving copies of documents at agreed dead letter drops in the city.

In 1984, Carney was posted back to the USA, serving at San Angelo military base in Texas, but still could not stand life in the Air Force. In the following year he deserted. He contacted the East Germans in Mexico and was flown from there to East Germany. Here he was put to work intercepting and translating US military telephone conversations.

Carney was decorated for his efforts and provided with a flat and a car in East Berlin. However, in 1991, after the fall of the Berlin Wall, he was abducted from Berlin in a daring raid by US Air Force agents and brought back to the West.

Jeffrey Carney was tried by a military court for espionage and desertion and sentenced to twenty years' imprisonment. He was released after serving eleven years only to find that, in the new political climate, the East Germans did not want him back. He eked out a living as a labourer in an Ohio factory.

Gerry Irwin, on the other hand, did not defect to the Russians; he claimed to have been in contact with extraterrestrial beings. When he later disappeared, there were rumours that he had been abducted by the aliens he had encountered. A more prosaic US Army posted him as a deserter.

On 28 February 1959, Irwin, a missile technician, was returning

to his base at Fort Bliss after a leave period in Idaho. He had driven
a few miles past Cedar City when he allegedly saw a glowing object
descending in a field to one side of the road.

Wondering if an aircraft had been forced down, Irwin pulled up.
He scribbled a note saying: 'Have gone to investigate possible plane
crash. Please call law-enforcement officers.' Leaving the message on
the window screen of his vehicle he ran off to help.

Irwin's note was found on his abandoned car and a search was
instigated by the Cedar City sheriff's office. Irwin's unconscious
body was found lying in a field. The soldier was taken to a hospital
where nothing amiss was found with him; his condition was diag-
nosed as 'hysteria'. When he came round he claimed that his jacket
was missing.

Irwin was then flown to a military hospital at Fort Bliss and kept
under observation for a few days. He was released as being fit for
duty but a while later he fainted. He woke up the next day and
asked dazedly, 'Were there any survivors?'

For a month the soldier was kept under psychiatric observation.
Upon his release he caught a bus back to Cedar City and returned to
the field in which he had been found unconscious. Irwin claimed
to have found his missing jacket. He then made his way back to the
sheriff's office in Cedar City, who returned him to Fort Bliss.

Again Gerry Irwin was placed in hospital. Once more he was
released. On 1 August 1959, he did not report for duty and was
posted missing as a deserter. Irwin was never seen again, although
he became something of an icon in the world of so-called mysterious alien contacts.

23

'I AIN'T GOT NO QUARREL
WITH THEM VIET CONG!'

*I have a different leadership style than the guys who have done this job.
My job is to catch deserters. And that's what I do.*
– Chief Warrant Officer James Averhart, Commander, Marine
Absentee Center, 8 March 2006

The struggle for Vietnamese freedom from French colonial rule
lasted for eight years, from 1946 to 1954. By 1953, Communist
leader Ho Chi Minh and his Vietnamese guerrillas controlled two-
thirds of the country. General Henri Navarre, in charge of French
forces, decided to build a large fortified camp at Dien Bien Phu in
a valley surrounded by mountains near the border with Laos, from
which the French could mount attacks from within the Vietnamese
lines. With all supplies and reinforcements only arriving from the
air, the French built an airstrip.

Hundreds of French paratroopers were dropped to defend the
fortress, together with construction engineers and some Algerian
and South Vietnamese troops. Later the garrison was reinforced
with infantry troops and soldiers of the French Foreign Legion.
Eventually the garrison strength amounted to some 16,000 men.

Before the French could finish constructing their fortress the
North Vietnamese general Vo Nguyen Giap surrounded Dien Bien
Phu with 40,000 men and laid siege to the camp with heavy artillery. Within a short time the French defenders were fighting for
their lives.

The besieged French troops began to suffer heavy losses and
morale sank. Eventually a number of men announced that they

would fight no more; they were going to desert. However, such a tight grip did the North Vietnamese have on the roads and tracks in and out of the fortress that there was nowhere for the malcontents to desert to. Sulkily, while their companions fought on, throwing back after attack, the deserters formed their own camp within a camp, surging out occasionally to steal food from their preoccupied comrades and sometimes engaging in pitched battles with them. They even commandeered the brothels, which had been set up for the Algerian troops.

It was estimated that at its peak the deserters' camp, known as Nam Yun, contained over 2,000, perhaps as many as 4,000, men of different nationalities, all of whom refused to join their comrades at the barricades. The French officers were too busy with their men repelling attacks to have time to bother with the shanty-town deserters.

Eventually the French surrendered Dien Bien Phu. Over 10,000 men, including the deserters and one nurse, were marched 500 kilometres into captivity. Three months later the surviving prisoners were repatriated. By this time there were only 3,280 remaining. The rest, already weakened after the two month siege, died of disease, heat exhaustion and malnutrition.

In 1954, after the surrender of Dien Bien Phu, an agreement was reached by which Vietnam was divided into two halves. South Vietnam was supported by the West and the northern half of the partitioned nation by the USSR and its allies. Three years later the two parts of the segregated country were at war. The aim of the northern half, under its lead Ho Chi Minh, was to unify the nation, while the USA struggled to keep Communism at bay in south-east Asia.

Many Americans at home were opposed to what they regarded as a continuation of the French colonial war in Vietnam. There were widespread riots in cities and on university campuses, protesting against the conflict. This attitude was typified by the refusal of the world heavyweight boxing champion Cassius Clay, later known as Muhammad Ali, to be conscripted, saying, 'I ain't got no quarrel with them Viet Cong!' He was stripped of his title for the stand he had taken.

Even inside the US armed forces there were vociferous complaints about the validity of the war. This led to desertions and, eventually, to a series of organised escape routes for those servicemen and women who did not wish to fight in Vietnam.

In 1962, the Russians secured a propaganda coup when they helped four US sailors, Richard Bailey, John Barilla, Michael Lindner and Craig Anderson, desert in Japan and reach Sweden, where many other deserters and draft-dodgers were already living. They were all twenty years old or younger and served on the US *Intrepid*, moored off Yokohama.

The four disaffected seamen contacted a KGB-backed organisation in Japan. Calling itself the National Committee for Peace and Freedom in Vietnam, it was specifically designed to approach low-ranking servicemen and persuade them to desert. They issued leaflets to Americans on leave or recuperating from wounds suffered in Vietnam. Once the four men had got in touch with the committee and stated their desire to leave, the escape machinery swung into action on their behalves.

The four deserters left their vessel on shore leave and were at once taken to the homes of anti-Vietnam campaigning Japanese citizens. After being given shelter for a few days they were sent on to the port of Hokkaido and put aboard a Japanese fishing vessel. Out at sea they were transferred to a small Russian border patrol vessel and taken north to a larger Russian ship, which deposited them on the Russian island of Sakhalin. They were then moved to Moscow and put up in a hotel.

The Russians had no intention of keeping the seamen, who were of no military use to them, or even of interrogating the men. They did, however, squeeze all the political mileage they could out of the situation, issuing press statements and putting the men on display at interviews, where the absconders stated that they were opposed to the aggressive war in Vietnam. The deserters were then sent on by a commercial airline flight to

Sweden, where they joined the organised US defectors' colony in residence there.

The National Committee for Peace and Freedom in Vietnam was closed down by the Russians in 1968 after US Intelligence operatives tracked down the escape route which had been used so successfully.

A number of US soldiers fled before they could be sent to serve in Vietnam; other young citizens left the country to avoid conscription into the armed forces. Jack Todd, born in 1946, was one of the 12,000 US deserters who fled to Canada during the Vietnam campaign. Nebraskan-born, he had been a prominent athlete and at the age of twenty-three was working as a sports writer on the *Miami Herald* newspaper.

Todd had assumed that he would be drafted and probably sent to Vietnam, but began to have his doubts about the prospect when a traumatised friend recently returned from service in the field told him about the horrors of the war and begged him to avoid the army at all times. Todd still entered the service and completed his basic training near Seattle, although he was beginning to have doubts about the validity of the US's cause in Vietnam. The realism of the details of his military training sickened him.

When he was sent home on Christmas leave at the end of 1969, Todd made the decision to desert and sought sanctuary in Canada, like so many others. It was estimated that in addition to the deserters another 40,000 young Americans had crossed the border to avoid being conscripted.

Todd's life as a deserter was not easy. He lived rough among other exiles before he secured a job on a Vancouver newspaper. Over a period of years he made a reputation as an award-winning sports writer for the *Montreal Star*.

While he was in Canada Todd renounced his American citizenship. He paid several brief visits back home but, when President Carter announced a general amnesty for Vietnam deserters, Todd was not eligible and could not return home again, even for his mother's funeral. Later he condemned his decision to desert as 'absurd', especially after he learned that he had been slated for a posting as a military journalist to Germany, not Vietnam.

A leader in the fight to avoid service in Vietnam was Richard Perrin, who was several years younger than Todd. He deserted from the US Army in 1967, fled to France and formed an organisation urging soldiers to resist the Vietnam War. Perrin had been influenced by the Civil Rights movement as he was growing up in Vermont and was drafted into the army in 1967. Here he met Private Andy Stapp, a soldier who had been court-martialled for distributing anti-war leaflets. To get him away from Stapp, Perrin was posted to Germany. By this time Perrin disliked the whole army experience so thoroughly that he deserted.

Perrin left his army base near Heidelberg and took a train to Paris, where he linked up with other US Army deserters. He published the *Resistance Inside the Army* journal, which is considered the first underground GI newspaper.

In 1969 it became apparent that France was no longer a safe haven for deserters. The French authorities feared that agitators like Perrin would encourage disgruntled US troops stationed in France to desert and cause problems. Perrin flew to Canada. He taught at a university and formed another group, the Regina Committee of American Deserters, which helped deserters from the US Army who fled to Canada. Six years later, when an amnesty for deserters was published, Perrin returned briefly to the USA to visit his parents, but continued to make his home in Canada.

There were relatively few desertions in Vietnam itself, but one marine who was suspected of voluntarily going over to the enemy was Robert Garwood, a prisoner of war who was later court-martialled and found guilty of consorting with the enemy.

Stationed at the Marine Base Da Nang in the Quang Nam province of South Vietnam, PFC Garwood was a motor pool driver. On 28 September 1965, he was not present in his billet when a bed check was made. The soldier was still absent the following morning and a search was instigated, with a reward offered for Garwood's recovery. At first it was thought that the driver might have gone absent without leave and would soon turn up, but then the military authorities received news that Garwood was a prisoner of war in North Vietnam.

There are two versions of how PFC Robert Garwood ended up in North Vietnamese hands: one provided by the soldier himself and the other pieced together by investigating officers of US Military Intelligence. According to Garwood, he was on his way to pick up an officer at the end of China Beach and bring him to the Marine base, when he got lost and ran into a North Vietnamese patrol. He claimed to have fought valiantly before being overpowered and dragged off, although accounts from Hanoi, north of the border, stated that the American had gone over voluntarily.

Later, reports came back to the US Intelligence authorities that Garwood seemed to have a great deal of personal freedom and to be collaborating with his captors in prison camps and trying to intimidate other Americans. There were reports that he had broadcast for the Viet Cong on Radio Hanoi, urging American prisoners of war to stop terrorising the people of Vietnam.

When most US prisoners of war were released in Operation Homecoming in 1973, Garwood did not return with the others. At debriefings a number of accusations were made against the former driver. It was asserted that he had enjoyed the attentions of the Viet Cong and had even accepted a commission in their army. After the war ended he lectured in 're-education' camps to captured former South Vietnamese officers.

Little more was heard of the soldier until 1979, when he contacted an official of the World Bank in Hanoi, passing him a note identifying himself and stating that he was willing to come back to the USA. The American authorities asked for his return and Garwood was repatriated.

In 1980, after a number of delays, during which he was extensively debriefed, Garwood was tried and accused of a number of offences under the Uniform Code of Military Justice. Some of the charges were dismissed but after a 92-day trial extending over eleven months, he was found guilty of collaborating with the enemy and striking an American prisoner of war. He did not take the stand to give evidence and he was not convicted of desertion. He was reduced to the lowest rank, forfeited pay and allowances and was given a dishonourable discharge from the US Army.

An unusual case of suspected desertion during the Vietnamese conflict was that of Andrew Lee Muns. In 1968, Muns, who was born in New Jersey in 1943, was serving as the payroll officer on the USS *Capon*, a refuelling ship based at Subic Bay in the Philippines, serving far from the action in the Vietnam War. He had been onboard less than a month when, on 17 January, Ensign Andrew Lee Muns was reported as missing from his vessel. A total of $8,600 had been taken from the safe of his office. Enquiries were made and it was assumed that the young officer had stolen the money and then deserted.

In 1976, the family asked for the ensign to be formally declared dead. This was agreed to by the New Jersey authorities, although his body was never found. His relatives were denied the US flag customarily presented to the next of kin on such occasions, because in this case the officer had not received an honourable discharge. His relatives had hoped in vain to drape the flag over the empty coffin. Andrew Lee Muns's family always refused to believe the allegations. After a gap of almost three decades, in one last desperate effort to discover the truth, his sister Mary Lou Taylor turned to the internet for help. She posted messages on a website devoted to Vietnam veterans, asking anyone serving on the *Capon* in 1968 at the time of her brother's death, to contact her.

Although he seldom used the internet, one of Andrew Lee Muns's fellow officers, who had shared an office with Muns, saw the message and got in touch with her. He admitted that it had been completely out of character for the young ensign to have stolen money. The sister made further enquiries and discovered that another $51,000 in the safe at the time had not been taken.

Mary Lou Taylor intensified her efforts. She went through the records of the trial, found the agent who had originally investigated the disappearance and even tracked down the widow of the captain of the *Capon* in 1968. This last witness stated that her husband had always suspected that the ensign might have been murdered.

The sister's persistence caused the Naval Criminal Investigation Unit to reopen the case, thirty years after it had been officially closed. Many crew members of the time were tracked down and interviewed. Again and again former seamen and officers stated that they had never believed that Ensign Muns had left the *Capon* voluntarily in 1968.

Eventually the investigating officers closed in on a petty officer who had served in the payroll office with Muns when he had vanished. The man was now working as an estate agent in Missouri. Under interrogation he broke down and said that Muns had caught him stealing money from the safe. The petty officer had strangled the young officer and hidden his body in one of the vessel's oil tanks.

In March 2001, a grand jury indicted the former petty officer for murder. However, at a later date a judge ruled that the accused man's constitutional rights had been violated during his questioning and that his confession was not admissible evidence.

Mary Lou Taylor said that she did not care what happened to the accused man. Her brother's good name had been vindicated. He could now be given an honourable discharge.

Despite the continued absence of a body, Ensign Andrew Lee Muns was buried with full military honours in Virginia's Arlington National Cemetery in June 2001.

The deserter who went absent for the longest period during and after the Vietnam War was undoubtedly Mateo Sabog. Sabog, a master sergeant of Hawaiian extraction with twenty-four years' service, had been serving in Vietnam when he disappeared in 1970. He left the 507th Transportation Group with orders to report to Fort Bragg in North Carolina, but never appeared there. This puzzled the authorities as the sergeant had only a few more months to serve before he could leave the service legitimately. Nevertheless, he was posted as a deserter and all but forgotten.

In 1994, a war-graves team working in Vietnam was shown a grave which the Vietnamese said might contain Master Sergeant Sabog's body. The missing man's relatives were informed of the discovery but were then told that the remains were definitely not those of the master sergeant's. His name was subsequently inscribed on the Vietnam Veterans' Memorial in Washington.

Several years later Sabog, now in his seventies, walked into a Georgia social security office and demanded his benefits. Searches revealed that he was whom he claimed to be. Further investigations showed that the master sergeant had flown back from Vietnam, but had gone to ground when he reached California. He had then assumed the name of Robert Fernandez and had for a time lived a nomadic existence as an odd-job man. Finally, he had settled in Rossville as a carer for an old woman and her family. Only when this work came to an end did he seek his social security benefits.

Mateo Sabog never gave a convincing reason for his decision to desert the US Army. His case was given careful consideration by the military authorities and, in view of his age and the fact that he had been so close to completing his time in the army when he had gone absent, no action was taken against him.

In 1998, readers of several international news magazines and viewers of at least one major US television news programme were shocked to discover that during the Vietnam War there had been a concerted effort to kill US Army deserters with nerve gas. There was only one problem with the news stories. They were completely untrue.

According to the news items, in 1970 a military campaign called Operation Tailwind had been aimed at a Laotian village sixty miles from the Vietnamese border, which was supposed to house ten to fifteen US Army deserters. These so-called deserters were alleged to have passed on information to the Viet Cong and to have been operating as an autonomous bandit group.

As a preamble to an attack on the village, the news stories continued, the deserters had first been attacked with canisters dropped from the air. These bombs had contained a deadly nerve gas known as sarin. The next day, after the gas had done its deadly work, Green Berets had landed to kill any survivor.

The news items caused a sensation. It was the first time that the USA had admitted to using nerve gas in the war. Intrigued, other journalists began to investigate the stories. Soon the original news items began to disintegrate. Operation Tailwind had indeed taken place, but the 'village' had been a North Vietnamese headquarters on the Ho Chi Minh trail, known as Binh Tram. The operation had been a diversionary attack to confuse the North Vietnamese so that another US assault could be launched in South Laos.

There had been no US deserters in the area, and although tear gas had been used in the raid, no nerve gas bombs had been dropped. The Operation Tailwind deserters had been a figment of a journalist's imagination.

US involvement in the Vietnam War ended in 1973, with the final success of Ho Chi Minh, when the country was unified once again.

A number of deserting soldiers, sailors and airmen have claimed that they have left the military scene for reasons of conscience; some have meant it. One of the first examples of religious beliefs prompting desertions occurred during the spread of Christianity at the time of the Roman Empire. A number of troops were converted to Christianity and observing the commandment 'Thou shalt not kill', felt that they could no longer serve in the army and began to desert. Not wishing to antagonise the Romans unnecessarily, the Church authorities urged its members in the army not to desert but to serve as good soldiers and make every effort to convert their fellows.

24

'DIED DELUDED'

Sir, I'm Sergeant Jenkins, and I'm reporting.
– Sergeant Robert Jenkins, Korean deserter, coming home in 2005 after
the longest recorded absence of any deserter in the modern US Army

When Iraqi forces invaded the neighbouring emirate of Kuwait in 1990 on the pretext that the latter country was illegally drilling for oil underground across its borders, the following year a coalition force headed by the USA clashed briefly with sections of the Iraqi Army and drove them out of Kuwait. Air and ground fighting over the border of Iraq followed before hostilities ceased and Kuwait's independence was guaranteed. The Americans referred to the campaign as Operation Desert Storm.

When it became obvious that the coalition forces were going to triumph, thousands of Iraqi troops deserted. Some 13,000 men were estimated to have fled to northern Iraq, which was controlled by the Kurds.

The most prominent Iraqi deserter was Lieutenant General Hussein Kamel al-Majid, the son-in-law of Iraqi President Saddam Hussein. In 1995 he defected briefly to Jordan and offered to provide the West with details of Iran's weaponry capabilities.

Kamel was in charge of Iraq's military industrial complex and for a time was responsible for his country's nuclear programme. As a soldier he displayed particular brutality during the Iraqi occupation of Kuwait. With his wife, Saddam Hussein's daughter, and their four children they lived in style in a large house in the presidential complex on the banks of the river Tigris.

On the night of 7 August 1995, Hussein Kamel and his wife,

together with his younger brother Saddam Kamel and his wife (also a daughter of Saddam Hussein), fled across the desert in a fleet of black Mercedes and arrived at the border of neighbouring Jordan and asked for asylum. In all there were thirty people in the party.

King Hussein granted the absconders asylum while the American Intelligence services tried to discover whether it was a genuine defection or some sort of ploy on the part of President Saddam Hussein. It was thought that the two brothers had deserted because Saddam Hussein's elder son, Uday, had started curbing their power. Hussein Kamel provided the Americans with details of Iraq's weapons systems, but these were blunted when Saddam Hussein issued over 10,000 documents giving the United Nations even more information on the chemical, biological and ballistic missiles systems of his country. The Iraqi leader condemned the defections, comparing Hussein Kamel with Cain and Judas, saying that he would be 'stoned by history'.

Kamel's defection to the West did not have much impact. The information he provided was not particularly helpful and Iraqi freedom organisations did not trust him because of his previous close affiliations with President Saddam Hussein. Attempts by the US authorities to sponsor such defectors' movements were ruined by the infiltration of Saddam Hussein's double agents. Realising that King Hussein of Jordan did not really want them in his country, the two brothers grew increasingly unhappy in exile.

In February 1996, Kamel and most of his fellow deserters returned to Iraq. It has not been ascertained whether Saddam Hussein promised them immunity or if they returned because threats had been levelled against all the family members remaining in the country. Once back in Iraq, the two deserters were separated from their wives and children.

Soon after their return, Kamel and his brother Saddam were gunned down and killed in a raid on their homes, in which rocket-propelled grenades were fired into the buildings. The officially named culprits were members of their families, shamed by the brothers' original desertion, but the killings were believed to have been sanctioned by the President.

Only one American soldier was accused of desertion in Iraq during this conflict. His name was Clarence Davis. After a troubled childhood, including several spells in juvenile homes of correction, Clarence Davis enlisted in the US Marines because, after committing yet another offence, a judge had given him a choice of that or going to prison.

Davis was posted to Iraq and at the start of Operation Desert Storm he told his commanding officer that he would not kill any Iraqis. He was arrested, kept in a military prison and then court-martialled for desertion and refusing to obey an order. He was refused the services of a civilian lawyer because, it was stated, it would cost too much to fly one out from the USA. Davis was sentenced to a term of imprisonment and sent back to serve it at Fort Lejeune in North Carolina. Clarence Davis was released in 1993, after serving almost three years. A year later, in February 1994, he took his own life.

A number of reserve officers and men refused to serve in the Gulf War. The case receiving the most publicity was that of Yolanda Huet-Vaughn. Simultaneously she was practising as a doctor in Kansas City, was a part-time captain in the US Army Reserve Medical Corps, and also the mother of three young children. The daughter of a Mexican doctor, Huet-Vaughn had come to the USA with her parents when she was five years old. She had joined the Army Reserve as a medical student.

In 1990, she refused orders to report to her unit to serve in the Gulf War. She stated that she considered the war immoral, inhumane and unconstitutional. Declaring that she was a conscientious objector, Yolanda Huet-Vaughn refused to report to her unit when called upon to take part in Operation Desert Storm. She spoke out publicly against the war, appeared on a television programme and protested at an anti-war rally in Washington DC. She then surrendered to the authorities in a blaze of publicity at a multi-racial church service. She was arrested as a deserter.

Yolanda Huet-Vaughn was court-martialled at Fort Leonard Wood in the remote Ozark Mountains in Missouri. Captain Huet-Vaugn was allowed to testify on her own behalf but was not permitted to explain her reasons for refusing to serve in Saudi Arabia. She was convicted of desertion and sentenced to two and a half years' imprisonment, forfeiture of pay and dismissal from the service. She served eight months of her sentence at Fort Leavenworth before the decision was overturned on the grounds that she had not been allowed to call witnesses during her trial. She was released in November 1993. Professionally she was censured and fined $5,000 by the Kansas Board of Healing Arts.

After her release, Yolanda Huet-Vaughn continued to campaign against war and appeared often on television and at public meetings.

Ten years later, the United States claimed that Iraq was not complying with the wishes of the United Nations inspectors looking for weapons of mass destruction. Saddam Hussein refused to accede to a demand from the USA's President Bush that he and his sons go in to voluntary exile. US and British troops invaded the country, Iraqi forces were defeated and Saddam Hussein was captured and put on trial.

Once more, thousands of Iraqi troops deserted. It was also estimated that a number of troops deserted in the USA rather than be sent to Iraq. By the beginning of the twenty-first century military authorities in both Great Britain and the USA became very worried by the increasing number of desertions in their armies.

In 2005, in answer to a tabled parliamentary question, the UK's Ministry of Defence revealed that while only 100 soldiers had deserted in 2001, this figure had risen to 150 in 2002, 205 in 2003 and 530 in 2004. Lawyers representing different soldiers who had absented themselves from their duties attributed the rise to forces discipline, barrack-room bullying and the possibility of being sent on active service to Iraq. Some of the soldiers claimed that they had done so for ideological motives and refused to believe official propaganda about the causes of the conflict. One of these deserters in 2006 said he refused to 'die deluded'. In the USA, military officials admitted that at least 5,500 servicemen had deserted since the outbreak of the war.

The only major accusation of desertions from other forces involved a rather embarrassing episode concerning the Czech Army. When the USA threatened to invade Iraq in 2003, a handful of Czech soldiers stationed in neighbouring Kuwait incurred the opprobrium of many of their fellow countrymen by accepting an offer to hurry back home before any shots were fired.

The soldiers were part of the 250 strong Radiation, Chemical and Biological Protection Company, stationed at Camp Doha, about twenty miles from Kuwait. They were stationed there as a part of the US-led 'Enduring Freedom' operation in the Gulf area. The role of the unit, should war break out, was to be called into action to combat the effects of weapons of mass destruction, detecting and issuing warnings about any radiation emanating from over-head aircraft and to carry out decontamination procedures. As a part of their duties the soldiers also took part in exercises under simulated battle conditions in temperatures which in the summer time could rise to 40 degrees Celsius. The camp area was reasonably well equipped for the comfort of the soldiers, with shops, a cinema, a recreation centre, a library and television reception.

In January 2003, after the troops had been in Kuwait for five months, the Czech Minister of Defence, Jaroslav Tvrdik, paid a visit of inspection to the facility. When he talked to the men he was disturbed to hear that a number of them were worried about the prospective US invasion of Iraq. The soldiers complained that they were under a great deal of psychological pressure because of the impending conflict.

The minister said that any Czech soldiers who were really worried could return home. To his surprise twenty-seven of them accepted his offer. Seven of the troops were so eager to leave that they packed their gear, threw it into the back of a jeep and headed for the airfield where Jaraslov Tvrdik's jet was waiting to take the minister home.

In their anxiety to get a lift back on the aircraft, the soldiers drove so fast that they crashed into a civilian vehicle on their way to the airport. Several of the men were injured but they all made their way on to the aeroplane to be taken home, while the other soldiers opting to be sent home waited to be transported in a more leisurely fashion.

News of the flight of the less than magnificent seven caused such an uproar in Czechoslovakia that five of the original twenty-seven changed their minds about leaving. The seven soldiers who returned were accused of being cowards and deserters. The headline in one Prague newspaper read, 'Czech soldiers crumble, head for home'. Tvrdik announced that hundreds of other members of the Czech Army had volunteered to take the place of their colleagues in Kuwait.

During the Falkland Islands campaign in 1982, the actions of a young British soldier came under scrutiny. Guardsman Philip Williams was cut off from his unit for over a month during the fighting against Argentinian troops. When he returned to his battalion he was accused of cowardice and bullied by his comrades. As a consequence he later went absent without leave, until he was arrested by the police.

Williams was born in a village near Lancaster in 1964. After he left school he worked at a number of dead-end jobs, including gutting chickens, working on a farm and labouring in an indoor market. He then joined the Scots Guards. At the age of eighteen he was posted to the Falkland Islands with the 2nd Battalion after the Argentinian invasion.

Williams saw action during the attack on Mount Tumbledown. During this battle he volunteered to collect casualties under heavy artillery fire and help bring them back down the hill. There was an explosion. When the guardsman recovered consciousness he was lying alone on the hillside, amid Argentinian corpses.

Unaware of how much time had passed, Williams wandered aimlessly for a while. He spent about a month in a disused farmhouse, disoriented and confused. He drank from a stream and killed geese with a grenade, eating their flesh raw.

Eventually he set out to walk round the coast. Cutting inland he came across an isolated farmhouse. The occupants told him that the war had ended in victory for the British forces and that his unit had already sailed for home. The military authorities were contacted and Guardsman Williams was flown by helicopter to Port Stanley. He was kept there for several weeks while he was interrogated by the Services Investigation Branch. Then he was flown to Ascension Island to await the arrival of the transport vessel carrying the rest of his battalion home.

After more debriefings, Williams was flown home with the rest of the battalion to Chelsea Barracks in London. With the other troops he was greeted as a hero and sent home on six weeks' leave. At first things went well. Then a headline in the *Manchester Evening News* cast doubts as to the veracity of the guardsman's story. It read, 'A Deserter? Not Me, Says Soldier'.

The implications of the story, which Williams denied vehemently, opened the floodgates. He started to receive anonymous letters and telephone calls accusing him of cowardice in the Falklands. Matters got worse when he returned to his barracks. Fellow guardsmen accused him of having deserted and on several occasions he was beaten up by his comrades.

When Williams went on Christmas leave that year he did not return to his unit. Instead he went to live with an aunt in Morecambe, until the local police arrested him and handed him over to a military escort. Back at Chelsea Barracks, Williams suffered a nervous breakdown and was taken to a military hospital. Upon his return to Chelsea, he was discharged from the army. He was nineteen years old.

One peacetime desertion in Great Britain attracted attention because it involved champion boxer David Barnes. Barnes, who was born in Manchester in 1981, joined the army at fifteen. He hated the discipline of service life but began to make a name for himself as an amateur boxer. Managers began to approach him to turn professional and Barnes soon realised that he could make more money fighting for cash than he could as a soldier.

Barnes walked away from his unit and began boxing professionally under an assumed name, soon running up seven consecutive victories. He was taken on by Frank Warren, a leading manager, who was unaware that his protégé was on the run from the army.

Barnes did so well that Warren arranged for the welterweight to travel to the USA for a bout. It was only when Barnes had to apply for a passport that the fighter confessed that he was a deserter. He agreed to give himself up and Bryan Hughes, Barnes's trainer, drove him back to Aldershot, to the barracks whence he had deserted.

Barnes was sentenced to six weeks' detention at Colchester Military Prison, where he worked as a gymnasium cleaner. He served his time, left the army and continued his boxing career. In 2003, Barnes, twenty-one years old, married and with two children, won the vacant British welterweight championship on a points decision.

Deserters became front page news again in 2002, when Sergeant Charles Robert Jenkins, who had taken flight in Korea more than three decades before, became the object of attention once more.

Little had been heard about the missing sergeant for more than thirty-five years. In 2002, five Japanese citizens, the survivors of thirteen Japanese citizens who had been kidnapped at various times and taken to North Korea by intelligence personnel who needed them to teach their agents the Japanese language and customs, were allowed to return to Japan from North Korea.

One of the returned citizens was a woman, Hitomi Soga, then forty-three years old. Her story was an incredible one. In 1975, she had been shopping with her mother on Sado Island in the Sea of Japan when the two women had been kidnapped and taken to North Korea. Hitomi Soga never saw her mother again.

While she was in North Korea the girl asked if she could be allowed to learn English. The teacher she was allocated was Robert Jenkins, the American deserter. They later married and had two children, both girls who, in 2002, aged nineteen and seventeen, were studying at the Pyongyang University of Foreign Studies.

On returning to Japan, Hitomi Soga said that she wished to remain but that she was not sure whether her family would be allowed to join her there.

Alerted to the presence of Jenkins in North Korea, efforts were made to contact him. A Japanese diplomat saw him in Pyongyang and asked the American if he wished to return home. Jenkins replied that he was afraid to come back in case he was punished as a deserter. In 2002, relatives of Hitomi Soga appealed to the US government, requesting that Jenkins be pardoned and allowed to rejoin his wife.

Jenkins was allowed to return. On 11 September 2005, the longest-missing deserter in the US Army reported to Camp Zama, a US Army base outside Tokyo, and saluted Lt Colonel Paul Nigara, provost marshal of the US Army in Japan. At his subsequent court martial, the 64-year-old Jenkins pleaded guilty to desertion and aiding the enemy. He was sentenced to thirty days' confinement (later reduced to twenty-five days), forfeiture of all pay and benefits and a dishonourable discharge. It was widely suspected that such a lenient sentence had been awarded in return for Jenkins telling the authorities all that he knew about North Korean spying activities.

25

TIPPING POINTS

I pledge to save wayward and wilful boys from the sad and certain conse-quences of ignorance and sin.
– Governor T. W. Birkett of North Carolina promises in 1916 to display tolerance and leniency for the forty Ashe County military deserters in his state who had decided to hide out in the hills until the end of the First World War

For 6,000 years most deserters attempted to put as much distance between themselves and any obligation to serve as they could. The manner of their desertions have varied. Some diehards had made up their minds to desert long before they were swept into the armed forces. Frankie Fraser was conscripted on a number of occasions but never stayed longer in a unit than it took him to escape and continue his life of crime. There were hundreds like him.

Some enterprising recruits, by dint of careful planning, actually made a profit out of deserting. During the American Civil War, the bounty jumpers on both sides became professional deserters, although the wealthier Union states made more use of the system than the cash-strapped Confederates.

Governments and individual states offered financial inducements to civilians to enlist. An average bounty of this nature was in the region of $100, although the wealthy Rhode Island offered $350 to each of its citizens volunteering to serve for at least two years.

This was a signal for a large number of men to sign up for service all over the country, taking their bounties, deserting at once and then applying again in another state, and so on. Some of the shrewder bounty jumpers even remained in a unit for a few weeks, waiting to be transported by their units at the army's expense to another part of the country, before absconding there and searching for the next recruiting office.

So profitable did this form of premeditated desertion become that criminal organisations sprang up to organise bounty jumping on a large scale. The city of Chicago became a particular hub of such institutions. A broker would recruit down-and-outs from the bars and streets, arrange for them to sign on at army recruiting centres, if necessary assist them with the logistics of their departures, usually within twenty-four hours, and meet again, when the brokers would take a percentage of the bounties of the members of their gangs.

One notorious organiser of this sort was Edward Jones. Not only did he facilitate the desertions of the bounty hunters under his supervision, he also showed a hands-on approach to their activities by enlisting and departing from eight separate military units. His career was only brought to an end when he tried to cheat some of his fellow jumpers out of the payments due to them. The aggrieved men, under a cloak of anonymity, reported their broker to the police. Jones was arrested at his hotel and handed over to the military. He spent the rest of the war years in a military prison at Camp Douglas.

Bounty jumping could be lucrative, but it was also perilous. During the war, over 140 of its practitioners were executed. They even had a song written about them in 1866:

The Bounty Jumper's Lament

In my prison cell I stand, thinking of you Mary Ann
And the gay old times we had in the days before
When my sock was lined with tin, and I thought it was no sin
For to jump a bounty every week or more

Chorus
Tramp, tramp, tramp, the guard is coming.
Even now I hear them at my door.

So goodbye, my Mary Ann, you must do the best you can,
For I'll never jump a bounty any more.

At the other end of the scale from the calculating recruits who had never intended to remain among the ranks, came those who fled impulsively because an opportunity to leave suddenly presented itself. In 1861, *Harper's Magazine* published the confession of Private William Henry Johnson, a young Union soldier about to be executed for desertion on 13 December 1861. Johnson was twenty-three and had been serving in the Army of the Potomac. He rode out one evening to water his horse. He wrote later:

> I had not the slightest idea of deserting up to a few minutes before I started in the direction of the enemy's lines ... It was then that I conceived the idea of deserting. I thought that I could ride right up to the rebel pickets and inside the enemy's line, go and see my mother in New Orleans...

Johnson was caught almost at once by a returning patrol. He was shot by a firing squad in a field outside Alexandria, near Washington.

Most deserters, however, whatever their reasons for defecting, built up to their departures gradually, after months and sometimes years of consideration and planning, fuelled by developing grievances. In such cases each man's attempt to leave was usually triggered by one defining event, which served as a tipping point, impelling the deserter finally to screw up his resolution, forsake inertia, take action and go. A study of these tipping points can do much to summarise the motives, reactions and even in some cases the ultimate fate of deserters in all periods, climes and conditions.

A number of soldiers have been motivated to desert by news of an event which might affect them or provide them with an opportunity to better their conditions. An early example of this occurred with the death of Alexander the Great in 323 BC. During his conquests, the great ruler had attempted to secure his position by founding military settlements in the areas he had conquered and left behind. In order to keep the main force of his army together, he had peopled these fortresses with those he regarded as dispensable: mercenaries, soldiers reaching retirement age, the wounded and the ill. Some of these settlements were situated in ill-favoured parts of the world, and the troops left behind by Alexander had a hard time making comfortable lives.

One of these outposts was Bactria, in central Asia. The area consisted mainly of deserts on the edge of the Hindu Kush mountain range, where there were great extremes of climate. When the depressed and homesick garrison there heard rumours of Alexander's death, its members felt that they were no longer bound by their promises to their former commander to stay behind and guard their remote area. Three thousand of them, mostly Macedonians, abandoned the settlement and started marching back home. The appearance of these deserters alarmed the citizens of Macedonia so much that the Macedonian Army was sent to sally out and slaughter the deserters.

It has always been easier for the discontented to leave military units if they hear of the existence of people or organisations willing to assist them in their efforts to get away. Sometimes the knowledge that help is available has been the final inciting incident for hesitating would-be deserters, as was evinced during the Vietnam War when dozens of organisations designed to encourage and aid deserters from the US Army came into being.

Such enticements to cast aside arms, however, had occasionally been available to deserters over a period of several thousand years. They were even in existence during the time of the Roman Army.

For a time Romans had attempted to temper discipline with mercy as far as dealing with their deserters were concerned. They even conceded that a few instances could be used in mitigation at the trials of absconders. These included illness, family problems and even going in pursuit of a fleeing slave.

However, as the size of the empire increased, the size of the army also grew, and more and more foreigners were recruited as troops to put down revolts in an increasing number of areas; the military authorities grew far less tolerant about soldiers who disappeared without permission from their legions, especially the ones who were not citizens. Recruits from outside Rome itself began to be treated increasingly harshly. Officers mistrusted these additions to their ranks so much – regarding them as untrustworthy barbarians – that their deployment even began to affect military tactics. Roman commanders hesitated to include night marches in their strategies, as these gave discontented legionaries too many opportunities to escape under cover of darkness.

Matters in this area came to a head in 167 AD, when Aemilius Paullus, a general and consul, rounded up foreign deserters from his ranks. To display his displeasure, he chose a rather bizarre method of execution: at a public celebration to mark a victory, the general had the deserters lie on the ground in a line, where they were trampled to death by a herd of elephants.

Far from cowing the foreign legionaries, such a horrific reaction only made many of the foreign legionaries only more anxious to leave the service of Rome. Unofficial organisations designed to help these particular Roman soldiers sprang up to aid different races, especially Germans. The knowledge that they would not be alone if they left led to a considerable increase in desertions among the soldiers recruited far from Rome.

As time passed, commanders began to factor in the statistics of potential desertions among their ranks into their overall plans of action. Knowing that up to a third of their troops might be AWOL from any campaign, generals subtracted this number in advance from their forward planning. This had no effect on deserters continuing to leave.

A major contributory cause of sudden absences among the ranks was receiving bad news from home. This could be achieved by the simple act of receiving a distressed letter from loved ones.

An example of this came about at the court martial of Private Edward Cooper of the Confederate Army during the American Civil War. When asked at his subsequent trial why he had absented himself from the battleground, the private produced a note he had received from his wife. In it she said that she and their two children were starving and that if Cooper did not return soon she feared that the three of them would die. The note had a great affect on the court; it was said that some of the judges reading it wept. Nevertheless, Private Cooper was still sentenced to death. Later this punishment was commuted to imprisonment.

Serious recurring reasons for leaving abruptly during different conflicts of various eras were not having been paid for up to eighteen months, quitting in disgust because the rifles and other weapons issued did not work, and being conveyed to battle grounds by armed guards because the troops concerned were not trusted to fight unsupervised.

There have also been many examples of overstressed troops suddenly impelled to leave on the spur of the moment for what from a distance could be judged to have been quite trivial reasons. In the annals of courts martial, recaptured absconders have given in all seriousness as reasons for their departures an absence of cooking utensils in their camps and lack of other soldiers of a like mind and similar interests to talk to around camp fires at night.

After the Russian forces entered Afghanistan in 1979, one of their radio operators deserted because he could not get satisfactory treatment for an injured leg. Gennady Tsevma went over to the Mujahideen guerillas on an impulse, to seek better medical attention.

A more chilling reason for deserting summarily was given by a Prussian officer serving in the Seven Years War. Commenting on the abrupt rise in desertions after a battle in which men had seen their comrades badly injured or suffer during an epidemic sweeping their camps, he said: 'The main causes of the prevailing and heavy desertions is to be traced to the fear of soldiers that they will fall ill and then be virtually buried alive in one of our overcrowded hospitals.'

Records show that due to shortages of men, no matter what the reasons for their absences deserters were often given a second chance in action. Many of them, like the poet Vernon Scannell, behaved with great courage when they returned to the front line. In his short story *The Veteran*, war novelist Stephen Crane depicts an old soldier who confesses to having run away during his first battle. When asked how it was that later in the war he came to serve so bravely, the veteran replied simply, 'I had to get used to it!'

Some, however, simply never could.

SELECT BIBLIOGRAPHY

Allison, William and John Fairley, *The Monocled Mutineer* (London: Quartet, 1978)

Anon., *A German Deserter's War Experience*, translated by Julius Koettgen (New York: Huebsch, 1917)

Arthur, Anthony, *General Jo Shelby's March* (New York: Random House, 2010)

Atkinson, Rick, *An Army at Dawn: The War in North Africa, 1942–1943* (London: Abacus, 2004)

Babington, Anthony, *For the Sake of Example: Capital Courts Martial 1914–18, The Truth* (London: Leo Cooper, 1983)

Barber, Noel, *The War of the Running Dogs: The Malayan Emergency, 1948–1960* (London: Collins, 1971)

Barnes, James, *Yankee Ships and Yankee Sailors: Tales of 1812* (New York: Macmillan, 1897)

Boadt, Lawrence, *Reading the Old Testament: An Introduction* (New York: Paulist Press, 1984)

Breitman, Richard, *The Architect of Genocide: Himmler and the Final Solution* (New York: University Press of New England, 1991)

Brooks, Graham, 'Captain Kidd,' in James J. Hodge (ed.), *Famous Trials 8* (London: Penguin, 1963)

Burford, Kate, *Burt Lancaster: An American Life* (London: Aurum, 2000)

Chadzynski, Martin and Carli Laklan, *Runaway!* (New York: McGraw-Hill, 1979)

Clark, Alan, *Barbarossa: The Russian-German Conflict, 1941–1945* (London: Hutchinson, 1965)

Clisby, Mark, *Guilty or Innocent? The Gordon Bennett Case* (North Sydney: Allen & Unwin, 1992)

Connell, Evan S., *Son of the Morning Star: General Custer and the Battle of the Little Bighorn* (London: Pavilion, 1985)

Cooper, Janet (ed.), *The Battle of Maldon: Fiction and Fact* (London: Hambledon, 1993)

Corr, Gerard H., *The War of the Springing Tigers* (London: Osprey, 1975)

Davidson, Louis B. and Edward J. Doherty, *Strange Crimes at Sea* (London: Neville Spearman, 1957)

de Koven, Reginald, *The Life and Letters of John Paul Jones*, Vol. 1 (New York: Scribner, 1913)

Dear, I. C. B. (ed.), *The Oxford Companion to the Second World War* (Oxford: Oxford University Press, 1995)

Elphick, Peter, *Singapore, the Pregnable Fortress: A Study in Deception, Discord and Desertion* (London: Hodder & Stoughton, 1995)

Fishgall, Gary, *Against Type: The Biography of Burt Lancaster* (New York: Scribner, 1995)

Foot, M. R. D., *SOE in France: An Account of the Work of the British Special Operations Executive in France 1940–1944* (London: HMSO, 1966)

Foxall, Raymond, *The Amateur Commandos* (London: Hale, 1980)

Gaylin, Willard, *In the Service of their Country: War Resisters in Prison* (New York: Viking, 1970)

Geraghty, Tony, *March or Die: France and the French Foreign Legion* (London: Grafton, 1986)

Granger, Stewart, *Sparks Fly Upwards* (London, Granada, 1981)

Groom, Winston and Duncan Spencer, *Conversations with the Enemy: The Story of P. F. C. Robert Garwood* (New York: Putnam, 1983)

Hallam, Elizabeth (ed.), *Chronicles of the Crusades: Eye-Witness Accounts of the Wars between Christianity and Islam* (London: Weidenfeld & Nicolson, 1989)

Hastings, Max, *The Korean War* (London: Joseph, 1987)

Hayes, Thomas Lee, *American Deserters in Sweden: The Men and their Challenge* (New York: Association Press, 1971)

Hillier, Fay, *Ooh, You Are Awful … But I Like You: The Life Story of Dick Emery as told to Fay Hillier* (London: Sidgwick & Jackson, 2001)

Hough, Richard, *The Potemkin Mutiny* (London: Hamish Hamilton, 1960)

Huie, William Bradford, *The Execution of Private Slovik: The Hitherto Secret Story of the Only American Soldier since 1864 to be Shot for Desertion* (London: Jarrolds, 1954)

Jeal, Tim, *David Livingstone* (London: Heinemann, 1973)

Jensen-Stevenson, Monika, *Spite House: The Last Secret of the War in Vietnam* (New York: W. W. Norton, 1997)

Kaplan, Justin, *Mr Clemens and Mark Twain: A Biography* (London: Jonathan Cape, 1967)

Keeton, J. W. and John Cameron, *The 'Veronica' Trial: Notable British Trials* (London: Hodge, 1952)

Kemp, Peter and Christopher Lloyd, *The Brethren of the Coast: The British and French Buccaneers in the South Seas* (London: Heinemann, 1960)

Kessler, Ronald, *Escape from the CIA: How the CIA Won and Lost the Most Important KGB Spy Ever to Defect to the U.S.* (New York: Pocket Books, 1991)

Kray, Reginald, Ron Kray with Fred Dinenage, *Our Story* (London: Sidgwick & Jackson, 1988)

Krivitsky, Walter G., *I Was Stalin's Agent* (London: Hamish Hamilton, 1939)

Lewis, Norman, *Naples '44* (London: Collins, 1978)

Lord, Graham, *Just the One: The Wives and Times of Jeffrey Bernard* (London: Sinclair-Stevenson, 1992)

MacPherson, Myra, *Long Time Passing: Vietnam and the Haunted Generation* (New York: Doubleday, 1984)

Maude, H. E., *Of Islands and Men: Studies in Pacific History* (Melbourne: Oxford University Press Australia, 1968)

Murphy, Brendan M., *Turncoat: The Strange Case of British Sergeant Harold Cole, 'The Worst Traitor of the War'* (San Diego: Harcourt, 1987)

Nicolle, David, *Nicopolis 1396: The Last Crusade* (Oxford: Osprey, 1999)

Phillips, Norman, *Guns, Drugs and Deserters: The Special Investigation Branch in the Middle East* (London: Werner Laurie, 1954)

Prasad, Devi, *They Love It But Leave It: American Deserters* (London: War Resisters' International, 1971)

Read, Piers Paul, *The Train Robbers* (London: W. H. Allen, 1978)

Reynolds, Bruce, *Bruce Reynolds: The Autobiography of a Thief* (London: Bantam Press, 1995)

Richardson, Charlie with Bob Long, *My Manor* (London: Sidgwick & Jackson, 1991)

Rowse, A. L., *Bosworth Field and the Wars of the Roses* (London: Macmillan, 1966)

Royle, Trevor, *Civil War: The Wars of the Three Kingdoms 1638–1660* (London: Little Brown, 2004)

Scannell, Vernon, *Argument of Kings* (London: Robson, 1987)

Seward, Desmond, *Richard III: England's Black Legend* (London: Country Life, 1983)

Sexton, Rae, *The Deserters: A Complete Record of Military and Naval Deserters in Australia and New Zealand, 1800–65* (Magill: Australian Maritime Historical Society, 1985)

Shaw, Roy with Kate Kray, *Pretty Boy* (London: Blake, 1999)

Stanford, J. K., *Tail of an Army* (London: Phoenix House, 1966)

Swigget, Howard, *March or Die: The Story of the French Foreign Legion* (New York: Putnam, 1953)

Talbot Rice, Tamara, *Byzantium* (London: Rupert Hart-Davis, 1969)

Thomson, James Pringle, *The Jacobite Rebellions: 1689–1746* (London: G. Bell, 1914)

Todd, Jack, *The Taste of Metal: A Deserter's Story* (Toronto: HarperCollins 2001)

Tucker, Spencer C. and Frank T. Reuter, *Injured Honor: The Chesapeake-Leopard Affair, June 22, 1807* (Annapolis: Naval Institute Press, 1996)

Wahlert, Glenn, *The Other Enemy: Australian Soldiers and the Military Police* (Melbourne: Oxford University Press Australia, 1999)

Weale, Adrian, *Renegades: Hitler's Englishmen* (London: Weidenfeld & Nicolson, 1994)

— —, *Patriot Traitors: Roger Casement, John Amery and the Real Meaning of Treason* (London: Viking, 2001)

West, Richard, *The Life and Strange Surprising Adventures of Daniel Defoe* (London: HarperCollins, 1997)

Williams, Philip with M. S. Power, *Summer Soldier* (London: Bloomsbury, 1990)

Williams, Robert Neville, *The New Exiles: American War Resisters in Canada* (New York: Liveright: 1971)

Windrow, Martin and Jeffrey Burn, *The Waffen-SS* (London: Osprey, 1999)

Wycherley, George, *Buccaneers of the Pacific* (London: Rich & Cowan, 1935)

Yousaf, Mohammad and Mark Adkin, *The Bear Trap: Afghanistan's Untold Story* (Lahore: Jang Publishers, 1992)

Ziegler, Philip, *London at War, 1939–1945* (London: Sinclair-Stevenson, 1995)

INDEX

Also available from The Robson Press

TOMMY AT WAR
John Sadler & Rosie Serdiville

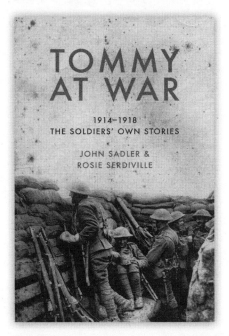

2014 marks the centenary of the outbreak of the Great War, arguably the definitive conflict in the history of Europe. Never before or since has such a great swell of popular sentiment produced such a patriotic rush to arms. In the trenches and on the battlefield, British soldiers united with their allies to fight valiantly for the cause.

John Sadler and Rosie Serdiville disclose the poignant and emotive experiences of war, in the front line and behind, from men and women of every class and background. Combining rich anecdote and unique testimony, the stories of those that passed through the ordeal of war reveal remarkable tales of horror and suffering, but also the comradeship, exhilaration and adventure of the Western Front.

336pp hardback, £20
Available now in all good bookshops or order from
www.therobsonpress.com